Studies in the Gospel of Mark

MARTIN HENGEL

Studies in the
Gospel of Mark

FORTRESS PRESS   PHILADELPHIA

Translated by John Bowden from the German. The original articles appeared as follows:
1. 'The Gospel of Mark: Time of Origin and Situation' = 'Enstehungszeit und Situation des Markusevangeliums', in *Markus-Philologie. Historische, literargeschichtliche und stilistische Untersuchungen zum zweiten Evangelium*, ed. H. Cancik, WUNT 33, J.C.B. Mohr (Paul Siebeck), Tübingen 1984, pp. 1–45.
2. 'Literary, Theological and Historical Problems in the Gospel of Mark' = 'Probleme des Markusevangeliums', in *Das Evangelium und die Evangelien*, ed. P. Stuhlmacher, WUNT 28, J.C.B. Mohr (Paul Siebeck), Tübingen 1983, pp. 221–265

Excursus Reinhard Feldmeier, 'The Portrayal of Peter in the Synoptic Gospels' = 'Die Darstellung des Petrus in den synoptischen Evangelien', in *Das Evangelium und die Evangelien* (see 2. above), 267–71
3. 'The Titles of the Gospels and the Gospel of Mark' = *Die Evangelienüberschriften*, Sitzungsberichte der Heidelberger Akademie der Wissenschaften, Philosophisch-historische Klasse, 4, Carl Winter: Universitätsverlag 1984.

Appendix
   (a) 'Wolfgang Schadewalt', by Maria Schadewaldt
   (b) 'The Reliability of the Synoptic Tradition' = 'Die Zuverlässigkeit der synoptischen Tradition', *Theologische Beiträge* 13, 1982, 198–221
With additions by the author to his own articles

Library of Congress Cataloging in Publication Data
Hengel, Martin.
   Studies in the Gospel of Mark.
   Articles translated from the German by John Bowden.
   Includes indexes.
   1. Bible. N.T. Mark—Criticism, interpretation,
etc.—Addresses, essays, lectures. I. Title.
BS2585.2.H44   1985   226'.306   85–4508
ISBN 0–8006–1881–5

1730C85 Printed in the United Kingdom 1–1881

To
Henry Chadwick
Regius Professor of Divinity
in the
University of Cambridge
on the occasion of his sixty-fifth birthday

71219

Contents

Preface

Truly great texts never age. Such texts keep finding – or rather, winning – new readers, even when they are at odds with the spirit of the age and changing intellectual fashions; even when they are thought to be outdated, 'exhausted', with nothing important left to offer.

Great texts constantly invite rediscovery. Their riches are inexhaustible in the truest sense of the word, and precisely for that reason they are always far in advance of their readers. It is well worth being invited by them to make yet more discoveries.

It is our theories about these texts that grow old – often rapidly, and rightly so. We love to present them with arrogant claims, asserting, for example, that we understand texts better than their authors. It is all too easy for our theories simply to project our own prejudices and desires on to the texts. The modern, perhaps even radical and provocative, theory or method is not necessarily the one that does justice to the text, and sometimes it could well be that certain ancient traditions, all too familiar to us, come much nearer to the intention and the historical reality of a text than the most recent theories. The danger of misinterpretation is particularly acute where we apply our methods and attempts at explanation in an all too one-dimensional and limited way, or are over-hasty in making dogmatic assertions, failing to note both the profound depths in a great text or the complexity of its historical ramifications. One-sidedness, whether radical of naive, is no virtue, above all in the interpretation of ancient texts.

The Gospel of Mark is one of these very great texts from the ancient world, and it is worth our while devoting all our energies to it, It is a text that we never master; we always continue to sit at its author's feet. Here it is worth remembering the motto of the Swabian exegete I. A. Bengel, which was the motto of the Nestle Greek Testament up to its twenty-fifth edition: *Te totum applica ad textum. . . rem totam applica ad te.* We should not forget it.

The history of the interpretation of Mark since the discovery of the priority of the Gospel 150 years ago is a model deterrent against one-track approaches. This is most evident from the way in which the author of the Gospel has been portrayed. The Tübingen school still saw him as a late epitomator; Heinrich Julius Holtzmann and his followers down to Albert Schweitzer regarded him as the only historically reliable 'biographer' of Jesus; while William Wrede made him a constructive dogmatic theologian. By contrast the form-critical school believed that they had to demote him to the status of a mere collector and redactor, and recently he has been seen as an unknown Gentile Christian as opposed to the Jewish Christian from Jerusalem presented by tradition. Thus scholarly research has moved primarily in contrasts. Was he a simple, not to say primitive, narrator or a theological 'didactic poet', essentially sophisticated and freely producing his own theological portrait? Was he a story-teller of the miraculous who produced *theios aner* legends? Or a committed polemicist against the glorification of Christ as a divine man? Did he himself invent the messianic secret or take it over from the community tradition, or did this notion emerge later, from the pen of a foolish redactor? Did he want to tell Jesus stories in the form of history, or was he a strict preacher of a *theologia crucis*? Is his work a unity or full of glosses? Do we have to reckon with an 'Urmarkus' as well as with the evangelist? To whom was he closer, Peter or Paul? Or neither of them? And finally, to end with, the crucial question: has his work anything at all to do with the real man Jesus of Nazareth or is it purely a mythical construction, historicized 'theology'?

The abundance of theories, contradictory in either appearance or reality, might reduce us to resignation: *ignoramus, ignorabimus,* we do not know and shall not know. But it can also be a challenge. In the last resort, the reason why what seems to be so simple and short a work allows of so many different and extreme interpret-ations – each of which often has one or more grains of truth – must be the riches and depth of its content. And could not the fascination exercised by this small work ultimately be associated with the fascination exercised by Jesus of Galilee himself?

The studies contained in this volume certainly do not claim to be able to answer the riddle of this unique work, the earliest Gospel that we have. They are only preliminary studies, approximations, which aim to deal with certain historical and theological aspects of the Gospel and to clear away some of the rubble left by mistaken hypotheses which obstruct the way to a proper understanding of this work. The title should really have been *Essays Preparatory to the Study of the Gospel of Mark*. That would indicate that if we really attempt to 'immerse' ourselves in the strange world of the ancient sources and attempt to draw on the scattered riches to be found in the parallels, analogies and references at our disposal, while at the same time listening to the Gospel itself, we shall bring some disputed questions nearer to a solution, and it will be possible to define the historical and theological context of the work more clearly than usually happens today. At the same time, among other things, this approach should show that at least some of the traditions of the early church about the Gospel according to Mark deserve more credence than is usually accorded them today.

The first study, 'The Gospel of Mark: Time of Origin and Situation', originally appeared in the symposium edited by H. Cancik, *Markus-Philologie*, WUNT 33, Tübingen 1984, 1–45. In it I have tried to determine more closely the time of origin and situation of the Gospel. I believe that in this attempt we can make more progress than with the three later Gospels. With some degree of probability, we may say that the work was written in Rome in 69, the year of fearful civil war which still antedated the capture of Jerusalem by Titus. Presumably chapter 13, which is decisive for dating, was composed under the impact of the disturbing rumours about *Nero redivivus*, who was seen as the Antichrist on the verge of appearing. This explains the lack of firm information about events in Judaea, though the author is directly interested in it as the place where Jesus died and as the centre of the final events which are about to happen. John Mark, a Jewish Christian from Palestine, wrote for a sorely tried community which a few years earlier had to suffer the first cruel persecution under Nero. This gives Jesus' call to persevere in discipleship until the parousia of the Son of Man a special emphasis in his Gospel, and at the same time it explains the pessimistic and realistic anthropology, which shows an awareness of how easily the people, like the disciples, can be led astray. Thus the evangelist does not see salvation in pious works but in utter trust in Jesus and in the certainty of forgiveness of sins, received as a gift through Jesus' sacrificial death.

This already brings us to the heart of the second study, 'Literary, Theological and Historical Problems in the Gospel of Mark', published for the first time in the collection edited by P. Stuhlmacher, *Das Evangelium und die Evangelien*, WUNT 28, Tübingen 1983, 221–65. Pastor R. Feldmeier, who was my assistant at that time, contributed a short excursus, 'The Portrayal of Peter in the Synoptic Gospels' (267–71), and I have added that here.

In this article my starting point is the contrary assessments of the Second Gospel in the two most recent German commentaries, those by R. Pesch and W. Schmithals. I myself attempt to evaluate the Gospel as a kerygmatic biographical historical account, which is at the same time a well-constructed, dramatic narrative work of art. Quite recently, in his lecture, 'Ein Heide las das Markusevangelium' (A non-Christian Reading of the Gospel of Mark), which he gave on the occasion of his honorary doctorate in Tübingen, Günther Zuntz demonstrated in an impressive way that this short work is a 'masterpiece of amazing originality' (in H. Cancik, ed., *Markus-Philologie*, 205–222). The exciting book by the well-known actor Alec McCowen, *Personal Mark*, London 1983, also presents Mark clearly as a dramatic author: not as a free poet who gives full rein to his imagination, but as a brilliant narrator of the story of Jesus. 'He is not a sentimental man. He likes facts. He does not linger over second-hand information' (p. 15). Is it not remarkable that this 'dramatic' work composed for reading in worship could in our day inspire a celebrity to give it a dramatic performance?

Irenaeus could already be cited as evidence for the Gospel as a work of art: *Etenim cum omnia composita et apta Deus fecerit oportebat et speciem Evangelii bene compositam et bene compaginatam esse* ('But as God has made everything in harmony and with good proportions, so to it was necessary for the form of the Gospel to be harmonious and well structured', *Adversus haereses* 3, 119). Mark himself was well aware of this and achieved it impressively in his own work.

If only we could see how much we sin against the spirit of this book with our theological boredom and pedantry! Above all else, for Mark reliable traditions, close to history, and consummate narrative art are not opposites; nor are the proclamation of Christ and stories about Jesus; nor theological interest and historical truth. The evangelist shows his stature and sovereign mastery by the very fact that he manages to produce a real *coincidentia oppositorum*, which goes a long way towards explaining the very different judgments on his work. He is in basic opposition to any one-sided attempt at interpretation, to what I would venture to call premature explanation, because his work is *theopneustos* (II Tim. 3.16), 'permeated by the Spirit of God', in the deeper sense of the word, because in it we can sense something of the primitive Christian *pneumati theou agesthai* (cf. Rom. 8.14), 'being moved by the spirit of God'.

So behind the Gospel there is a theological authority from primitive Christianity and not the amorphous collectivity of an unknown community. That means that we must also ask questions about the author and his historical situation – and that means asking whether the note by Papias is true and whether the author was close to Peter. Here we can place more confidence in the evidence of 'John the elder' on which the disputed note by Papias is ultimately based than on most modern hypotheses.

The third study, 'The Titles of the Gospel and the Gospel of Mark' begins from a phenomenon in the earliest sphere of influence of the Gospel of Mark to which scholars so far have paid little attention, namely the titles 'Gospel according to Mark, Luke', and so on. These are unique in antiquity, and in all probability can be traced back to the earliest Gospel, being connected with its function in liturgy and its dissemination in the early Christian communities. In this connection I also discuss the questions of early Christian libraries, the amazingly strict discipline in copying, and the liturgical reading for which the Gospel of Mark was originally written. It is from the influence which the Gospel of Mark exercised here, in that we owe to it the fixed title 'Gospel' for an account of the activity and death of Jesus and thus the genre of Gospel generally, that we can see most impressively the revolutionary significance of the earliest Gospel for the history of the church and theology.

All three studies have extensive documentation and references to further literature; here texts from the ancient sources have usually been more important to me than an exhaustive list of secondary literature, which today has grown beyond all bounds. As far as I have felt it necessary, I have quoted important texts in the original, and I am grateful to my publishers for making this possible. Sometimes the notes have taken on the character of brief excursuses; this is because the studies themselves go back to lectures, and I have kept the form of lectures so that they are more readable. Readers can choose how intensively they want to read them.

I have added, to end with, a lecture by the great philologist Wolfgang Schadewaldt, because in a quite distinctive way he takes my preparatory studies forwards towards their real goal, namely the question of the relationship between the earliest Gospel and its real subject-matter, the person of Jesus of Nazareth.

When some years ago I was able to read the manuscript of the lecture through the kindness of Schadewaldt's widow, Frau Maria Schadewaldt, the daughter of the Zürich New Testament scholar Arnold Meyer, I was deeply moved, since the thoughts expressed in it came so close to the results of my own research. Unfortunately I was unable to hear Wolfgang Schadewaldt when in the last years of his life he was discussing the question of 'The Reliability of the Synoptic Tradition' with Tübingen theologians, because at the time I was still teaching in Erlangen. At my request, Frau Schadewaldt then wrote an introduction to her husband's lecture and had it published in *Theologische Beiträgen* 13, 1982, 198–223. She kept the form of the lecture, which addressed the audience directly, and indeed provoked them, in no way toning it down. That is also the form in which it has been translated into English. The lecture is to some degree the legacy of a significant philologist who speaks to us out of his comprehensive knowledge of ancient literature, especially from the early and classical periods (and indeed out of his knowledge of the great authors of European literature generally). This is a legacy which is particularly important for us theologians who are so fond of regarding ourselves as 'critical'. Perhaps our emphatically critical attitude is no more than a cloak for our relative uncertainty, indeed ignorance and limited perspective. Although we may not follow in every respect the urgent appeal of Wolfgang Schadewaldt to read the Synoptic Gospels with more understanding, he can teach us theologians one thing: respect for the stature of the texts with which we deal day by day.

Finally, I must express my thanks to John Bowden for his admirable translation and to Frau Anna-Maria Schwemer and Fräulein Monika Merkle for reading the proofs of the English text so carefully.

Tübingen, February 1985   Martin Hengel

I

The Gospel of Mark:
Time of Origin and Situation

...illum Galbae	τοὺς μὲν οὖν
et Othonis et Vitellii	χρόνους ἐξακριβῶσαι
longum et unum annum	χαλεπόν ἐστι[1]

As a biographer, when writing his *Lives* of the heroes of the earliest days, Plutarch is fond of complaining about the difficulties of chronology. Thus according to him there is no information about Lycurgus which is not the subject of controversy, 'but least of all is there unanimity about the time in which the man is said to have lived'.[2] The cares of historians are still the same today, and unanimity does not seem to have become any greater. That is particularly the case with history 'transfigured by piety', the kind of history with which Plutarch was in fact occupied in his own way when he wrote the *Lives* of Heracles,[3] Theseus, Romulus, Numa and Lycurgus; he may have felt the distance which separated him from their times long past in the same way as we do when we think of that 'time when a command went out from Caesar Augustus'. Even where scholars believe that they have attained a large measure of unanimity in the darkness of earliest Christianity, where, as Overbeck pointed out, there is always the danger that 'all cats are grey',[4] the invigorating wind of doubt keeps suddenly rising again and compels us to think afresh. That is also the case with the earliest Gospel.[5] For example, those who call themselves critical scholars have recently arrived at the unanimous opinion that the Gospel was composed anonymously, and in all probability was written by a Gentile Christian.[6] By contrast, I have tried below to demonstrate that the information from the early fathers of the second century is less questionable and doubtful than these relatively recent conjectures.[7]

There also seems again to have been some movement in the dating of the Second Gospel. The most recent introductions and commentaries make a fine show of unanimity in conjecturing an origin in the period after the destruction of Jerusalem, i.e. somewhere in the years after the August of 70.[8] However, J.A.T.Robinson has suggested the period between 45 and 60 in his stimulating book *Redating the New Testament* (1976), which is provocative because it questions so much that is taken for granted.[9] In a fine article, Günther Zuntz suggests a period immediately before the end of Caligula's reign on the basis of Mark 13.14ff. He argues that Mark 13.14 refers to the statue which the megalomaniac emperor wanted to set up in the temple, and Caligula was murdered on 24.1.41.[10] So-called 'conservative' scholarship stands in between – sometimes rather to its surprise; scholars here regard as most probable a date after the Neronian persecution, but before the end of the second temple.[11]

1. The tradition of the early church

The remarkable thing in connection with the origin of the Gospel which later came to be least regarded in the early church and was hardly commented on is that in fact we have the earliest and most detailed information about it;[12] moreover, this information was controversial as early as the end of the second century. On the one hand we have Irenaeus with his famous survey in *Adv.Haer.* 3,1,1:

> Matthew composed his Gospel among the Hebrews in their own language, while Peter and Paul proclaimed the Gospel in Rome and founded the community. After their death Mark, the disciple and interpreter of Peter, transmitted his preaching to us in written form. And Luke, who was Paul's follower, set down in a book the gospel which he preached. Then John, the Lord's disciple, who had reclined on his breast, himself produced the Gospel when he was staying at Ephesus, in the province of Asia.[13]

Already for Irenaeus, the predominant sequence of Gospels as early as his time was based on the chronological order of their composition. The Hebrew Gospel of the apostle Matthew is the earliest, followed by the Gospel according to Mark, a disciple of Peter. Irenaeus evidently received both reports from Papias,[14] whose work he knew; in fact he understands Papias' note to mean that Mark wrote his Gospel from recollections only after the death of Peter (and Paul). Had this happened during the lifetime of Peter, we would have expected a reference to his approval, which was expressly stressed a little later by Clement and probably also by Tertullian.[15] However, Papias, who for his part in turn refers back to a report by the presbyter John, says nothing of this. Irenaeus has understood him correctly. We could, of course, at a pinch follow Harvey in interpreting Irenaeus' μετὰ δὲ τὴν τούτων ἔξοδον in the sense of 'after their departure',[16] but this does not make very much sense. Moreover, ἔξοδος in the sense of 'departure, death' is accepted terminology in the Bible and early Christianity.[17] Although Irenaeus does not mention Nero's persecution and the death of the two apostles in Rome in so many words, he does seem to have known this tradition. We find it in the Acts of Peter and Paul, which were written about the same time, in Tertullian, and already very much earlier in I Clem. 5.1-6.2.[18]

We also find the same tradition about the origin of the Gospel after Peter's death in the so-called 'anti-Marcionite Prologue' to the Gospel of Mark, the earlier and simpler version of which runs as follows:

> ...Mark declared, who is called 'stump-fingered' because he had short fingers in comparison with the size of the rest of his body. He was Peter's interpreter. After the death of Peter himself he wrote down this same gospel in the regions of Italy.
>
> *Marcus adseruit, qui colobodactylus est nominatus, ideo quod ad ceteram corporis proceritatem digitos minores habuisset. Iste interpres fuit Petri. Post excessionem ipsius Petri descripsit idem hoc in Italiae partibus evangelium.*[19]

Even if we do not follow de Bruyne and Harnack in putting this puzzling and disputed text actually before Irenaeus, the information contained in it does seem to be old. Regul has rightly doubted de Bruyne's theory of an anti-Marcionite edition of the Gospels in Rome, provided with the prologues in question, but he was not in a position to give a satisfactory explanation of the origin of this simple prologue to Mark. The designation of Mark as *colobodactylus* shows that he did not simply copy Irenaeus; we find the term elsewhere only in Hippolytus[20] and – perhaps also like the *in Italiae partibus* (= ἐν τοῖς τῆς Ἰταλίας μέρεσιν, i.e. *in Italia*)[21] – it indicates an original Greek form; the independence of the terminology also points in the same direction. So we must reckon with the possibility that this archaic prologue is based on a distinctive tradition independent of Irenaeus. The second form of the prologue, which is in part in direct contradiction, shows the influence of Eusebius' later version and the attempt at a balance. Thus it is a clear redaction of the original version, which seemed to be inadequate.

Now that means that according to the earliest tradition of the church we can arrive at, the origin of the Gospel of Mark is to be put at the earliest in the period after the death of Peter in the Neronian persecution.

Presumably this tradition from Papias and Irenaeus rests on an old

tradition which we can trust. For the usual explanation, that Papias'
note about Mark was meant to guarantee the apostolic derivation of
the Second Gospel, is not convincing. His comments on Mark (and
on Matthew) are far too detached and critical for that.[22]

So it is no wonder that towards the end of the second century the
tradition emerges that Mark already wrote his Gospel in Peter's
lifetime and with his knowledge. In his *Hypotyposes*, book 6, Clement
of Alexandria reports a tradition of 'the old presbyters' according to
which the two Gospels with genealogies, i.e. Matthew and Luke,
were written first. However, the Gospel of Mark was composed in
the following way:

> When Peter proclaimed the word publicly in Rome and presented
> the gospel in the power of the spirit, the many people there asked
> Mark to write down what had been said, because he had long been
> a companion of Peter and had remembered his words. Mark did
> this and handed over the Gospel to those who had asked for
> it. When Peter learned of this he neither intervened with an
> admonition nor encouraged it.

Thus for Clement, the apostle has the possibility of examining the
work, but he holds back. This is presumably so that the last work
which follows, composed by the apostle John on the prompting of
his disciples, and caught up in the Spirit, as a πνευματικὸν εὐαγγέλιον,
can shine out all the more clearly. In this way it has much better
credentials than that of Mark, the disciple of the apostle, which Peter
only tolerated.[23]

As this 'intermediate solution' was still too restrained, in a para-
phrase of the Clement tradition Eusebius makes Peter experience the
origin of the Gospel by a revelation of the Spirit: 'He was delighted
at the zeal of the men and authorized the work for reading in worship
by the communities.'[24] Even before Eusebius' correction of Clement's
account, which he no longer found adequate, Origen endorsed the
authority of the Gospel of Mark still further. In contrast to Clement's
sequence of Matthew, Luke, Mark, John, Origen understands the
sequence of the Gospels which was already fixed in his time (like
Irenaeus before him) as the chronological order of their origin. So he
writes at the beginning of his commentary on Matthew: 'The (Gospel)
according to Mark was (written) second, as Peter instructed him' (ὡς
Πέτρος ὑφηγήσατο αὐτῷ).[25]. Later hypotheses about the Gospel of
Mark make the guidance a command or a formal dictate of the
apostle.[26] Yet others, by contrast, have the Gospel of Mark origina-
ting in Alexandria, and no longer in Rome.[27]

The composition of the second Gospel even during the lifetime of the prince of the apostles would necessarily lead to an essentially earlier date. It would in fact make it about twenty-five years older. In his *Church History* and the *Chronicles* – which are earlier; indeed the Christian part of them forms the chronological background to the *History*[28] – Eusebius presupposes such an early date.[29] This may go back to the Chronicle of the World composed by Sextus Julius Africanus.[30] Eusebius reports that Peter came to Rome in the time of Claudius to combat Simon Magus there; he had already refuted Simon in Judaea. Justin already told in his *Apology*, after 150, how this father of all the heresies had seduced the Romans in the time of Claudius by his magical powers, so that they worshipped him as God.[31] The apostle's companion, Mark, had then written the Gospel in the way described above. After that he is said 'to have been sent to Egypt and to have been the first to proclaim the Gospel which he had written',[32] with resounding success. As evidence Eusebius cites the Therapeutae; i.e. in his view Philo depicts the life of the first Christian-ascetical communities in Alexandria in *de vita contemplativa*. The whole passage is rounded off in a synchronism: 'From Philo, however, we have word that he came to Rome under Claudius and was an associate of Peter, who preached at that time to the inhabitants there.'[33]

The *Chronicon Hieronymi*[34] confirms this information, in that it makes Peter come to Rome after the founding of the community in Antioch in the second (according to some manuscripts even in the first) year of Claudius (24.1. AD 42 to 23.1. AD 43). He was bishop there for twenty-five years. A year later, in the third year of the ruler, we find: *Marcus euangelista interpres Petri Aegypto et Alexandriae X̄P̄m adnuntiat.* To some degree in agreement with this, later chronographers and a number of hypotheses about Mark claim that Mark composed his Gospel in Rome 'ten years after the ascension'.[35]

The calculation is relatively simple. Starting from the synchronism in Luke 3.1 dating the emergence of John the Baptist in the fifteenth year of the emperor Tiberius (AD 28/29) and on the presupposition that according to the Fourth Gospel the ministry of Jesus lasted for three years, the *Chronicon Hieronymi* puts the passion of Jesus in the eighteenth year of the emperor (AD 32/33 – passover of 33). The second year of Claudius (accession 24.1. 41) is 'about' ten years later.

A still older parallel tradition, of which there is already evidence in second-century sources, reports that the apostles went out all over the world twelve years after Easter. Accordingly, in some hypotheses we find the variant that Mark conceived his Gospel twelve years after the Ascension.[36] If we follow the one-year synoptic chronology, to which according to Clement the supporters of Basilides already appealed,[37] and assume that the year of the passion was the sixteenth year of Tiberius (AD 29/30), the twelve years takes us back to about 42. The historical roots of this unique tradition certainly *also* lie in the round or sacred numbers ten or twelve, but that is not the whole story; we can find further stimulus in Acts 12.17, where in connection with the persecution of the earliest community in Jerusalem by Agrippa I at the time of the passover in 42 (or 43), it is said of Peter, after he is freed from prison, in an enigmatic way: ἐπορεύθη εἰς ἕτερον τόπον. The persecution which presumably resulted in the expulsion of Peter and probably other disciples from Palestine, i.e. from the sphere of Agrippa I's rule, marked a deep division in the history of earliest Christianity. The tradition of the twelve or ten years could therefore be connected with this break.[38]

Eusebius also reports that Mark died in the eighth year of Nero (AD 62),[39] even before Peter. The prologue to Theophylact's Commentary on the Gospels is able to end by giving the dates of the composition of all four Gospels: Matthew wrote eight years after the Ascension, in Hebrew, for the Jewish Christians, and John translated his Gospel into Greek. Mark wrote after ten, Luke after fifteen and John after thirty-two years – after he had critically read the other three Gospels – 'and he made good what they had omitted'.[40]

Thus there may have been a number of variants in the legend of the origin of the second Gospel which developed and were harmonized. In the Acts of Peter, which were written round about the time of Irenaeus towards 180, Peter visits Rome first under Nero, after Paul's departure for Spain. On his first visit to the house community of the senator Marcellus he comes '*et uidit* evangelium legi'. He rolls up the scroll and declares: *qualiter debeat sancta scribtura (sic!) domini nostri pronuntiari. quae gratia ipsius quod coepimus*, scribsimus, *etsi adhuc uobis infirma uidentur, capaciter tamen (add. scripsimus,* see E.Hennecke/W.Schneemelcher/R.McL.Wilson, *New Testament Apocrypha*, II, 302) *quae perferuntur in humana carne inferre*.('You must know how the holy Scriptures of our Lord should be declared. What we have written by his grace so far as we were able, although it seems weak to you as yet [we have written] according to our powers, so far as it is endurable to be implanted in human flesh.') Here Peter himself appears as the author of the one written Gospel. There are no more details about where, how and when this came into being. The author of the Acts of Peter, towards the end of the second century, obviously could not envisage a community without a written Gospel, even in the apostolic period.[41]

2. Indications in the Gospel itself

Historically speaking, these traditions from the early church hardly take us further. Even if, as I believe, the 'Elder' in the Papias quotation gives us an indication which historically is to be taken seriously, it does not give us a clear date. In other words, the time of the composition of the second Gospel must be inferred from the indications given by the second evangelist in his work.[42]

First of all, we must establish the *terminus ad quem* and the *terminus a quo*. The view of the old Tübingen school,[43] which regarded the evangelist as a late *pedisequus et breuiator*[44], 'follower and abbreviator', of the earlier Matthew, has now been almost completely abandoned. It survives only in some fundamentalist circles. The fact that it is now established that Mark is the earliest Gospel puts certain limits on late datings of this kind.

With an experienced sense of proportion, A. Jülicher set boundaries which scholars have largely recognized:[45]

If Mark is the evangelist, the work must have been composed by 75 at the latest. Not much earlier, because the need for such a Gospel was not felt so early and because it took a number of decades for the material in the Gospel to arrive through the interweaving of authentic reminiscence and pious legend at the finished texture which amazes us in the Gospel of Mark (cf. also the forecast in 13.10). But it can hardly be later, since for example according to 13.30 the beginning of the last woes will be experienced before the end of Jesus' generation, cf.9.1. There is a dispute as to whether Mark is already living after the destruction of Jerusalem. Some passages in ch.13 sound rather as if he was living at the beginning of the Jewish War, though 13.1f., 24 – the last verse especially in comparison with Matt.24.29 – clearly point to the time after 70.

Up to the last clause, with qualifications I could go along with him. The dispute as to whether the Gospel was written before or after the destruction of Jerusalem is still unresolved.

Since the *terminus a quo* is harder to determine, we begin with the simpler *terminus ad quem*. Here Matthew and Luke, who are writing some time after AD 70 (see 18 below), presuppose the text of Mark, and indeed in the form in which we have it today. On the basis of a comparison of the Synoptic Gospels, an Ur-Markus hypothesis seems superfluous and improbable. The minor agreements can be explained, without exception, as a result of stylistic improvements or common oral tradition.[46] Above all, both evangelists found the same offensive ending in their Marcan model (Mark 16.8). A secondary redactor of Mark would surely first of all have removed this abrupt and offensive ending. The clear difference in content from their common source in the two great Gospels also presupposes some distance in time: at least a number of years and more likely one or two decades.

In addition Jülicher mentions a number of indications which are given in terms of the evangelist's own time.[47] Thus Mark 9.1: εἰσίν τινες ὧδε τῶν ἑστηκότων οἵτινες οὐ μὴ γεύσωνται θανάτου ἕως ἂν ἴδωσιν τὴν βασιλείαν τοῦ θεοῦ ἐληλυθυῖαν ἐν δυνάμει ('There are some standing here who will not taste of death before they see the kingdom of God come with power'). In other words, the evangelist expects that only some – no longer most – of Jesus' audience (cf. Matt. 8.34: τὸν ὄχλον σὺν τοῖς μαθηταῖς) will still experience in their lifetime the parousia of the Son of man, which was mentioned immediately beforehand. By contrast, about 53-54 Paul can say in his enumeration of the witnesses of the resurrection that 500 brethren saw the Risen Christ at one time, ἐξ ὧν οἱ πλείονες μένουσιν ἕως ἄρτι, τινὲς δὲ ἐκοιμήθησαν ('most of whom are still alive, though some have fallen asleep'). Here the majority are still alive, and only 'some' have died. The outcome of this expectation – a disappointing one – is indicated in John 21.21-23, about AD 100: here there is only one person, the mysterious beloved disciple, who was expected to experience the parousia, but the Lord had only said to Peter, ἐὰν αὐτὸν θέλω μένειν ἕως ἔρχομαι ('if it is my will that he remain until I come'). But he would not. So in the end people were disappointed. Thus chronologically the Gospel of Mark seems to stand between John and I Corinthians. I Clement 44.2f. is also typical of a later situation about AD 95-100. According to it, most of the ministers appointed by the apostles are either already dead or have grown old. The author himself belongs to the third generation. On the other hand, this author speaks of the Neronian persecution of 64, which in my view is also reflected in Mark, as still being an event of his generation (5.1f.). Thus his work, behind which stands the Roman community, may be about thirty years later than the Gospel of Mark, which presumably was also written in Rome (see below 28ff.)

In a similar way to Mark 9.1, in Mark 13.30 the Marcan Jesus affirms in his great testament and farewell discourse that the generation of Jesus' contemporaries will not pass away, i.e. will not die, before they themselves all experience the end-events which have been described earlier, including the parousia of the Son of Man.[48] Matthew, who where possible follows his Marcan model as an authority – an authority which in my view is ultimately dependent on Peter – takes over these formulae with minor changes.[49] Luke, in a less apocalyptic mood, tones them down somewhat.[50]

In Mark 15.21 Simon of Cyrene, the man who bears the cross, is identified – quite unusually – not by his father's name but by his sons Alexander and Rufus, probably because these are still known to the audience of the Gospel. Matthew and Luke, however, omit both names; they no longer know what to make of them.[51] Here, of course, we could point out that the passion narrative is the earliest part of the Gospel, even 'pre-Marcan', but in that case why did not Mark delete the names – like those who took over his Gospel – if they no longer meant anything to him?[52] On the other hand, Matthew and Luke add the title 'governor' when Pilate is first mentioned only by name in Mark, and conversely call the high priest(s) by name, whereas Mark contents himself with a simple Πιλᾶτος (or ὁ ἀρχιερεύς) and presupposes that every hearer knows who is meant.[53] On this basis R.Pesch would date the very old main source of the Gospel which he postulates, the Jerusalem passion narrative (for him this begins as early as Mark 8.27ff.) in or before the year 37, back to the time when Caiaphas was still 'the high priest' – rather too bold a conclusion.[54] However, we may hardly put the Gospel later than a generation (i.e. thirty or forty years) after the Christ event.

On the other hand there can be no question that Mark, for all the rough-hewn quality of his account, which never, like say Josephus, claims to present 'scholarly history',[55] reproduces the 'historical contours' of Palestinian Judaism before the destruction of the second temple more accurately than the later evangelists. His work is still wholly orientated on this period. Jews, Pharisees and leaders of the people are not yet lumped together in a *massa perditionis* as in John; the 'scribes and Pharisees' are not yet a stereotyped, uniform group as in Matthew. Rather, the scribes, who appear as a distinctive class, often come to Galilee from Jerusalem, which before 70 was the unrivalled centre for study of the Torah.[56] The 'scribes of the Pharisees'[57] accordingly appear as the leading intellectual group of the Pharisaic party. In Galilee they are therefore mentioned less frequently than the Pharisees, who no longer play any substantial role in Jerusalem.[58] Mark, however, introduces the Pharisees along with the ascetical disciples of John the Baptist, who are still completely within the framework of Judaism, and thus characterizes both groups as representatives of a rigorous piety.

By contrast, the Sadducees, the representatives of the priests and lay aristocracy in Jerusalem, who came to an end with the destruction of Jerusalem, are completely absent from Galilee,[59] though there are Herodians – in the territory of Antipas – who allied themselves with the Pharisees against Jesus and were able to put a politically dangerous catch-question in Jerusalem.[60] The Sadducees in Jerusalem deny the resurrection, and precisely for that reason their rejection by Jesus is noted with approval by a scribe.[61] The real opponents of Jesus in Jerusalem are not the Pharisees, but the representatives of the supreme political and religious institution, the members of the Sanhedrin, represented by three groups: the ἀρχιερεῖς, i.e. the members of the leading high-priestly families (these were the main opponents), the πρεσβύτεροι, the representatives of the lay nobility, and the γραμματεῖς, those learned in the Torah, who need not all have been Pharisees.[62] After 70 this whole pluralistic political and religious landscape, which Mark depicts quite accurately in broad outline, was destroyed. No New Testament author portrays the different groups in Jewish Palestine at the time of Jesus as accurately and as true to their time as Mark. Towards the end of the first century Matthew and John show a new Judaism, completely dominated by Pharisaism. Luke, the historian, still preserves some historical knowledge, but from a certain distance.[63]

Thus in contrast to the later Gospels the Gospel of Mark is in no way orientated on the situation which had changed so radically after 70, but on the religious and political circumstances of Jewish Palestine under the procurators – one might also say, on the circumstances of Jesus' own time. Even the political unrest of the last twenty-five years before the destruction of the temple after the death of Agrippa I (44) has not left its mark there – if we disregard Mark 13.

This is also confirmed by the picture of the disciples: Peter has a dominant position in the foreground, even more so than in the later Gospels,[64] and behind him, already clearly at a distance, are James and John the sons of Zebedee.[65] In the lists of disciples, which always form a hierarchy, there is James, whom Mark mentions nine times and always puts before John, despite his early death in 42 or 43, in second place immediately behind Peter. Here Mark has retained a very old order of names which for him was already 'historical'. Matthew abbreviates this frequent mention of the sons of Zebedee in three places, Luke in six,[66] while Luke 8.51; 9.28 change the order to reflect the later importance of John.[67] The fact that in comparison with the other Gospel Mark mentions the Twelve most often as a clearly defined élite of disciples appointed by Jesus fits this observation;[68] indeed in the old enumeration of the witnesses of the resurrection (I Cor.15.4f.) they are mentioned directly after Peter, though they relatively soon lost their leading role in Jerusalem. There is as yet no sign of the later circumstances in the community; the term ἀπόστολος appears only once, with the indeterminate meaning 'messenger' (Mark 6.30). There is no trace of church order and hierarchy, where above all we should include the predominant role of James the brother of the Lord in Jerusalem after Peter's flight (Acts 12.17), although Mark, as Mark 6.3 attests, knows James well. In terms of the history of earliest Christianity Mark – as a rule – reflects more the early period, before the move to the Pauline mission to the Gentiles and the 'caliphate' of James the brother of the Lord in Jerusalem.[68a] All these observations go against the view, popular today, that the Gospel of Mark is a theological 'didactic poem' which simply expresses circumstances in the church shortly before or after the destruction of Jerusalem. It seeks deliberately to narrate past 'history' in the form of stories, artistically arranged and connected together.

However, despite this we should resist the temptation of too early a date: it is important to avoid both Scylla *and* Charybdis.

Certainly Jülicher's argument that 'it took a number of decades for the material in the Gospel to arrive through the interweaving of authentic reminiscence and pious legend at the finished texture which amazes us in the Gospel of Mark',[69] is intrinsically not all that convincing, for mixtures of 'authentic reminiscence and pious legend' could even develop in the lifetime of a hero. That is evident from the early development of the legend of Alexander, to which the court historiographer Callisthenes, who accompanied him on his Anabasis, made a powerful contribution, and which even included the miraculous, divine conception of this young conqueror of the world.[70] It is the same with the legend of Augustus,[71] and Lucian[72] also produces examples of the rapid formation of a legend and a credulity encouraged by eye-witnesses, to some degree in order to frighten his readers. Sulpicius Severus (c. AD 360-410/20) wrote his life of Martin of Tours (AD 316-397), bursting with miracles, presumably immediately after his death. He had visited the saintly bishop personally, two years before he died. Jonas of Bobbio, the author of the *Vita Columbani*, which takes no less a delight in miracles, entered the monastery of Bobbio, founded by the great monk, three years after the founder's death (AD 618). His work, which he wrote over a long period, was published in 643.[73] Despite its clear structure and its dramatic tension, Mark's work is the popular creation of a natural talent, and we must not ask of him that reflective detachment with which, say, Tacitus recounts the reports of eye-witnesses who were still alive in his time, attesting the healing miracles of Vespasian in Alexandria.[74] Miracle stories as Mark tells them could theoretically already have been current during the lifetime of Jesus.

In comparison with the Second Gospel, moreover, the message of

Paul, which can be traced back to the forties, gives the impression of having a more 'progressive' christology and soteriology. The example of Paul shows how quickly quite new religious developments could come about under the creative impulse of the eschatological and enthusiastic Spirit of God.[75]

Here, though, we must remember that the apostle to the Gentiles – unlike Peter and Mark – was from the beginning to some degree detached from the Jesus tradition. However, in his case too it was about twenty years before he wrote the first letter that we have, I Thessalonians, presumably in 50.

Despite what has been said so far, nevertheless a whole series of specific reasons tell against too generously early a dating, say, along the lines of Eusebius – and for a later dating, of the kind that I already hinted at in connection with Papias and which we find advocated in Irenaeus.

1. The linguistic problem perhaps bears least weight. Mark presupposes the complete translation of the Jesus tradition from Aramaic into Greek. In terms of language and content his work is extraordinarily coherent, and both literarily and theologically it gives the impression of being very mature. The clarity of Mark's writing, sure of its subject-matter, does not fit well into the earliest period of ferment after the birth of Christianity, when the events of a recent past were still vivid to many people, and they were expecting an imminent end with burning hearts. In the early period of this eschatological enthusiasm, prompted by the Spirit, there had been hardly any thought of a 'Jesus biography', but only of the proclamation by word of mouth of the new message of the coming of the crucified Messiah as Son of Man and judge of the world within a limited area, in Syria and Palestine.

2. Where we have parallels to the Logia source (Q), the sayings tradition in Mark usually gives the impression of being secondary, having been worked over more strongly.[75a] Accordingly I believe that the written collection of the sayings of Jesus as we have it, say, in Q, is substantially earlier than the second Gospel. One can probably also presuppose the existence of an earlier passion narrative which Mark has, though, fused into his work as a whole with brilliant narrative power. It is no longer possible to make a literary-critical reconstruction of it.

3. The references to the world-wide mission in Mark 13.10; Mark 14.9 seem to be an alien body, but they nevertheless belong from the beginning to the fixed literary content of the Gospel (see below 24f.). Their earliest conceivable point of origin is at the time of the expansion of the universal Pauline mission, i.e. *after* the so-called Apostolic

Council about 48. Even more understandable would be the time after the late fifties when others – in my view also including Peter – had already taken over this revolutionary world-wide concept of mission which indeed represented something new in antiquity.[76] For Mark, the question of the validity of the ritual law, over which there was such a fierce struggle at the time of Paul, is in principle no longer a problem and has clearly been resolved in favour of the mission to the Gentiles. The work is in fact obviously written for Gentile Christians. However, we cannot presuppose the existence of these in large numbers before the Pauline mission, and despite some points of contact, the Gospel certainly does not come from a disciple of Paul.[77] Mark 7.15, in my view an authentic saying of Jesus, to which Mark gives a prominent place, demonstrates the final break with the dietary regulations; Mark 2.23-28 and 3.1-6 show freedom towards the sabbath commandment based on christology, whereas Mark 15.39, with the quite astonishing confession of the centurion by the cross after the death of Jesus, reveals an approach to all peoples as the goal of Jesus' career.

4. Finally, the prophecy of the martyrdom of the sons of Zebedee made by Jesus refers to a fixed date (Mark 10.39). In the form in which it has come down to us, the saying is certainly formulated as a *vaticinium ex eventu*, i.e., it is presupposed that the hearer knows about the violent death, presumably of both disciples, and at least of one of them, information which is confirmed by a fragment of Papias:[78] ὅτι Ἰωάννης ὁ θεόλογος καὶ Ἰάκωβος ὁ ἀδελφὸς αὐτοῦ ὑπὸ Ἰουδαίων ἀνηρέθησαν: John the theologian and James his brother were killed by the Jews. This does not say that John was killed with his brother James by Agrippa I in AD 43, as E.Schwartz[79] supposed; because he was one of the three pillars (Gal.2.9), his death must be put later. As according to Papias both 'were killed by the Jews', we could presume (no more) that his death, like that of James the brother of the Lord, took place in Judaea in the turbulent sixties. We do not know any details.[80] He should no longer be identified with the unknown evangelist or the presbyter of the same name from Asia Minor.

5. However, this brings the Gospel nearer and nearer to the critical point of the year 70. Here the decision must be made above all in expounding Mark 13, the apocalyptic farewell discourse of Jesus, over which there is especial dispute; there the author first of all brings the reader down to his present and then moves on without a break to the pressing events of the end of the world. As at the end of Dan.11, where on the basis of the cessation of historical information and the transition to a utopian future we can fix the composition of

the work to the year 165,[81] so too in Mark 13 we have to attempt a date.

First, however, we need to examine some over-hasty interpretations of Marcan texts in connection with the year AD 70. E.g. Mark 12.9 (τί [οὖν] ποιήσει ὁ κύριος τοῦ ἀμπελῶνος; ἐλεύσεται καὶ ἀπολέσει τοὺς γεωργοὺς καὶ δώσει τὸν ἀμπελῶνα ἄλλοις, 'What will the owner of the vineyard do? He will come and destroy the tenants, and give the vineyard to others') certainly does not relate to the Jewish catastrophe of the year 70, but is the necessary conclusion to the parable, to some degree the answer which the hearer himself has to give to the question.[82] Mark 15.38, the rending of the veil of the temple, is not to be connected with the portents of the destruction of Jerusalem in Josephus, Tacitus, Talmudic accounts and other authors of antiquity, despite later exegesis in the church.[83] Nor does it represent the *evocatio* of the deity from the sanctuary which is doomed to destruction.[84] It marks the end of the cult, since the annual sacrifice of atonement in the Holy of Holies has become obsolete through the atoning death of the Son of God.[85]

3. References in Mark 13

(a) The destruction of the temple

So we can concentrate wholly on Mark 13. Here Jesus' prophecy on leaving the temple (v.2) is best taken as a *vaticinium ex eventu* of the destruction of the temple: βλέπεις ταύτας τὰς μεγάλας οἰκοδομάς; οὐ μὴ ἀφεθῇ ὧδε λίθος ἐπὶ λίθον ὅς οὐ μὴ καταλυθῇ ('Do you see these great buildings? There will not be left here one stone upon another, that will not be thrown down').[86] According to Josephus' account Titus commanded that the whole town and the temple should be razed to the ground (τήν τε πόλιν ἅπασαν καὶ τὸν νεὼν κατασκάπτειν). Apart from the towers of Herod's old citadel, Phasael Hippicus and Mariamne, it was all levelled so much 'that it gave visitors the impression that the city had never been inhabited.' However, the theme of complete destruction of hostile cities is extraordinarily frequent in Josephus.[87] Still, in Mark 13.2 it is striking that in contrast to the detailed description in Luke 19.41-44, Jesus does not speak of the destruction of the whole city but only of that of the temple; here the καταλύειν of the sanctuary is again put on the lips of false witnesses (Mark 14.58),[88] who attributed plans for such destruction to Jesus himself.

The question is whether Mark 13.2 is only conceivable as a *vaticinium ex eventu*: in my view the answer to this must be no. An eschatological tradition about the καταλύειν of the temple – whether by the Messiah or above all by the enemy of God – could only conceive the action as *radical* tearing down. In one way or another the destruction was an expression of divine judgment. The Antichrist, who according to Rev.17.15ff. will destroy Babylon-Rome, acts unknowingly as an agent of the divine wrath. The theme of judgment also underlies the 'trampling' of the temple forecourt and the holy city by the Gentiles in Rev.11.1,8. However, in this text, which was composed more than twenty years after the destruction of the temple, the altar and the sanctuary proper are spared. Conversely, long before 70 there were already predictions of the complete annihilation of the house of God, or depictions which could be interpreted as a prophecy of future destruction.

So the threat of the destruction of the temple had a long prehistory. As early as in Ps.74, which depicts the catastrophe of 587 BC in the form of the people's lament to God, the destruction of the temple is presented in a way which could be later understood as prediction. Accordingly, the exegesis of the early church interpreted this psalm as a prophecy of the destruction of the temple by Titus. The enemy have laid the sanctuary in ruins (thus the original Massoretic text, 74.3), set up their standards in it and torn it down and burnt it, thus 'desecrating the divine dwelling down to the ground' (74.4-7). Euthymius gives an apt interpretation of the 'violated to the ground' (εἰς τὴν γῆν ἐβεβήλωσαν): 'they tore down the temple to the ground in an impious and godless way' (754).[88a] The announcement of complete annihilation recurs in Jeremiah and in the apocalyptic tradition of Daniel.[89] The latter shows how virulent it became by the time of the Maccabees. In II Macc.14.33, the Seleucid general Nicanor threatens: 'If you do not hand Judas over to me as a prisoner, I will level this precinct of God to the ground and tear down the altar, and I will build here a splendid temple to Dionysius.'[90] Why should Mark or his tradents not have imagined a future destruction of the temple in a similar way (see below 17f.)?

However, the chain of threats against the temple goes further: according to Diodorus Siculus the friends of Antiochus VII Sidetes advised him to 'storm the city of Jerusalem', which was starved out and ready for peace negotiations, 'and utterly exterminate the people of the Jews', which according to ancient custom would have meant a complete destruction of city and sanctuary. In his generosity, Antiochus contents himself with dismantling the walls and taking hostages.[91] Granted, Pompey spared the temple which he had besieged and stormed, but on the rebellion after the death of Herod the oppressed Romans unthinkingly set alight the outer halls of the sanctuary, which were completely destroyed, and took possession of the temple treasure.[92] The temple was often under severe threat again under the procurators. The fate of cities like Carthage or Corinth was also all too well known to educated Jews;[93] the warning in John 11.48, καὶ ἐλεύσονται οἱ Ῥωμαῖοι καὶ ἀροῦσιν ἡμῶν καὶ τὸν τόπον καὶ τὸ ἔθνος ('And the Romans will come and destroy both our holy place and our nation'), expresses a fear which was alive throughout the whole period of the procurators in Judaea.[94] The great admonition which Josephus makes King Agrippa II deliver in Jerusalem immediately before the outbreak of the Jewish war ends with an urgent request to spare the holy places, 'for the Romans will no longer hold back when they have conquered these, since the sparing of them once before was received with ingratitude'.[95] Finally, reference should be made to the prophecies of disaster uttered by Jesus son of Ananias, who announced the destruction of city and temple in ecstatic cries from the time of the procurator Albinus to the besieging of the city by Titus (c. AD 63-70). Different 'prophecies' of the threat of the annihilation of the sanctuary and city must have been in circulation, as also counter-prophecies from the Zealots that the sanctuary was impregnable.[96] These examples should suffice: the announcement of the complete destruction of the temple in Mark 13.2 in no way presupposes the catastrophe of 70. Mark may have formulated this sentence simply in view of the threatening situation in Judaea from the time of the sixties by using early tradition stemming from Jesus himself.[97]

(b) Mark 13.13-39

Still less can any convincing reference to a past destruction of Jerusalem be found in the apocalyptic discourse from Mark 13.2ff. on. On the contrary, the section Mark 13.14-19 which scholars are fond of quoting in this connection does not fit at all into the situation at or after the destruction of the temple and the city or in the time of the siege, from July to September 70. The occupation and destruction of the city had been preceded long beforehand by the gradual occupation of Judaea – with the exception of the fortresses of Herodion and Massada. As early as 68, before the murder of Nero on 9 June, Vespasian largely had Judaea under control and isolated Jerusalem.[98] At that time an invitation to the inhabitants to flee into 'the mountains' of the wilderness of Judah must have seemed nonsensical, for the fugitives would run into the hands of either the Romans or the Sicarii in and around Massada; the latter were no less murderous, and offered resistance up to 73 or 74.[99] Rather, the country people fled *into* the city, in which a bloody civil war was raging, only ended by the advance of Titus.

The habitable land had largely been 'pacified' since the encirclement of the city by Titus – apart from the two fortresses. The few who had survived outside Jerusalem and had not been active Sicarii and rebels no longer had to fear for their lives; flight had become unnecessary, indeed even fatal. Like Vespasian before him, Titus sought, rather, to settle the refugees in secure places.[100] Thus it becomes clear that the author is writing away from Judaea and knows very little of actual events in the country – rather like those modern exegetes who want at any price to put the origin of the Gospel in Palestine or in its geographical proximity. The reference to the inhabitants does not fit into any authentic historical situation known to us. Therefore the old hypothesis, which keeps being put forward again, that here the evangelist was working over a Jewish-Christian flysheet from the time of the beginning of the Jewish War or the days of Caligula, is not convincing.[101] In my view the text has been thoroughly worked over by the evangelist (which is not to say that he has made it all up). At some points we can see the 'redaction' of the evangelist more clearly, and at others the 'tradition' that he is working over comes more to the fore, but it is impossible to reconstruct a coherent 'flysheet' which fits meaningfully into the historical events known to us. The description in vv.14-20 has to be forced if it is to be fitted into the picture which Josephus draws of the Jewish War, the sacking of the temple and city and the 'pacification' of the country. We might be more inclined to think of the megalomaniac attempt by Caligula to set up his statue in the temple in Jerusalem, but here too there are considerable tensions with the actual events.[102]

Rather, Mark 13.14-20 reproduces earlier pictures of apocalyptic terror of the kind that had been in circulation since the Maccabaean revolt, expressing the experiences of the people of the land under foreign invasion. The summons to flee immediately into the 'mountains' in v.14b is reminiscent of I Macc.2.28, where it is said of Mattathias after the murder of the Seleucid official and the Jewish apostate: καὶ ἔφυγον αὐτὸς καὶ οἱ υἱοὶ αὐτοῦ εἰς τὰ ὄρη καὶ ἐγκατέλιπον ὅσα εἶχον ἐν τῇ πόλει ('And he and his sons fled to the hills and left all that they had in the city').[102a] The onset of disaster happens much more quickly than was to be expected from the advance of a Roman army under Cestius Gallus, Vespasian or Titus, far less a Petronius in 39/40 (Mark 13.15,16). On the other hand, the date of the catastrophe still seems to be completely uncertain, so that people can ask God for it not to happen at an unfavourable point in time. If at all, this suddenness and uncertainty of the happening can only be compared with the parousia itself.[103] As Lars Hartman has rightly stressed, the disaster threatens to erupt as suddenly as the annihilation of Sodom by fire from heaven.[104]

The decisive verse Mark 13.14 therefore also has nothing to do with the siege[105] or capture of the temple by Titus in 70. The event depicted at one point by Josephus, when the Romans, after capturing the burning temple, set up their standards in the eastern court (the Court of the Women) and there acclaimed Titus emperor,[106] cannot therefore be connected with this verse, because only at this point is there a summons to immediate flight.[107] However, the chances of fleeing from the city, which are not mentioned in the text, had already become nil at that stage, since Titus had set up the *circumvallatio* round the city. Moreover, the masculine perfect participle ἑστηκότα,[108] with its unusual construction *ad sensum*, points more to the beginning of a permanent state of affairs associated with a specific person. By contrast, Titus left the burnt-out sanctuary, which later served as a camp for prisoners, and indeed Jerusalem, soon after the final victory.[109]

The whole verse is deliberately couched in enigmatic terms. It already gave difficulties to Luke and Matthew, the earliest interpreters. Luke, who omits the formulation, has replaced it with a reference to the siege and threatened destruction of Jerusalem (Luke 21.20) and corrected the summons to flee from Judaea into the hills, which he has taken over, by an appropriately topical addition advising the inhabitants of Jerusalem to leave the city and the people of the country not to flee there (Luke 21.21). Here the experiences of the cruel catastrophe of the year 70 – in contrast to Mark's account - are incorporated into the eschatological discourse: the majority of the numerous refugees from Galilee and Judaea who sought refuge in Jerusalem perished in the city, and the rest became prisoners of Rome.[110] Behind the ἐκχωρείτωσαν (Luke 21.21) there could be a reference to the flight of the Christians to Pella.[111]

Matthew is writing some time after Luke,[112] who is nearer to the catastrophe of 70 than he is. Correcting and interpreting Mark, he says that the 'abomination of desolation' prophesied by Daniel 'is standing in the holy place' (ἑστὸς ἐν τόπῳ ἁγίῳ, Matt.24.15); by this he probably means the temple – now destroyed. Using formulations taken over from Mark, he expresses his expectation that the future time of distress and the messianic woes will begin from there. The double τότε with the future (Matt.24.14b, 21), which has been added, shows that for him these are still to come.

However, in Mark, the Danielic βδέλυγμα τῆς ἐρημώσεως[113] there clearly conceals a person, as is shown by the masculine ἑστηκότα, which Matthew corrects. The person is occupying a place which is not his due. The announcement is so exciting for the evangelist that he warns the reader to pay special attention.

By his appearance at the 'place which is not his due' this person signalizes the complete unbroken presence of the messianic woes; again a quotation from Daniel is used to describe this last and supreme time of distress.[114] The ἑστηκώς can therefore only be the *eschatological adversary of God himself*, the 'final tyrant' and '*Antichrist*', whose appearance is described clearly by a text which presumably stands very close in time, II Thess. 2.3f.:[115] καὶ ἀποκαλυφθῇ ὁ ἄνθρωπος τῆς ἀνομίας, ὁ υἱὸς τῆς ἀπωλείας, ὁ ἀντικείμενος καὶ ὑπεραιρόμενος ἐπὶ πάντα λεγόμενον θεὸν ἢ σέβασμα, ὥστε αὐτὸν εἰς τὸν ναὸν τοῦ θεοῦ καθίσαι ἀποδεικνύντα ἑαυτὸν ὅτι ἐστὶν θεός ('And the man of lawlessness is revealed, the son of perdition, who opposes and exalts himself against every so-called object of worship, so that he takes his seat in the temple of God, proclaiming himself to be God'). I.e., before the parousia of the Son of man there will be a last intensification of the eschatological distress, sparked off by the revelation of the Antichrist, and he will be clearly and finally identifiable when he himself is enthroned in the temple, thus 'proclaiming himself to be God'. By his cryptic reference, Mark is simply indicating the appropriation of the sanctuary by the enemy of God, though he only speaks cryptically of the accursed one standing ὅπου οὐ δεῖ (Mark 13.14).

The connection between the destruction of the temple announced in Mark 13.2 and the revelation of the representative of the 'abomination of desolation' in Mark 13.14 remains unexplained. That there is a connection here for Mark follows from the question by the two pairs of brothers who represent the closer circle of disciples (Mark 13.4): πότε ταῦτα (this is certainly to be related to Mark 13.2) ἔσται καὶ τί τὸ σημεῖον ὅταν μέλλῃ ταῦτα συντελεῖσθαι πάντα; 'What will be the sign when these things are all to be accomplished?'); in my view Mark 13.14, with the stress on ὅταν δὲ ἴδητε ('when you see') itself contains a reference to this 'sign' for which the disciples ask. Hence, too, the quite extraordinary invitation to the reader, which goes right beyond the framework of a mere report.[116] Now that means that Mark is probably thinking that the appearance of the enemy of God in the holy place will presumably result in the complete annihilation of the sanctuary; here again the obscure formulations of Daniel lie in the background.[117] According to the fifth Sibylline, this enemy will try to 'destroy the city of the blessed completely, at the summit of his power'; however, according to Jewish hope, he will be prevented from doing this by the Messiah sent by God (166ff.). But Mark does not go further into this question because the fate of the Jerusalem sanctuary, whose representatives had rejected Jesus' messianic 'visitation'[118] by delivering him over to death, no longer has any further interest for him: it has become the place of judgment, i.e. of utter devastation, and the last tribulation will start from there.

So the event described in Mark 13.14 has not yet taken place. The previous disastrous events, wars, earthquakes, famines, indeed even the previous persecutions (Mark 13.7f.,9ff.), do not yet represent the dawn of the last $\theta\lambda\hat{\iota}\psi\iota\varsigma$, but only the $\dot{\alpha}\rho\chi\dot{\eta}\,\dot{\omega}\delta\dot{\iota}\nu\omega\nu$. As in II Thess.2.1ff., the author warns against expecting the parousia itself, i.e. the real end, in the imminent future, for the present distress of the community does not yet represent its climax. II Thess.2.3 indicates that first of all the great apostasy, caused by the $\ddot{\alpha}\nu\theta\rho\omega\pi\sigma\varsigma\,\tau\hat{\eta}\varsigma\,\dot{\alpha}\nu\sigma\mu\dot{\iota}\alpha\varsigma$, must come; in Mark 13.14, accordingly, there is the 'desolator'. For both, the place of this 'revelation' of cruelty is the sanctuary in Jerusalem. However, for the evangelist this catastrophe is relatively imminent, so that the attentive reader can guess who this enemy of God will be. If the evil one has established himself in the holy place, then the last distress is dawning without delay on the holy land, to some extent as a diabolical miracle, which can only be escaped – like the catastrophe of Sodom (see above, 18) – by immediate flight into the safety of the hills.[118a] It may be that the evangelist, who already uses cryptic language in Mark 13.14, wants the following lively imperatives in vv.15-18, characteristic of apocalyptic, and which in fact tend, rather, to veil the real situation of his community (and of the Jewish-Christian church in Palestine in his day), to be understood allegorically as in Rev.12. There is also a summons to a comparable flight in Rev.18.4. The people of God is to flee from Babylon, which is threatened by destruction through the Antichrist, so that it does not have to be involved in its sins and punishment. Specific historical events cannot be established within this view of the future. It is also striking that in the real $\theta\lambda\hat{\iota}\psi\iota\varsigma$ Mark notes only the fact *that* it will happen, and does not elaborate in any way *how*. That also matches his procedure elsewhere.[119]

All this, though, only helps us to reject a wrong dating of the Gospel to the time after 70, for it is extremely improbable that Mark should have written after the destruction of Jerusalem by Titus without clearly referring to it. The content does not suggest in any way that it was written after this catastrophic year. The question of a closer definition of the time of composition, assuming it to be before 70, still has to be answered.

(c) Mark 13.6-13

If we are to make more progress, we must also consider more closely the context, Mark 13.6-13 (and 21-23), in which Mark describes the actual situation of his community (or the church of his time as a whole).

It seems strange that he encloses the whole large section about the intensification of the messianic woes (vv.8-19) within the double warning against pseudo-Messiahs and pseudo-prophets, which is further stressed by the βλέπετε at the beginning (v.9) and the end (23,cf.33): in his eyes the danger from within of being led astray is even greater than persecution and physical distress from outside the community. So he has to give an emphatic warning against corruption within the church. Now that means that he is writing at a time when the community had been robbed of its great formative authorities by martyrdom – Paul and James presumably in AD 62 and Peter in AD 64 – when apocalyptic enthusiasm overflowed and at the same time there was a danger that the community would be leaderless.

Josephus tells us a good deal about Jewish messianic prophets and charismatic political activists.[120] The first person to whom he gives a name, Theudas, appeared as early as the middle of the forties, soon after the death of Agrippa I,[121] and the last in about AD 73 in Cyrenaica.[122] By contrast, Mark is thinking primarily of Christian false teachers, though Klostermann rightly asks whether 'Christian pseudo-Christs are not an intrinsic contradiction'.[123] We might therefore also suppose that the reference was to figures like Simon Magus, who in fact did make an appearance in Rome (see above, 5). Here Christian and Jewish elements are still partially mixed, as also elsewhere in Mark 13. Judaism and Christianity are not yet so cut off from each other as they are in Matthew and John. Presumably Christians were also influenced by Jewish messianic and syncretistic hopes. However, this warning does not contribute in any way to dating; it remains too indefinite.

Stereotyped apocalyptic themes follow in vv. 7 and 8: ὅταν δὲ ἀκούσητε πολέμους καὶ ἀκοὰς πολέμων ('And when you hear of wars and rumours of wars'), but that does not yet mean the end. Things will get even worse, ἐγερθήσεται γὰρ ἔθνος ἐπ' ἔθνος καὶ βασιλεία ἐπὶ βασιλείαν ('For nation will rise against nation, and kingdom against kingdom'), i.e. political chaos, a war in which everyone fights everyone else, will break out.[124] Earthquakes and famines will provide the necessary apocalyptic accompaniment, but even that is only the 'beginning of the woes'.

Of course we can simply dismiss this reference as apocalyptic horror literature without any historical significance, but that is perhaps treating it too lightly. For Mark with his qualification that this is only the 'birth-pangs of woes' is probably addressing Christians who regarded the contemporary 'wars and rumours of wars' as a sign of the dawn of the τέλος, and thought that the climax of the ὠδῖνες had been reached and indeed passed. So these verses do not fit well into a time of undisturbed – or even restored – imperial peace.

In itself, the time between Tiberius and Nero was a time of marked peace. In none of the years down to Nero's death on 9.6. AD 68 were there chaotic wars to pose a universal threat.[125] The outbreak of the Jewish War, which began with a rebel victory over Cestius Gallus, the governor of Syria, in autumn 66, and was connected with the hope of a Parthian intervention, did not change this situation much. In the wider context of the empire a small fire in the East did not amount to much. Things suddenly changed at a stroke with Nero's suicide as a result of the rebellion of Vindex, Galba and the Praetorian guard. The bloody civil war which now broke out, and which cost three further emperors their lives in one year (Galba, 15.1 69; Otho, 16.4. 69; Vitellius, 20.12. 69), and the rebellion of the Batavians along with other tribes in Germany and Gaul, further unrest in Britain, Africa, on the lower Danube and in Pontus, not to mention the smouldering Jewish war, gave the impression that 'the world was coming off its hinges'.[126] It should, of course, be added that Vespasian and his generals were again completely masters of the situation in all parts of the empire by autumn 70 at the latest. This also tells against putting Mark after 70. From that time on, the apocalyptic interpretation of the contemporary tumults of war rejected by Mark 13.7f. had no specific point of reference.

From this perspective it seems sensible to shift Mark 13.8f., and thus the final redaction of the Gospel of Mark generally, to the year of terror, 69. There was a conflagration in various corners of the empire, and most threateningly in Italy itself. At the beginning of his *Histories* Tacitus describes conditions in almost apocalyptic colours: 'I am beginning a work which contains a wealth of catastrophes, bitter battles, fierce rebellions, indeed acts of terror in times of peace: four princes were murdered, three civil wars were waged, even more wars abroad and not a few which were both...'[127]

Klostermann, who mentions this text, is quite right in saying that here the evangelist is 'simply following a scheme',[128] but he is evidently writing in a situation where other Christians thought that his apocalyptic scheme was now becoming 'bloody reality', i.e. that the end was very near, whereas Mark deliberately plays things down (ἀλλ' οὔπω τὸ τέλος) and describes the catastrophes dawning in his time as merely 'the beginning of the woes'. Earthquakes and famines, which round off the series of terrors, occurred periodically in the Mediterranean. Given the relatively few reports which have come down to us from antiquity, it is, however, striking that we have three references to earthquakes in Italy in AD 68 and reports of unrest over famines in Rome towards the end of Nero's rule. Prophecies of the imminence of a world catastrophe were also circulated in pagan circles towards the end of Nero's reign, whether to the effect that the empire would perish in civil war after nine *saecula* or that catastrophe threatened because the last ruler of Rome was a matricide.[129]

In vv.9-13, the evangelist's gaze turns from the political and cosmic confusion to the fate of the community, which moves him more than the murder and death among the Gentiles: 'But watch for yourselves!' Verse 9 depicts the 'history' of the persecution in the form of a climax of a kind that we can also recognize from Acts. It begins with condemnation by the Jewish authorities, who inflict the traditional penalty of scourging;[130] then follow accusations before the Roman provincial authorities, the procurators in Palestine or the governors like Gallio in Corinth,[131] and finally the emperor himself appears as judge.[132] Paul appealed to him, and was probably executed in Rome in AD 62; in 64 Nero accused the Christians of setting fire to Rome to divert suspicion from himself: *ergo abolendo rumori Nero subdidit reos et quaestissimis poenis adfecit, quos per flagitia invisos vulgus Chrestianos appelabat* ('Consequently, to get rid of the report, Nero fastened the guilt and inflicted the most exquisite tortures on a class hated for their abominations, called Christians by the populace'). That those called by the people *Chrestiani* – i.e., in an ironic word-play, 'doers of the right'- are 'hated because of their abominations' and are accused of being *odium humani generis*, the object of universal hatred, fits in amazingly well with Mark 13.13 καὶ ἔσεσθε μισούμενοι ὑπὸ πάντων διὰ τὸ ὄνομά μου ('And you will be hated by all for my name's sake'). Mark is the first person in the New Testament to speak in this way of universal hatred against the Christians.[133] This remark, which concludes the whole section on persecutions (vv.9-13), is not primarily connected with the dispute which disrupts families in v.12, but is a plerophoristic characterization of the contemporary situation in Mark's community.[134] Is it not obvious that here Mark has in mind those cruel events of 64, when there was the first mass killing of Christians (cf. v.12: καὶ παραδώσει... εἰς θάνατον, and the concluding καὶ θανατώσουσιν αὐτούς)? We know of no comparable persecution in the forty years before and the hundred after.[135] The emphatic theology of suffering and the cross in the Gospel has its very specific *Sitz im Leben* here.[136] Even if the *institutum Neronianum* against the

Christians claimed by Tertullian is historically difficult to demonstrate,[137] in the years after this fearful event the Christians in Rome – and not only there – must have feared new bloody mass persecutions. Pliny's letter to Trajan shows that about forty years later, the persecution of Christians by the highest organs of state was a matter of course. This began – albeit with varying degrees of intensity – with the Neronian persecution. The 'fact' that Christians were to be persecuted under the law was no longer in question for Pliny; he merely wanted an opinion from the emperor on how it was to be carried out.

Here the preceding v.12 marks a clear intensification over against the description of the forensic situation in v.11. The formulation of the verse is based on Micah 7.6 and the prophetic apocalyptic tradition.[138] It is certainly not limited to denunciation and betrayal among blood relations,[139] but involves the *family of the church*. Therefore in v.12a we must suppose that – perhaps under torture[140] – one brother believer betrays another and hands him over to the executioner. One could again refer to Tacitus for this: *Igitur primum correpti qui fatebantur, deinde indicio eorum multitudo ingens... convicti sunt*, 'so they first arrested those who openly confessed (that they were Christians) and then on their evidence an enormous crowd ... was condemned.'[141]

Thus despite its framework of traditional stereotyped apocalyptic formulae, the text in Mark refers to very specific events, so cruel that the community could only understand them in the light of apocalyptic prediction. After the death of the great leader figures, they encouraged an intensified expectation of the end among the oppressed Christians, against which the evangelist wanted to issue a warning.

At the same time Mark can spare himself any martyrological elaboration because – as in his passion narrative – he is not concerned to describe the inhuman suffering of the Christians. Rather, he wants to show that the persecution of the community from the beginning leads to *confession*, and represents the other side of the 'world-wide', eschatologically motivated mission. Therefore Mark 13.10 is not a secondary insertion which breaks up the context; the καί has adversative character,[142] and the verse could almost be translated, 'However, the gospel must first ...'. This relation between persecution and confession becomes paradigmatically clear at the climax of the whole Gospel, i.e. at the death of Jesus. The centurion at the cross, the commander of the execution squad, becomes the first 'confessor' (Mark 15.39).[143]

The confession before the judges, prompted by the Holy Spirit (v.11), to some degree represents a special version of the πρῶτον δεῖ κηρυχθῆναι τὸ εὐαγγέλιον ('first the gospel must be proclaimed); the dark underside is the denunciation and betrayal among the brothers (v.12). What is asked for is perseverance in faith, whether in the face of the threat of martyrdom or in the face of the dawn of messianic woes lasting until the parousia: ὁ δὲ ὑπομείνας εἰς τέλος οὗτος σωθήσεται ('but he who endures to the end shall be saved'). The latter is possible through the miracle performed by God, who has shortened the time of the last and most fearful distress from the beginning of creation for the sake of believers (vv.19f).

The time in which the evangelist is living is coloured by the vivid experience of fearful persecution, an expanding mission, the danger of being led astray, and the tumult of war threatening the whole empire; this tumult is misunderstood by Christians as a sign of the end which is already dawning. Jerusalem is not yet destroyed, but it is probably threatened, though the evangelist has only fairly vague ideas of what is going on there. The climax of the time of distress is still to come, but it is to be expected relatively soon, when the Antichrist, whose features are already becoming evident, takes over the sanctuary in Jerusalem in order to desecrate and destroy it.

But how is the Antichrist to be understood in Mark?[144] What role is expected of him? The figure of the eschatological enemy of God is primarily shaped by the picture which the Daniel apocalypse paints of Antiochus IV Epiphanes and his actions. This also has an influence on Mark 13.

Only a few years or decades after Mark, his portrait takes on completely new and additional features in Jewish and Christian sources, the Fourth and Fifth Sibyllines and Revelation (13.18; 17.11f.,16), as a result of expectations of the *Nero redivivus* who emerges from the Parthian east with tremendous power.[145] The most interesting description of him is that in the Fourth Sibylline, probably written soon after the eruption of Vesuvius on 24/25.8.79 (128ff.). There, immediately after this catastrophe, the matricide Nero, who has fled to the Parthians (119ff.), sets out with a mighty army against the West and crosses the Euphrates (137ff.), in order to plunder the Roman empire. There is no longer any interest here in the temple in Jerusalem, destroyed by Titus (115ff.,125ff.). The end itself, however, only comes when as a result of these events all piety disappears from the earth (152ff.), and takes the form of God's fiery judgment (161ff.,175ff.). The question is whether Mark does not already presuppose this expectation of the *Nero redivivus*: in fact for him the cruel crimes of Nero – not least the persecution of his fellow Christians – and his religious arrogance were still very much in the present.

The following considerations must remain hypothetical. The

reader may decide for himself whether they do not nevertheless explain this difficult text and thus at the same time the historical context of the second Gospel better than other hypotheses.

Nero killed himself on 9.6. AD 68. However, as Suetonius reports, there were Romans who 'now set up pictures of him clad in senatorial robes on the orator's tribunal, or now presented edicts as though he were still alive and would soon return, to the great discomfort of his opponents.' Would not the Christians in Rome have been numbered among these his *inimici*, who needs must fear his return?[146] Some months later, still under Galba, as we hear from Tacitus, 'Achaea and Asia were seized by a false terror, as if Nero were about to arrive; various reports were in circulation about his death, so that an increasing number of people made up stories and even believed that he was still alive.'[147] A slave from Pontus collected a great following, on the pretext that he was Nero, at the beginning of 69, held court on the island of Cythnos in the Cyclades, tricked a centurion of the Syrian army who was on the way to deliver an address of submission to the Praetorians in Rome, and aroused wild expectations: 'as a consequence terror increased: in their desire for rebellion and hatred of the existing situation, many people were emboldened to mention the name very frequently.'[148] Calpurnius, appointed by Galba to be governor of Pamphylia and Galatia, happened to land on the island with two triremes: 'Deliberately adopting a demeanour of mourning and appealing to the loyalty of his soldiers, Pseudo-Nero asked (the two ships' captains) to take him to Syria or Egypt.'[149] Calpurnius overpowered the pretender's ship by a stratagem and had him killed without establishing his identity – perhaps he might indeed have been Nero. His head was brought to Rome. According to the Excerpt of Zonaras, Dio Cassius reported that the aim of the false Nero was to reach the Syrian army, the greater part of which was in Palestine.[150]

This expectation of a *Nero redivivus* was particularly associated with the East as the starting point for a new rule over the world.[151] Ten years later, in 79, a further Pseudo-Nero from Asia Minor, who had first of all enjoyed much success in his homeland and then fled from the Roman authorities over the Euphrates, was received by the Parthians with open arms.[152] The almost contemporaneous Fourth Sibylline Oracle shows that behind this development there was an earlier, already well-formed and widespread expectation. The Christians, not least in Rome after the great persecution – must have been far more excited at the expectation of a return of Nero than over the civil war with the struggle by individual senators, governors and commanders for power. At all events, the old Galba seemed to be no more than an interlude. It was natural to think that the power of evil, with diabolical help, would establish itself at the head of the army in Judaea and take control of the sanctuary into his power. Later, the Fifth Sibylline and Revelation depict the Antichrist as a successful commander who overthrows all resistance; he comes from the East and not only attempts to seize the Holy City but ultimately destroys even Rome itself.[153] Here old expectations in the book of Daniel and the threat to the temple by the divine claims of Caligula were bound up with the earliest expectations of the first serious persecution of the Christians.

In addition, in an enthusiastic way Nero himself had been interested in the East and its mysterious religions. He often planned to travel in the East and ultimately wanted to escape there.[154] Astrologers are said to have prophesied his expulsion from Rome and 'rule over the East', some even 'specifically over the kingdom of Jerusalem'.[155] According to a rabbinic account Nero fled and became a proselyte, so that he did not have to destroy the temple.[156]

Against this background we can understand the expectation that the Antichrist would soon take possession of the sanctuary. As Nicanor once threatened – if we want to relate Mark 13.2 to it (see p.15 above) – he would rase it utterly and thus put himself in God's place, at the same time beginning a reign of terror with the persecution of all the faithful, which could only be avoided by an immediate flight 'into the hills'. εἰς τὰ ὄρη is again a phrase from the apocalyptic tradition and cannot be identified with a historical flight to Pella or anywhere else. In Rev.12 the woman, i.e. the community, flees before the snares of the dragon εἰς τὴν ἔρημον (v.6), which is almost synonymous, and there, like the persecuted Elijah, is fed by God. This is basically the same tradition.

There is no longer any need to describe all the horrifying dimensions of the last eschatological time of distress unleashed by the 'revelation' of the Antichrist at the scene of the sanctuary; the θλῖψις οἵα οὐ γέγονεν τοιαύτη ἀπ᾽ ἀρχῆς κτίσεως... ἕως τοῦ νῦν is sufficient indication of the final intensification. In this way the evangelist certainly also connects the expectation of an indescribable visitation by the enemy of God, further surpassing all the persecutions which lie in the past, with every other possible kind of plague depicted for us by Revelation in accordance with the tradition of the Jewish Christian community. For Mark the allusion to the well-known formula of Dan.12.1 is enough: *sapienti sat*. It is enough to know the fact; the elaboration of the manner of its happening can be dispensed with. People had already had their object lesson on that in AD 64. It was enough to know that things would get even worse. At the same time, this is an explanation of the special message to the reader in v.14b. Here is no reference from an earlier apocalyptic flysheet, long obsolete, which had slipped in by mistake; rather, the author points his finger to the dawn of the real distress, which must not surprise and overcome the community, and thus to the inhuman author of it who is to be expected, and whom the community already knows.

It must be in a position to pay attention to the *real* signs of the times, persevere steadfastly in the present tribulation, which will become even worse in the near future (v.13b),[157] and simply await its Lord who is to come (v.20). Therefore it must not be misled by false revealers, messianic pretenders and pseudo-prophets (vv.5f.,20ff.), otherwise it will not survive this time of distress.

So I believe that in contrast to the other Gospels, we can determine the time of the composition of the second Gospel relatively accurately, as also its author and the tradition which shaped him.[158] It presumably came into being in the politically turbulent time after the murder of Nero and Galba and before the renewal of the Jewish War under Titus, i.e. say between the winter of 68/69 and the winter of 69/70. The destruction of the temple is not yet presupposed; rather, the author expects the appearance of Antichrist (as *Nero redivivus*) in the sanctuary and the dawn of the last, severest stage of the messianic woes before the parousia.

The striking encipherment of the statements in ch.13, especially in 13.14, is understandable in view of the tense political situation. Like the other earliest Christian writings, the earliest Gospel was part of the underground literature, for oral and written prophecies *de salute principis vel summa rei publicae* were prohibited on pain of death in the time of the empire. Mark 13 contained such a prophecy.[159]

4. The origin of the Gospel

Finally, something should be said about the *place of origin* of the Gospel. It has already become clear that along with the tradition of the early church and the whole of earlier scholarship, I presuppose this to be Rome. The constantly repeated assertion that the work was written in Syria-Palestine – most recently, Antioch has also been mentioned – has no really serious basis.[160] It has become a bad habit among New Testament scholars to repeat erroneous opinions unchecked so long that they become a general assumption. One factor in particular which tells against Palestine and Syria is the complete ignorance of the situation in Judaea between 66 and 69. In Syria, as the anti-Jewish pogroms in numerous cities, including Damascus, show, people watched developments in Judaea very tensely; from there they seemed especially threatening. Hardly anything of that can be traced in Mark 13. It is utterly unrealistic. Rather, the Gospel of Mark, not least Mark 13, is written at a clear geographical distance from Palestine, for Gentile Christians, who have no inkling of the real political situation there. The fact that it nevertheless has countless features of Palestinian Judaism is connected with the fact that it was written by a Jewish Graeco-Palestinian, John Mark, who was a missionary companion of Peter for some time. Numerous Latinisms[161] point to an origin in Rome; these cannot simply be dismissed with a reference to the language of the Roman administration in Palestine. The explanation in Mark 12.42 of the widow's mite as λεπτὰ δύο, ὅ ἐστιν κοδράντης, indicates a place where the Greek τὸ λεπτόν (νόμισμα) was not understood and had to be interpreted as the Roman *quadrans* (a quarter of an *as*). Luke omits Mark's explanation. In Plutarch, on the other hand, the Roman *quadrans* is explained for the Greeks.[162] We find a similar position in Mark 15.16, where it is said that the soldiers took Jesus ἔσω τῆς αὐλῆς, into the interior of the prefect's residence, i.e. the former Herodian palace, where Mark adds the Latin explanation ὅ ἐστιν πραιτώριον, which would have been quite unnecessary for Greek-speaking Gentile Christians in the East.

The remarkable thing about the Gospel of Mark is that it contains not only more Aramaic formulae than any other original Greek literary text,[163] but also more Latinisms. Such an accumulation of Latinisms is unusual in comparison with other writings. At best one could point to the Shepherd of Hermas, which was similarly written in Rome. The whole matter needs a thorough investigation, for which there is no more room here. However, in conclusion I would like to give a further indication.

In Mark 7.24, in 'the region of Tyre' (τὰ ὅρια Τύρου), a woman comes to Jesus. Mark strikingly gives her two descriptions: Ἑλληνίς, Συροφοινίκισσα τῷ γένει (Mark 7.26). Ἑλληνίς to describe the language and the ethnic Φοινί(κι)σσα would have been enough by themselves. If the Gospel came from Syria, Συροφοινίκισσα, which in that case would be geographically vague, would seem nonsensical. Not so in Rome. There it was possible to make a clear distinction between the much more familiar Carthaginians, as Λιβυφοίνικες in Carthage, and the Phoenicians, who belonged to the province of Syria. In Roman satire (Lucilius, Book 15, fr.496f.; Juvenal 8,159f.) and in Pliny the Elder, *Natural History* 7,201, and in Latin inscriptions in Italy and in Africa, *Syrophoenix* therefore appears as a special indication of origin.[164] On the other hand it is totally absent from the numerous *gentilicia* on the Egyptian papyri.

Thus in the case of the earliest Gospel we are in the happy position of being able to define a historical point of origin with more accuracy than in the case of the later Gospels. It was written in a time of severe affliction in Rome after the persecution of Nero and before the destruction of Jerusalem, probably during AD 69, the 'year of revolution'. More use should be made of this in its interpretation than has so far been the case.

II

Literary, Theological and Historical
Problems in the Gospel of Mark

1. A disputed Gospel

No Gospel has occupied scholars so intensively over the last decade as that of Mark, and nowhere has the discussion been more heated than in connection with it. In Germany, four extensive commentaries have appeared one after the other in rapid succession, and the irreconcilable differences between them show up the dilemmas of research into Mark. The monumental two-volume commentary by Rudolf Pesch[1] regards Mark as the 'conservative redactor'[2] who for the most part uses written sources – here Pesch parts company with the early form-critical approach – and works on his traditions sparingly and with restraint, refraining from ambitious literary and theological elaboration. Therefore for Pesch the Gospel of Mark is the main source for a reconstruction of the activity and passion of Jesus.

At the opposite extreme to this stands the radical 'redaction-critical' commentary by Walter Schmithals.[3] He throws overboard the results of the form criticism of his own teacher R.Bultmann, which for long had hypnotized scholars,[4] and in a final, consistent development of the work of Wrede sees Mark as a poet and theologian creating his own composition; in his view, by using a minimum of tradition and under the influence of a non-Christian Galilean Jesus sect, Mark has produced something like a 'Jesus romance' with a marked theological profile. Here he was the first to introduce into the earliest history of Christianity the problem of the narrative Jesus tradition. Having spoken of 'Mark', though, I must correct myself: the evangelist was not this creative theological genius; that role was played by the unknown author of a basic document. Schmithals attributes all that is 'fine and good' to the latter; the evangelist himself largely corrupted this unique outline by introducing the messianic secret and many other follies.

For all their basic differences, the authors of both commentaries do, though, agree on one thing: in their almost unlimited confidence in the possibilities of literary criticism in the Second Gospel, a confidence which again dominates wide areas of New Testament scholarship today. Here we find ourselves taken back almost to the hey-day of dissection into literary sources, in the nineteenth century, when attempts were made to extract an earlier 'Ur-Markus' or a number of sources from the present Gospel. Thus Schmithals makes a razor-sharp division between 'light and darkness', the basic document and the additions by the 'dumb fool' Mark; with no less confidence, Pesch extracts the many written sources of the evangelist, especially the pre-Marcan passion narrative, deriving from the Jerusalem community of the late thirties. This, he believes, begins as early as Mark 8.27ff. Here he feels that we are on rock-hard historical ground.

The third commentary by Joachim Gnilka and the fourth by Josef Ernst[5] attempt, each in its own way, to find a balance between the extremes, which is not always easy. One could describe them both with Ovid's words, *medio tutissimus ibis* – you are safest in the middle.[6]

2. A collector or a creative theologian?

(a) Redaction criticism and form criticism

All in all, we might say that the tendency of scholars, above all in the USA, but also in France and Germany, is towards a purely redaction-critical approach, sometimes supplemented by structuralism, which neglects traditio-historical and historical questions. Even more radically than in Bultmann's time, many scholars believe that it is impossible in practice and a sign of antiquated methodology to ask historical questions about the earthly Jesus. One might almost suppose that, in the case of the earliest Gospel, views take a similar direction to that which has long been prominent in the case of the Gospel of John: i.e., the concern is only with the theological 'bias' of the author and perhaps still with the sources which he used. Insufficient attention is paid to the fact that the author is not writing a theological treatise or even a polemical work which seeks to contest belief in miracles or a *theologia gloriae*,[7] but is narrating history, or more exactly, that he is describing the activity of Jesus, from his call to his messianic office to the message of the resurrection given by the angel at the empty tomb – in a manner that can well be compared with a biography, which at that time could take many different forms.[8] Those who heard the Gospel of Mark and the subsequent

Gospels simply understood them as unique 'biographies' which bear witness to the career and teaching of the unique Messiah and Son of God, Jesus of Nazareth. No one in antiquity thought that the Gospels were a literary genre of a quite new and special kind. It was not the literary genre that was unique but the person described in it and his work of salvation.

This kind of 'biographical' narrative, which is not connected with an ongoing chronology – that only emerges after the entry into Jerusalem (Mark 11.1ff.) – but consists of 'small units', i.e. brief anecdotal scenes which are joined together by brief transitional passages and between which individual groups of logia are sometimes interspersed, certainly has parallels in antiquity, both in the 'Jewish' and in the 'Hellenistic' sphere. However, I cannot go into that question in more detail here.

In this connection it is crucial to note that the collection of material, which recalls the rabbinic collections of anecdotes (Aboth of R.Nathan) or some Old Testament narrative cycles (the Samson, David, Elijah and Elisha stories), indicates that Mark is not presenting romantic fiction, freely composed, with a theological colouring, but is working with material from tradition. An expert in Semitic popular tradition like Julius Wellhausen demonstrated that clearly, well before the discovery of form criticism. In Mark, we look in vain for the 'revelation discourses', so typical of the Fourth Gospel – even in Mark 13 he uses predominantly pre-existing tradition. This bond with earlier individual traditions distinguishes Mark quite fundamentally from later romantic apocryphal testimonies like the Protevangelium of James, the Infancy Gospel of Thomas or the so-called Acts of Pilate, and for that very reason a *radical* redaction-critical approach cannot do him justice. Here form criticism still has an important task. Mark does not simply want to invent something new; he wants to find an appropriate way of expressing the Jesus tradition, which is binding on him. Here Pesch is quite right; the question is simply in what form Mark had the tradition, whether in written sources which can still be reconstructed by literary criticism or in oral form, already shaped kerygmatically by worship. The 'pre-Marcan collections' which people are nowadays fond of discovering in the Second Gospel – e.g. in Mark 2-4 – cannot in any way go back to a written source by another author. What is supposed to be 'critical' scholarship simply posits things here which cannot be proved. The fact that long after Mark there was still a wealth of oral traditions about Jesus, many of them, of course, with a dubious form, is shown not only by Papias' zeal as a collector, but even more by the hyperbolic remark in John 21.25. *Radical* redaction critics basically do not know what to make of this kind of account; on the contrary, it is striking how in their concern to dehistoricize Mark's narrative they have recently found themselves led into an unbounded allegorization of the material, as they have to attribute to it a deeper, unhistorical, symbolic-dogmatic significance.[9]

On the other hand, though, the form-critical approach which has long prevailed has misunderstood the theological and literary competence of the second evangelist. Because he wrote in such a simple unliterary style, and with often apparent artlessness strung together individual pericopes one after the other; because the literary framework of the Gospel, which demonstrably comes from him, was amazingly simple, he was seen even more than the authors of the first and third Gospels, rooted more strongly in literary convention, as the 'collector and redactor'.[10] Rudolf Bultmann goes so far as to claim that: 'Mark is not sufficiently master of his material to be able to venture on a systematic construction himself.'[11]

(b) The arrangement of a dramatic narrative

In fact more recent investigations have again disclosed how marvellously Mark has arranged his Gospel. This is not a completely new insight. Adolf Jülicher, who was relatively critical of form criticism, already came to the conclusion that 'The arrangement of the whole is well considered and effective.' Of course we cannot echo Jülicher's other remark just as it is – 'for on the whole Jesus' life developed in the way in which Mark portrayed it.'[12] We simply know too little about this life as a connected whole.

However, one may say that Mark constructed his work as a dramatic narrative in several 'acts', which might almost be said to correspond to the laws of ancient tragedy as worked out by Aristotle in his *Poetics*. In the same way it has proved possible to rediscover in it the laws governing arrangement in ancient rhetoric. This markedly literary approach may seem to be alien to the material or even to amount to playing with the Gospel, but it does help us to a better understanding of the work, which has been misunderstood by radical form criticism.[13]

In this way a very clear construction has been discovered in Mark, full of inner tension and very consistent. I do not want to discuss here the numerous attempts at division, but largely follow the proposal put forward by F.G.Lang:[14]

The evangelist begins with a 'salvation historical' 'prologue' (1.1-13), which contains the appearance of John the Baptist and Jesus' baptism and temptation. As the last representative of the old covenant, already with an eschatological stamp, John the Baptist provides the external stimulus to the calling of Jesus to his 'messianic office'.

There follows as the 'first act' the account of the activity of Jesus in Galilee (1.14-3.6), before the appointment of the Twelve. At the beginning we find a rhetorical *propositio* comparable to the programmatic summary of the proclamation of Jesus in 1.14,15. This account comes to a dramatic conclusion in 3.6: the first resolve by the Herodians and Pharisees, as representatives of the spiritual and religious leaders, to kill Jesus, after a series of controversial discussions.

The 'second act' depicts the climax of Jesus' activity, beginning with the gathering of the crowds (3.7f.), the appointment of the Twelve and the great miracles. Here the chapter of parables, 4, signalizes the hardening of heart among the people which was produced by the preaching of Jesus. Mark 6.1-6, the outright rejection in Nazareth, is an important turning point; in this pericope Mark very skilfully introduces all the necessary biographical details about Jesus' profession and family which we did not have in the brief introduction of Jesus in 1.9. The 'second act' comes to a climax – in contrast to the external success of Jesus, but in analogy to 3.5 - with Jesus' reproach to the disciples that they completely misunderstand him, and indeed that their hearts are hardened (8.14-22) because they have not understood the significance of his authoritative teaching (1.22,27) and actions. Not only the leaders of the people, who have been Jesus' opponents from the start (3.5f.), and the crowds, but also Jesus' relatives and neighbours, indeed even his disciples, refuse to believe in him. It is this *universal* disobedience which necessitates Jesus' course towards a representative expiatory death. A novellistic digression about the execution of John the Baptist (6.14-29) is framed by the sending out of the Twelve. It demonstrates that there is no stopping the message of conversion for the sake of the coming kingdom of God, and is at the same time a pointer to the passion as the goal of the whole dramatic narrative. The miracle stories also move clearly towards a climax. They begin with a simple exorcism (1.23ff.) in the synagogue and reach their peak in the twofold feeding of the five thousand and the four thousand (Mark 6.35-44; 8.1-9).

The Gospel achieves its *peripeteia* in the third act, which to some degree brings the *anagnorisis*,[15] the disclosure of the messianic secret, in Peter's confession. F.G.Lang comments on this:[16] 'In stylistic terms, the erroneous views about Jesus are first reported (v.28) and then Peter confesses Jesus' true identity (v.29). This produces a new situation for the disciples: being in the know about Jesus, they have been sworn to silence (v.30). This leads to a new tension which is only resolved by Jesus' acknowledgment before the Sanhedrin of who he is (14.61f.). Moreover, up to 8.21 Jesus has external success, visible in his mighty acts and the advent of the crowd; 8.31ff. equally abruptly brings the *peripeteia*,[17] the sudden shift to "misfortune": in accordance with all the artistic rules... the announcement of the passion contains the element of necessity (v.31) and at the same time the element of surprise, in that Peter makes a protest against it (vv.32f.).' The intrinsic necessity of the course of suffering is manifest at the end of the 'third act' in 10.45 (see below, 142 n.24); Peter's confession as *anagnorisis* is matched in 10.46-52 by the messianic cry for help from the blind beggar immediately before the last stage on the way up to Jerusalem. It shows that the mysterious knowledge of Jesus' messianic authority has spread despite the prohibition – and it is precisely this that will be the cause of his doom in Jerusalem.

The *lusis* or *katastrophe*, the violent breaking of the knot that has been tied,[18] takes place in Jerusalem; it is directly prepared for by the 'fourth act' (11.1-13.37), with the entry, the cleansing of the temple and the controversies with representatives of different groups, and the final eschatological instruction of the disciples.

With 14.1, the final resolve of the leaders of the people to put Jesus to death, the 'fifth and last act' and the *pathos*[19] proper begin; in a paradoxical way this ends with the confession of the Gentile centurion that the crucified man is the Son of God (15.39).

The deposition in the tomb and the discovery of the empty tomb form the 'epilogue' (15.40-16.8); here the Galilean women, who hitherto had been completely passed over, keep the action going and form the bridge between the crucifixion and what happens at the tomb (15.40-42,47; 16.1ff.). One might almost be tempted to compare the appearance of the angel to the women at the empty tomb with the *Deus ex machina*[20] of the tragedies of Euripides, who ushers in the miraculous change that brings a happy ending.

Of course the division proposed here is not the only possible one; the ancient theories are not themselves agreed over the form of a dramatic *fabula*. One might think of only three 'acts':[21] 1.14-8.26; 8.27-10.52; 11.1-15.39. This, too, preserves the decisive points of the tying of the knot, the *peripeteia* and the *resolution*, connected with the theme of *anagnorisis*.

Be this as it may, in terms of extent, construction and inner drama the Second Gospel remains a work which can be illuminated in an amazing way by the rules which Aristotle established in connection with the successful form of literary mimesis. The statement from his *Poetics*, τὸ γὰρ καλὸν ἐν μεγέθει καὶ τάξει ἐστί,[22] can directly be applied to this work, which displays a compact, recognizable, well-ordered and thought-out form.

F.G.Lang and Standaert go one stage further and would even presuppose as the literary aim of the evangelist the well-known effect of φόβος καὶ ἔλεος, fear and pity, which according to Aristotle the tragedy should produce in the public.[23] However, in this work, which from the beginning was created for worship, and indeed in my view grew out of worship, we may not in principle presuppose any division between 'theological' and 'literary' aim. As a kerygmatic narrative the Gospel has only one aim: to evoke and strengthen faith; the literary aims of producing tension, exaltation and deep emotion are completely subordinate to this.

All in all, the form of the Gospel, composed in such a magisterial way, along with analogies between it and the dramatic *fabula* and rhetoric, should not lead us to questionable conclusions about the origin, education and intention of the author (see below, 46ff.). The dramatic element in his work is essentially different from that of Greek tragedy, for all its contacts with Aristotle's poetic theory. It is not a matter here of the intertwining of guilt and destiny, but of the presence of salvation precisely in the suffering and death of the Son of God - though this is misunderstood time and again.

(c) Arrangement and theological reflection

Almost every pericope and every logion has its well-considered place and its paradigmatic character. One could, for example, suppose that the soteriological significance of the death of Jesus as a representative atoning death was not of central importance for Mark because in the whole of the Gospel it is mentioned only twice, at 10.45 and 14.24. However, if we look more closely, we discover that both passages are stressed by the context: 10.45 brings to an end the whole instruction of the disciples before the entry into Jerusalem, which from 8.31 stands under the shadow of the suffering Son of Man, and 14.24, the saying about the blood of the covenant which is shed for many, marks the climax of the Last Supper scene. In other words, the position of the two texts in the wider context of the Gospel as a whole shows how unjustified such a judgment would be.[24]

The fact that Jesus forgives sins is expressed clearly only once, yet this is particularly important for the understanding of Jesus in Mark; that is the very reason why Mark has made it the theme of the first controversy with the religious leaders of Israel who are thinking to themselves in terms of the accusation which brings down on Jesus the death sentence from the Sanhedrin: 'He blasphemes God.' The first and last conflicts with his opponents agree in this verdict (2.7; 14.64).

We can only understand the significance of this action, which is narrated just once, at the beginning of Jesus' activity, in connection with the two statements about atonement towards the end, if we investigate the description of the overwhelming power of sin in Mark, which Jesus encounters through his activity and death. It does not just affect his opponents or the mass of the people, but equally the disciples, including their spokesman Peter, and indeed even the women who run from the empty tomb 'in fear and trembling' and do not obey the word of the angel (16.8).[25] Here sin apparently has the last word, and yet is already overcome by the atoning death of Jesus.

Mark does not narrate events and traditions simply by chance: what he selects and describes has a deeper significance, as a 'typical ideal', from the call of the disciples up to Gethsemane and the crucifixion of Jesus as king of the Jews. *However, this strictness in his overall plan does not simply dispense with historicity; Mark only reports history which has undergone the deliberate reflection of faith.*[26] Even apparent incidental remarks like 7.3f.; 13.10,14b; 14.9 and so on are significant as theological reflection. He does not create new narratives and sayings of Jesus in order to develop his own christology and soteriology, but uses a very deliberate process of selecting and ordering material in which hardly anything is left to chance.

In complete contrast to the form-critical approach, which saw the Synoptic Gospels – and here again Mark in particular – as a product of popular 'minor literature' growing up unconsciously, Standaert, in his investigation which is so surprising at many points, has conjectured on the basis of the discovery of dramatic or even rhetorical artifices in this mysterious work that the author had had a thorough training in rhetoric and literature. Only by his simple style did he accommodate himself to the capacity of his hearers to understand.[27] However, an analysis of biographical narratives from the Jewish Old Testament tradition, like Esther, Susanna, Judith,[28] the David and Elijah narratives and especially the Joseph story, could show that the rules of the well-ordered *fabula* which Aristotle brought to light were also valid outside the Graeco-Roman world.[29] The art of narrative is older, and does not necessarily presuppose academic education in the sense of Hellenistic rhetoric. That does not exclude the possibility that the rhetorical presentation of teaching, the capacity for lively narrative and refined discourse, could be learned in the Greek-speaking synagogue and the earliest community for missionary purposes.[30]

3. The fidelity of the dramatic narrator to history

It is clear from what has been said so far that the extremely different assessments of the Second Gospel by scholars rest on the fact that this work – probably more than any other New Testament writing, at least for the modern reader – is concerned with a *coincidentia oppositorum* which combines what German theological scholarship for a long time saw as an irreconcilable opposition: on the one hand narrative with dramatic tension, a clear theological and kerygmatic profile worked out with great literary skill, and on the other what for the circumstances of antiquity was a very respectable fidelity to tradition and history. All this is presented in an outwardly simple form and barbaric style. Mark certainly does not deal with his material more freely than, say, Plutarch. He selects examples from the tradition and shapes it, and of course he has a theological bias, but he does not simply have to invent things out of thin air. In him the separation of 'tradition' and 'redaction' is very difficult – if we leave aside the simple frameworks and stereotyped introductions – since like most of the writers of antiquity he adapts the material from the source or the tradition to his own style.[31] Precisely in so doing, he wants what he presents to be the gospel of Jesus Christ, εὐαγγέλιον Ἰησοῦ Χριστοῦ, that brings together two apparently irreconcilable things:[32] the narrative historical and biographical account and the proclamation of salvation as an address. Indeed, even for Mark, salvation did not lie in the changing theological constructions relevant to a particular period, but in what God had achieved for all men through his Son, the 'carpenter' Jesus of Nazareth (Mark 1.9; 6.3), from the Sea of Galilee to Golgotha and the tomb in the rock, in a relatively short space of time about forty years before he wrote.[33] This obliges the narrator *also* to report the event in the past as it is detached from the present – a present of which the evangelist is only too well aware.[34] The hearer is invited to turn aside, to spend some time with the preacher and miracle worker Jesus in distant, foreign Galilee, to stand beside him in the last battle in Jerusalem and take part in his passion, like the women, from afar. At that time, when the Son of God was delivered over to be ultimately forsaken by God, God himself founded the new covenant in his blood and sealed it through the resurrection of the dead.

In his account, which retells a past event, Mark expresses in detail what Paul seeks to express in extremely concentrated form, focussed on a single point, through the aorists of his confessional formulae and the reference to the cross of Jesus – though that should not be wrongly understood as a mere theological cipher. He describes the action of God in his Christ which took place in the past once and for all, and which preceded all the re-action of believers.[35] We could regard the statement in Rom.5.8, 'God showed his love for us in that Christ died (ἀπέθανεν) for us while we were still sinners' as a heading for the whole of the second Gospel. For this 'passion narrative with extended introduction'[36] is from the beginning directed towards the death of Jesus, since that alone is the real foundation of the salvation of believers. Therefore particularly in Mark this can be said to be integral to the 'lived life of Jesus'.[37]

Here lies the fundamental difference from the logia tradition, which Mark knows in a very distinctive form and takes for granted as being familiar to his audience. That he is writing later than the collection of sayings of Jesus in the so-called logia source follows from the fact that where he is working with individual traditions and logia which also appear in Q, his version is always more developed and later. One might almost say that he is writing the theologically necessary complement to such a collection only of the sayings of Jesus, which has become inadequate from the standpoint of the post-Easter community because – as Q shows – it lacks the kerygma of the death and resurrection and also an explicit christology. In my view this is an indication of the age and originality of such collections; the basic material in them could go back to the Hellenists in Jerusalem and they are probably already presupposed by Paul. Quite apart from the passion narrative, Mark introduces predominantly what is lacking in the logia source: miracle stories, controversies and teaching specifically directed towards the disciples.[38] The sayings tradition which Mark incorporates was, of course, substantially different from the so-called Q source which Matthew and Luke used; therefore it cannot simply be said that he knew Q in the form that we find in Matthew and Luke. However, he was familiar with the sayings tradition of Jesus, though he included only relatively little of it in his Gospel. Because Mark put what we miss in the sayings tradition, the kerygma of the passion and christology, at the centre of his 'story of Jesus', he could describe it not as λόγια κυρίου, i.e. 'words of (the revelation of) the Lord', but with good reason as εὐαγγέλιον Ἰησοῦ Χριστοῦ (see below 53, 58, cf. 72, 82f.).

At the same time, however, that means that he is not writing his account of Jesus to captivate the reader, to satisfy a need for historical information or to admonish and improve him morally - although according to the standards of antiquity he also does all this. Still less does he want to satisfy pious desires for sensation through narrating the miracles of Jesus, any more than he wants to counter an exaggerated desire for miracle. Jesus' actions are quite ambivalent; they provoke the accusation that he is in league with the devil, i.e. is a magician, and they do not produce permanent, constant faith even in the disciples. Against the background of the *dynameis* of Jesus, the hardness of heart which affects everyone without exception appears all the more terrifying. For the evangelist the miracles are a reference to the messianic *exousia* of Jesus and an expression of the eschatological fulfilment of prophetic promises. Both these things cannot be understood in terms of the worn-out catchphrase *theios aner*.

Of course this is not to forget the reference to the present experience of his community, the direct address to his readers or hearers. The terrifying example of the disciples is at the same time a warning, and the invitation to self-denial, discipleship and taking up the cross cannot escape any hearer. The fatal error in the interpretation of the Gospels in general and of Mark in particular has been that scholars have thought that they had to decide between preaching and historical narration, that here there could only be an either-or. In reality the 'theological' contribution of the evangelist lies in the fact that he combines both these things inseparably: he preaches by narrating; he writes history and in so doing proclaims. This is to some degree the *theological* side of that *coincidentia oppositorum* which marks out his work. At this point he has the model of Old Testament historiography before him, where this unity of narration and proclamation is often visible.

The immediate reference to the present becomes clear above all in Mark 13, the so-called synoptic apocalypse, which for Mark represents the testament, the eschatological farewell discourse of Jesus. In this way it contains something like an extremely abbreviated 'church history in a nutshell', which leads up to the time at which the author was writing, presumably shortly before the destruction of Jerusalem.[39] The last word of Jesus, 'What I tell you' – i.e. the four disciples who are standing around Jesus, seated (13.3) on the Mount of Olives, looking at the temple – 'I say to all, "Watch!"' (13.37; cf.14.38), shows that in the time of the evangelist the saying of Jesus addressed to the disciples in the Gospel has become a saying for a persecuted and threatened church which is eagerly awaiting the parousia of the Son of Man.

4. The messianic secret

Following William Wrede, scholars have been fond of describing the 'messianic secret' as the key to understanding the second Gospel. There is some degree of justification in this, but the perspective must not become too one-sided. Thus it can be said with a pinch of salt that the question of the messianic authority and mission of Jesus gives the whole work its unity and that the theme of hiddenness is an essential part of it. However, all this is not artificially foisted on recalcitrant material, but is bound up with the innermost nature of the event that is described. Moreover, the whole complex has far more layers and is much more complicated than has been long assumed. Thus the way of Jesus to the cross, his expiatory death for the many and the disciples' taking up the cross is just as important for Mark as the deliberate veiling of Jesus' messianic claim before the people. Only in suffering does the Marcan Jesus manifest his messianic status in the full sense. Messianic status and representative suffering belong indissolubly together.

More recent research has long been at odds over the unity, extent and significance of the so-called messianic secret precisely because of these complications in the matter.[40] In the strict sense it applies only to two direct statements by Jesus: the first command to the disciples to be silent, after Peter's confession (8.30) and before the first prediction of the passion, and the second, when they are coming down the mount of revelation (9.9), to those with him, that they are to 'tell no one what they had seen until the Son of man had risen from the dead'. For Mark these are the consequences of the tremendous fact that the Messiah and Son of God did not reveal himself immediately in 'the glory of his Father with the holy angels' (8.38) but obediently trod the way of the cross. For contemporary Judaism, as for the ancient world generally, this was an unheard-of and thoroughly offensive idea, which the disciples *could* not understand because it contradicted the traditional messianic expectation of salvation.

It is significant that from 9.13 on, the theme of the 'messianic *secret*' fades completely into the background, at least outwardly, and in essence has already been done away with from the time of Bartimaeus' confession in Jericho (10.48) of Jesus as 'Son of David'. This time the *disciples* want to prevent the public confession, while Jesus positively accepts the cry. The situation has changed. The question of authority (11.28) already indicates that the leaders of the people know of Jesus' claim and want to use it to lure him out into the open; the high priest's question (14.61) is no longer a surprise: it simply puts into words ideas which have long been in the air and could already have motivated the accusation connected with the saying about destroying and rebuilding the temple (14.58). The surprise was Jesus' clear, unsurpassable confession of his unique status. There is no support in the text for the disclosure romance which Schweitzer wove around the unveiling of the messianic secret, to the effect that Judas had betrayed it to the leaders of the people. Mark does not present the whole matter as mysteriously as that. Indeed, already from Mark 9.11 onwards there is no longer any injunction to the disciples to keep silent.

The other ingredients of the so-called messianic secret that Wrede constructed do not form a real unity, so they no longer call for any questionable overall theory, which in any case cannot be worked out strictly; these elements first of all have to be explained on their own terms. It goes without saying that Jesus rejects the acclamation that comes from the supernatural knowledge of the demons; he is in a battle with them. Here one could refer to James 2.19: 'the demons believe and tremble'. But their special knowledge, expressed in the call of the Stronger One who conjures them out, is inappropriate, and therefore they must be put to silence. The powers of evil cannot be legitimate witnesses to Jesus' divine sonship.[41] At the same time, Mark wants to use this theme to demonstrate the contrast between the people and the disciples, who do not yet know Jesus' status, and the invisible world of the spirits, who from the beginning have recognized Jesus as their messianic conqueror.

The commands to keep silent after healings, which are not maintained consistently, are meant to make clear that as a miracle worker Jesus wants to remain hidden. He wards off the press of the masses, in contrast to the popular miracle workers and magicians of the Hellenistic and Roman period, who could often be encountered in the Jewish sphere as well.[42] Both the command to keep silent at exorcisms and the prohibition to those who are healed against proclaiming their healing aloud may thus go back to the behaviour of Jesus himself.

As H. Räisänen has shown, the so-called theory of parables (4.10ff.), i.e. that Jesus speaks in riddles to harden the heart of the people, has even less direct connection with the messianic secret. It is meant to explain the fact – which later caused offence to the community – that despite the teaching and the miracles of Jesus, the people did not recognize him in true faith but rejected him. They could not believe, because they did not understand Jesus' proclamation in 'riddles'.[43]

The hardening of heart and misunderstanding among the disciples in connection with Jesus' way to his passion are also to be separated from the messianic secret proper: they correspond to the lack of illusion in the anthropology of the evangelist, who in his narrative, and without special terminology, brings out something that was also familiar to Paul. One could refer to Rom.3.22ff. as a commentary on that: 'for there is no difference' (in Mark between the disciples and the people),[44] 'for they have all sinned and fallen short of the glory of God, and are without merit justified by his grace through redemption in Jesus Christ.' As I have already said (given contemporary exegesis of Mark one cannot repeat this often enough), it is no coincidence that the instruction of the disciples ends with the logion about the service of the Son of Man – Servant of God for the many (10.45), and that at the heart of the Last Supper we have the saying about the blood of the covenant which is shed (14.24). Marcan soteriology is based on these two sayings. Even self-denial and the discipleship of the cross are only possible under this sign: the logion 8.37, 'for what may a man give as ransom for his life?', which concludes the whole complex, indeed points to the necessity of the sacrifice of Christ, as does 10.27, the answer to the terrified question of the disciples, 'then who can be saved?': 'With man it is impossible but not with God.'

Hardly anyone still puts forward in its original form Wrede's famous theory, taken over by Bultmann,[45] that Mark stressed the messianic secret so much because the evangelist (or the tradition with which he was working) wanted to conceal the fact that in reality Jesus had no messianic self-awareness. The 'messianic secret' is usually no longer explained by an attempted historical reconstruction but as an expression of specifically Marcan theology, predominantly his *theologia crucis*. However, the Marcan theology of the passion does not need such secondary expedients.[46] Quite apart from that, there is the question whether one may simply attribute to the redactional work of the evangelist all the *very* different components which are combined under the handy formula of the messianic secret. They are too complex, indeed too disparate for this. Certainly all this can *also* be subsumed under the umbrella phrase 'the mystery of Jesus and his way of suffering'. But this 'mystery of Jesus' is not a secondary theory imposed by Mark on the whole tradition; its real basis lies in the mystery of the earthly Jesus himself.

In my view the phenomena of the messianic secret – in contrast to Wrede's theories, reduced and disparate – are best explained in terms of the tradition with which Mark worked. This tradition was still aware of Jesus' messianic claim, the reality of which should not be doubted, since otherwise, historically and in terms of their content, the whole of his activity up to his passion, which is without parallel in the history of ancient religion, not to mention the development of the earliest christology after Easter, would be incomprehensible. We have no indication whatsoever from the history of tradition that the status of Messiah in Judaism was connected in any way with the resurrection of a righteous man or prophet from the dead. Therefore it is hard to derive the messianic status of Jesus simply from the resurrection appearances. Appearances of the dead in a transfigured form and messianic status are two completely different things. Christology cannot be derived solely from the resurrection event – no matter how it is interpreted. The root must be sought in Jesus' conduct and execution. Of course he did not express his messianic claim in a public proclamation, as in the Gospel of John, but at particular points, and indirectly, above all in instructing the disciples.[47]

In the last resort, the messianic secret goes back to the mysterious messianic authority of Jesus. So it is no invention of the gospel of the pre-Marcan community, but an expression of the mystery of Jesus himself which presses forward to the question of the Messiah. Mark expresses it in 4.41 by the question, 'Who is this, that wind and sea obey him?' The mystery of the messianic *exousia* of Jesus and the mystery of the kingdom in 4.11 are indissolubly connected in the historical person of Jesus himself.[48] The discrepancies in the individual statements go back to the disparateness of the traditions about Jesus with which Mark is working, and have their ultimate root there. With so unique a figure as Jesus, who bursts all historical frameworks, there could be no 'one-dimensional tradition', without tensions and apparent contradictions. His person and activity cannot be forced into the confines of ready-made christological theories.

5. The theological background of the author

(a) His relation to Paul

The soteriological contacts of the second Gospel with Paul, which have often been mentioned, should not lead us to make Mark directly dependent in his theology on the apostle to the Gentiles.[49] Where there are echoes, they go back to common 'pre-Pauline' traditions. There is hardly any trace in the Gospel of a direct connection between the two. The basic difference consists in the fact that Mark develops his εὐαγγέλιον Ἰησοῦ Χριστοῦ as a biographical account of Jesus, whereas Paul in his letters only expresses Jesus traditions very peripherally and formally. There is therefore no direct route from the Pauline gospel for the Gentiles, which is proclaimed in the preaching of the justification of the sinner by Christ, to the history of Jesus in Mark, though the evangelist not only knows but has worked out in a sublime way (2.13-17) the theme of the turning of the Son of God to sinners.

However, it is significant that in connection with the theme of Jesus and the sinners he does not echo the theme of the mission to the Gentiles in any way. The Jewish publicans are not a simple parable for 'the Gentile sinners' (Gal.2.15). The ministry of Jesus the Messiah is directed first of all to Israel. Nor is it possible to build any direct bridge to the evangelist from pre-Pauline formulae like I Cor.15.3f., which indeed the apostle explicitly terms *euaggelion*, for here nothing is said about the activity of Jesus before his death. In order to understand Mark better we must ultimately investigate his origin and his tradition.

(b) The Greek-speaking Jewish Christian from Jerusalem

Mark was a Greek-speaking Jewish Christian who also understood Aramaic. That is evident from the correct Aramaic quotations in his Gospel. I do not know any other work in Greek which has as many Aramaic or Hebrew words and formulae in so narrow a space as does the second Gospel. They are too numerous and too exact to be explained as the conventional barbarisms (ῥῆσις βαρβαρική) of the miracle worker and magician. This fact of itself makes it very improbable that the Gospel is to be derived from 'Gentile Christianity' (cf. Mark 3.17-19; 5.41; 7.11; 8.34; 10.46; 11.9f.; 14.1,32,36,45; 15.22,34). Most of these foreign-sounding words are omitted by Matthew and Luke. Presumably Mark came from Jerusalem; while he was unfamiliar with Galilee, he does know Jerusalem and Palestinian Judaism.[50] His 'deficient knowledge' of the geography of Galilee, which contemporary exegetes like to criticize, in fact simply shows up the latters' historical incomprehension: without a map it would be difficult even for a man of antiquity like Mark to establish his bearings in a strange area a good seventy miles from his home city, which he had presumably left long before he began to write his work, a strange area which he evidently had never visited.[51] As for his accounts of Jewish customs and historical circumstances, which are said to be not above criticism, it must be remembered that Mark does not mean to provide a historically accurate account in the modern sense, but presents Jewish customs polemically and tendentiously, i.e. in a vague and exaggerated way.[52] Nevertheless, alongside Josephus and Luke he is the most important source for Palestinian Judaism at the time of the procurators, in AD 6-70, and this fact is confirmed at many points by Josephus. Josephus seeks recognition as a scholarly and trustworthy historian, yet his carelessness is often shameful.[53] Mark does not have this ambition, so in this respect we should not ask so much of him.

(c) The Papias note

As information about the origin of Mark's work we have the note by Papias dating from about AD 120/130, i.e. the time of Hadrian; it comes from his 'five-volume' *Interpretation of the Lord's Sayings* (Λογίων κυριακῶν ἐξηγήσεις). It is often misunderstood and indeed mishandled in more recent scholarship, but in my view it must be taken very seriously.[54]

> This also the elder used to say. Mark, indeed, having been the interpreter of Peter, wrote accurately, howbeit not in order, all that he recalled of what was either said or done by the Lord. For he heard nothing of the Lord, nor was he a follower of his, but, at a later date (as I said) of Peter; who used to adapt his instructions to the needs [of the hearers], but not with a view to putting together the teachings of the Lord in orderly fashion: so that Mark did no wrong in thus writing some things as he recalled them. For he kept a single aim in view: not to omit anything of what he heard, nor to state anything therein falsely (Eusebius, HE 3,39,15).

Papias presumably received this report from the presbyter John, from Asia Minor,[55] the height of whose activity should be put roughly a generation earlier, about 70-100. In more recent times scholars have tended to dismiss this much discussed and much maltreated note as a secondary, apologetic vindication of the apostolic origin of the Second Gospel. In reality it represents the markedly *critical comments* of an author who rated oral tradition even higher than written works. The connection between Peter and Mark, which in fact goes back to the first century and is attested independently of the presbyter in I Peter 5.13,[56] cannot be a later invention in order to secure 'apostolic' authority for the Gospel. Moreover the main objection against the note in Papias, advanced by the representatives of the form-critical school, namely that the Second Gospel is not a literary work but a conglomerate of anonymous, popular and collective Jesus tradition, has now proved invalid.[57] But in that case, what are the reasons which compel us to deny this extremely distinctive note any historical value? Do not the numerous so-called critical judgments (which in fact are often radically uncritical) express a basically ahistorical zeal which has ceased to be concerned with what this mysterious text really says?

The second note, about the Gospel of Matthew, in fact plays down the authority of the First Gospel, written in Greek ('So then, Matthew compiled the sayings [of the Lord] in the Hebrew language; but everyone translated them (or interpreted them) as he was able'

(Eusebius, HE 3,39,16). It indicates that the First Gospel was not the original work of the apostle, but a secondary rendering of a basic Hebrew document. Therefore Pesch is wrong in his interpretation of the quotations from Papias when he supposes that Papias is providing an apologetic defence of the apostolicity of the Gospel of Mark and at the same time judging it by the better order of Matthew.[58] There is no indication that Matthew is arranged better, especially as in fact he followed the τάξις of Mark, which Papias found inadequate.

Moreover, the complaint about inadequate 'order' does not in fact relate to the literary arrangement, which in the Second Gospel is faultless, but to the historical and chronological arrangement of the material. Therefore we might assume that Papias had in mind the quite different chronology and order of the Fourth Gospel: he quotes Revelation and I John, and in the second book of his work reports a tradition of the killing of John and James, the sons of Zebedee, by the Jews; in addition there is much to suggest that he knew the Fourth Gospel.[59] Thus his sequence of disciples, Andrew, Peter and Philip, is matched by the call of the disciples according to John 1.40ff.; furthermore, in the preface there is also an absolute use of the term 'truth' which comes close to the Fourth Gospel (3,39,3 end): 'the commandments given by the Lord to faith, and reaching us from the truth itself' (τὰς παρὰ τοῦ κυρίου τῇ πίστει δεδομένας ἐντολὰς καὶ ἀπ᾽αὐτῆς παραγινομένας τῆς ἀληθείας). Moreover John in particular speaks of ἐντολαί of Jesus and the ἐντολὰς (or -ὴν) διδόναι (John 11.57; 12.49; 14.51,21,31; 15.10; I John 2.3f.; 3.22,23,24; 5.2f.);[60] the avoidance of the term apostle in the extant fragments and his predilection for 'disciples of the Lord' could also be connected with John. Moreover, it is difficult to attribute apologetic intentions to Papias about 120 or 130 (or even round about 110?): who would have doubted the authenticity of Mark or Matthew in his day? Gnostics like Basilides or Valentinus were keen to quote the church's Gospels, and according to Irenaeus docetic Gnostics even had a preference for Mark.[61] By contrast Marcion had not yet appeared. His separation from the community in Rome presumably only took place about 144,[62] and his wrath is directed less against the evangelists than against the original apostles like Peter and John himself.[63] Therefore Papias' work is quite unsuitable for offering a defence against Marcion. The Old Testament, the real point of dispute, plays no part in the fragments, and the observations about Mark and Matthew do not look like a convincing defence. This exceptional work must be earlier. In addition to a (hypothetical) predilection for the Fourth Gospel, we could also presuppose that Papias' criticism in essence stemmed from his predilection for the *viva vox* (ζῶσα φωνὴ καὶ μένουσα, HE 3,39,4), the living oral tradition in contrast to written documents, which in fact was already anachronistic. We also find this – though in a different way – throughout earlier Christianity among a number of Gnostic teachers and beyond, though of course in that case without any depreciation of the written tradition, which by then had become indispensable.[64] Evidently this avid collector of earlier tradition had information of both oral and written provenance, which went back one or two generations,[65] i.e. right to the time of the origin of the Gospels: in the case of Matthew about 90 and in the case of Mark probably about 69 (see above, 21–8). His main authorities were the presbyter John, who is connected with the Johannine corpus, and the presbyter Aristion, from whom perhaps the inauthentic ending to Mark derives (see below 71f.).

Papias' criticism of Mark starts from two points:

(*a*) He did not put the words and actions of the Lord in the right order, whether chronologically or in terms of subject matter (οὐ μέντοι τάξει); this basic criticism certainly goes back to the presbyter's tradition.

(*b*) He was not an immediate disciple of the Lord, but only of Peter; in other words his sources are only second hand.

The undertone of the criticism can also be seen in the explanations which follow: the lack of order in his work which is the object of criticism goes back to Peter's actions in shaping his oral teaching – understandably – to the needs of the hearers; in other words he presented the Jesus tradition in a disordered way by literary and historical standards and was uninterested in a collection (σύνταξις) of 'words of the Lord' with a good literary or chronological arrangement. Mark was not in error in writing down only some (ἔνια, as they had remained in his memory (ὡς ἀπεμνημόνευσεν).

The positive statements, that as far as Mark remembered the teaching of Peter he set this down on paper ἀκριβῶς, and that he *took trouble* not to leave out or falsify anything that he had heard,[66] are conventional in character: similar formulae appear almost as stereotypes in the prologues of historians.[67] Such a concession was a matter of course, which can be taken for granted in any reasonably well organized historian. Had Papias said less this would have been a *direct* dismissal of Mark.

Another striking point is the twofold stress on remembering. It corresponds with the stress on the remembering by the disciples in the Fourth Gospel (2.17,22; 12.16; 15.20; 16.4) and the concept of the ἀπομνημονεύματα τῶν ἀποστόλων which are later prominent in Justin; the difference is that Papias limits Mark's recollection to the subordinate proclamation of Peter: Mark is not a direct eye-witness.

It should no longer be denied that the 'recollection' of the authors (i.e. of their informants and those who handed material on to them) and not primarily the inventive creativity of anonymous early Christian prophets, communities, or even self-confident theological poets, played the normative role in the origin of the Synoptic Gospels. The authors are above all responsible for the selection and ordering of the material and for the linguistic and stylistic form that it is given.

(d) Mark and Peter

The dependence of the author on Peter, which plays a very important role in establishing the priority of Mark, but which today is usually completely ignored or even abruptly rejected, should be maintained: it makes a substantial contribution to our understanding of the Gospel.[68] It is also confirmed, independently of Papias, by Justin in his reference to Mark 3.16f. as supposed 'recollections of Peter'.[69] There are good historical reasons for what at first sounds an unusual piece of information, that Mark was Peter's interpreter. It is obvious that the Galilean fisherman Simon will never have learnt Greek thoroughly enough to have been able to present his teaching fluently in unexceptionable Greek.[70] The Greek Palestinian John Mark, whose house Peter visited first in the legend of Acts 12.12ff. after his liberation from prison, was presumably later his companion and indeed interpreter where that was necessary.[71] Peter's Greek will hardly have been pleasing to the fastidious ear of the ancient listener. The critical, educated reader might like to see for himself whether he has an unexceptionable *literary* command of German or French, and whether he is not grateful to a translator for help in preparing a report in a foreign language. (Although I myself speak English passably, I am nevertheless very grateful to have a first-class English translator, not only for my books, but also for English papers I have to read.) Did Peter have a better linguistic training than we do?

Given its essentially smaller extent, the Gospel of Mark mentions Simon Peter more frequently than the other Synoptic Gospels and also more frequently than John, if we leave out the chapter which is critical of Peter in the supplement, John 21. Simon Peter is mentioned 25 times in all.[72] Simon is the first disciple to be mentioned, in 1.16, directly after the *propositio* in 1.14,15, and quite unusually his brother Andrew is described as 'the brother of Simon' (on this cf. 15.21). At the beginning of Jesus' ministry, after the call of the first four disciples and the first exorcism in the synagogue of Capernaum, Jesus visits the house of the brothers – a report in the Gospel which falls outside its framework and seems very personal – and heals Simon's mother-in-law (1.29). In 1.36, unusually, the first group of disciples is described as Σίμων καὶ οἱ μετ᾽αὐτοῦ. Subsequently he stands at the head of all the lists of disciples, the Twelve and also the three and the four.[73] All this cannot simply be explained as mere convention; there must be profound historical reasons behind it. As the spokesmen of the Twelve Peter not only acknowledges the messiahship of Jesus but is also sharply rejected by him (8.29, 32f.); he is an embodiment of the disciples' lack of understanding and their failure.[74] He is the last disciple whom Jesus addresses personally in Gethsemane (14.37), the last who accompanies Jesus as far as the courtyard of the high priest's palace (14.37), indeed, even more, the last to be mentioned in the Gospel. The extraordinary formulation of 16.7, the angel's command to the women, 'Go and say to his disciples and to Peter...' (τοῖς μαθηταῖς αὐτοῦ καὶ τῷ Πέτρῳ) puts the name of the disciple who appears first in the Gospel at the end as well: this is an *inclusio*, through which the evangelist deliberately wants to stress this one disciple in a quite special way.[75] It can hardly be doubted that Mark is clearly stressing the unique significance of Peter, though without disguising his failure. Might this not be connected with the special origin of his tradition? On the other hand, some kind of later theological polemic against Peter or Jewish Christianity generally should not be read out of the Second Gospel, for – apart from the Fourth Gospel with its mysterious beloved disciple - we cannot see any other standpoint, whether of disciples or community, which would afford the authority for such polemic.[76] Matthew and Luke took over this stress on Peter from Mark and gave it rather more marked legendary elaborations (thus especially Matthew); the firm starting point is, however, to be sought in Mark, who is very close to Peter's martyrdom in Rome in 64 in both time and space. By contrast, John wants to limit the significance of Peter over against the unknown beloved disciple.

Certainly Simon Peter does not appear as a living individual, but as a type; however, that is part of the kerygmatic style of the narrator generally and affects all the people in the Gospel including Jesus himself: one can see how the material has been given kerygmatic form over a generation. That makes it all the more astounding how, despite all the narrative abbreviations, Mark nevertheless brings his vivid style to bear.[77]

Finally, it is striking that for Mark and his successors, James the brother of the Lord and the family of Jesus fade right into the background. Their existence is noted only in 6.3. However, the explanation of this is that from the beginning of the forties (cf. Acts 12.17; Gal.2.9) James had forced Peter out of his position of primacy in Jerusalem and that there were tensions here which were hardly less than those between Paul and his opponents.[77a]

There are yet other reasons for supposing that Petrine authority stands behind the Gospel of Mark. First, Mark's work was used by the historian Luke and also by Matthew, so self-consciously a Christian scribe, in a quite natural way as a guideline. The fidelity with which Matthew reproduces the whole of his Marcan model is particularly striking. Furthermore, the best explanation of the fact that the Second Gospel lived on in the church, although Matthew had taken over about ninety per cent of the material in it, is that the work of Mark was from the beginning bound up with the authority of the name of Peter. Furthermore, the only Gospel which deviates from the Marcan order fundamentally is the Fourth; in it the mysterious beloved disciple (said to be the author, 21.24) is always closer to Jesus than Peter, the guarantor of the Marcan-Synoptic tradition.

The Second Gospel probably developed out of living oral teaching and was composed for solemn reading in worship. The short cola, often with a rhythmic shape, point to oral recitation in the assembled community. The Gospel was written for the audience to listen to, and therefore is anything but an artificial literary composition written at a desk, stuck together from obscure written sources, countless notes and flysheets.[78] Here we should not simply project our own extracts and notes, our relatively mechanical 'scientific' ways of working, on to Mark. Behind this work there is neither a mere collector of amorphous popular 'community tradition' which was 'current' (how are we to imagine that) somewhere in the Gentile Christian churches, nor an anonymous, poetically inspired, Gentile Christian man of letters, but a theological teacher who himself must have been a master of the word and an authority in early Christianity. A Mr Nobody would hardly have undertaken the revolutionary innovation of writing a gospel. In my view the author was at the same time a disciple of the greatest apostolic authority in the earliest church. That could explain the initial success of his work.

On the other hand we should certainly not also assume some *slavish* dependence on the Peter tradition. The work of the Second Evangelist again puts its own personal theological stamp on that. For all their dependence, the deutero-Pauline letters Ephesians and Colossians, which come from unknown pupils of Paul, have a mark of their own, as does I John in comparison with the Gospel – not to mention Paul's disciple Luke. Certainly, about five years after the death of Peter and in the confusion of the civil war after Nero, a written Gospel from the hand of a disciple of Peter to point the way forward was the demand of the hour (cf. 27f.).

Unfortunately we know hardly anything about the theology of Peter, the most influential teacher, even in the Gentile Christian churches, alongside Paul. It would be attractive to attempt to reconstruct certain basic features from the Second Gospel, but this would rightly meet with objections from the start as being too imaginative a hypothesis. Here we must leave the question open.[79]

6. Mark's Work as Gospel

(a) Terminology

Nevertheless, perhaps I may be allowed a concluding hypothesis. Mark uses the term gospel, εὐαγγέλιον, seven times. At the beginning of his Gospel the εὐαγγέλιον Ἰησοῦ Χριστοῦ as an objective genitive means the gospel *about* Jesus Christ, i.e. the saving events of the ministry and death of Jesus in the 'biographical' work[80] that is now beginning.[81]

In the *propositio* in 1.14 Jesus appears in Galilee and proclaims the εὐαγγέλιον τοῦ θεοῦ. Here we have a *genetivus auctoris*, the good news from God, which is explained in v.15: 'The time is fulfilled and the kingdom of God is here.[82] Repent and believe in the gospel.' The good news of God is identical with the proclamation of the dawn of God's rule as the embodiment of the proclamation and activity of Jesus in Galilee. By contrast the gospel of Jesus Christ in 1.1 has an even more comprehensive character; it contains the *whole* saving event which begins with the forerunner, John the Baptist, and culminates in the death of Jesus for many and his resurrection. This is not yet to be found in all its fullness in Jesus' public announcement of the dawn of the kingdom of God alone. I.e. in contrast to the presentation of the proclamation of Jesus in the Fourth Gospel, in Mark there is still some tension between the preaching of God which begins in Galilee and the christological saving event which comprises the whole gospel, including the suffering and resurrection, indeed the promise of the parousia, of the Son of Man (8.34; 9.1; ch.13; 14.62).

Accordingly Mark does not use the term εὐαγγέλιον again in the first part of his account. On the other hand, it occurs twice in the instruction of the disciples after Peter's confession and the announcement of the passion: in 8.35 in the summons to self-denial, 'For whoever will lose his life for my sake and the gospel will save it', and similarly in 10.29, 'For no one has forsaken house (and family)... and fields for my sake and the gospel's who will not receive it again a hundred fold...'. The ἕνεκεν ἐμοῦ καὶ ἕνεκεν τοῦ εὐαγγελίου is a hendiadys: 'for Jesus' sake' at the same time means 'for the gospel's sake', and vice versa. Jesus is the content of the gospel. This refers back to the wider understanding in 1.1.

The last instances have an almost Pauline ring; 13.10 disrupts the connection between the little apocalypse and the announcement of persecution, 'but first the gospel must be preached to all peoples'. Here the gospel is the embodiment of world-wide missionary preaching.[83] In 14.9, at the beginning of the passion narrative proper, this Pauline-sounding traditional and kerygmatic understanding of εὐαγγέλιον is bound up with the narration of the story of Jesus, above all the passion narrative, so that such a narrative appears as an essential ingredient of mission preaching generally: 'Truly I say to you, wherever the gospel is *preached* throughout the world, what she has done will be *narrated* in memory of her.'[84]

This unique terminology, which connects the christological *kerygma* that we know from Paul indivisibly with the whole *story of Jesus* as the saving event, was certainly not the personal invention of Mark. Some examples like 1.1; 13.10; 14.9 may be his own redactional construction; in the other instances he probably went back to earlier tradition.[85] We should probably already presuppose this christological connection of a narrative about Jesus and proclamation with the term εὐαγγέλιον in a large number of communities even before the composition of Mark's work. We find it about a generation after Mark in a striking, well-moulded form, for example in Ignatius or even in the Didache, where in both instances there is already a hint of the transition to the written gospel.[86] Without this earlier terminology in numerous communities the term 'Gospel' would probably never have come into being as a designation for those four kerygmatic biographies that we find in the New Testament canon. Where does this nomenclature come from?

(b) Peter and the term *gospel*

In our earliest evidence, the letters of Paul, only one figure appears to us from the Twelve, the most intimate group of disciples, whose influence extended from Jerusalem, via Antioch and Corinth, to Rome. He was in a particular way the conversation-partner and missionary rival of the apostle to the Gentiles. Paul visited him for two weeks in Jerusalem, two or three years after his conversion and attacked him sharply in Antioch (Gal.1.18; 2.10ff.); he also caused difficulties for Paul in his own community in Corinth. He was a figure who more than any other could act as spokesman of the disciples in connection with the wealth of the Jesus tradition: Simon Peter. We will not go far wrong if we regard him – more than all the other disciples of Jesus – as the authoritative mediator of the Jesus tradition in the mission churches from Antioch to Rome. His original close connection with the Master contributed to his unique authority, as did the fact that he was first to see the Risen Lord.

On the other hand, we may regard it as certain that the word εὐαγγέλιον which Paul uses so often as the embodiment of the new message did not have first to be discovered by the apostle to the Gentiles, but goes back to the earliest Greek-speaking community in Jerusalem. Possibly, even, an Aramaic term underlies it, as the Targum on Isa.53.1 renders the Hebrew *smwᶜh* in the question 'Who has believed our report?' with *bswrth*', the Aramaic equivalent of εὐαγγέλιον, and the term is to be derived from the verb *bsr* = εὐαγγελίζεσθαι, which is used by Deutero-Isaiah to describe the proclamation of the message of victory in the dawn of the kingdom of God (40.9; 60.6; 61.1);[87] in connection with that it also plays a role in the proclamation of Jesus.[88] I Corinthians 15.1ff., where Paul describes the stereotyped kerygma of passion and resurrection as εὐαγγέλιον, which he himself has received as paradosis, also refers back to a very early pre-Pauline use of the word. Finally, Gal.2.1-10 suggests that the term εὐαγγέλιον or its Aramaic equivalent was also not unfamiliar to the Jerusalem authorities.[89] In 2.7 Paul stresses that his conversation partners had realized that 'I was entrusted with my Gospel for the Gentiles, as Peter was with the (gospel) for the Jews'.[90]

In the light of this, we have good reason to suppose that this term was also significant for Peter, though we no longer have any access to his preaching and his theology. It can hardly be doubted that he exercised enormous influence, which was hardly less than that of Paul. Of course, in contrast to Peter's influence, that of Paul was prolonged and revived by the collection and circulation of his letters. In Peter's case, by contrast, the recollection remained bound up with his person, his special Jesus tradition, and not so much with his own theology, which was probably simpler than that of Paul, the former scribe. Now if the term εὐαγγέλιον was also vital for Peter, then the Jesus tradition or the story of Jesus will have played a much greater role in it than with Paul. Perhaps Peter's speech to Cornelius with its account of the activity of Jesus (Acts 10.36-43) preserves a slight trace of this. Why should Luke, who sought to give the best theological portrait of Paul that he could in Acts 13.38f.; 20.24-36, not also have had some tradition about Peter? Possibly he was still aware that the word 'gospel' was not a term that Jesus used, so that he consistently deletes it four times in all from his Marcan model.[91] It is all the more striking that in Acts 20.24 Luke puts the word on Paul's lips with the significant formula that he has received from the Lord the ministry διαμαρτύρασθαι τὸ εὐαγγέλιον τῆς χάριτος τοῦ θεοῦ.

We find the second instance in 15.7, on Peter's lips: in the Cornelius story God has determined διὰ τοῦ στόματός μου ἀκοῦσαι τὰ ἔθνη τὸν λόγον τοῦ εὐαγγελίου καὶ πιστεῦσαι. One might almost suppose that in his last speech Peter is deliberately dismissed by Luke as a missionary to the Gentiles.

The point of contact between the term gospel and the Jesus tradition in Peter could explain why Mark uses this word in so evocative a way, which in part deviates from Paul, and secondly why in some communities εὐαγγέλιον was evidently used as a designation for the story and teaching of Jesus; also, finally, how the connection between the Jesus tradition and the term is manifestly rejected by the 'Pauline' Luke in his Gospel. The Johannine circle, as so often, went its own way in the terminology of its proclamation, and it can do without the newly-coined word as it can do without ἀπόστολος in the sense of 'messenger of Jesus'. We find it in I Peter 4.17 – a unique occurrence in the non-Pauline letters.

The special terminology which is becoming evident for the first time in Mark, and which involves the narrative Jesus tradition, would then finally have established itself despite all the resistance because in the last resort it still had behind it the old authority of the Petrine tradition, a tradition for which the historical tradition about Jesus and the good news belonged indissolubly together.

(c) Mark and the story of Moses

There is an even more profound reason why here in Mark – and to my mind in the Petrine tradition which underlies it – the story of Jesus, including the tradition of his words, is designated 'gospel'. *Judaism, too, knew a historical saving event: the exodus from Egypt under the leadership of Moses and the handing down of the Torah to Israel through Moses.* The Torah comprised not only the 613 prohibitions and commands,[92] but from Exodus to Deuteronomy a 'biography' of the man of God,[93] which among other things also contained the eschatological promise of a 'prophet' like Moses (Deut.18.19ff.), in Judaism very closely bound up with the expectation of Elijah.[94] As the first redeemer, Moses was a type of the second redeemer, and Elijah was the first manifestation of the *Moses redivivus*. As such, he was transported, and his return was expected. It is striking how deeply the Gospel of Mark is stamped with the Moses-Elijah typology. This begins with John the Baptist, who for Mark is the *Elia redivivus*; it is continued in the baptism and temptation of Jesus in the wilderness; and is evident in the parallel between Mark 1.15 and Ex.14.31,[95] which for Jewish tradition is the first climax of the saving event of the exodus and in the confession of the Song of Moses made manifest the faith of Israel and its acknowledgment of the kingly rule of Yahweh (15.18). This typology then emerges again clearly in some of the miracle stories, above all in their climax, the stories of the feedings, and reaches its real high point in the scene of the transfiguration with the appearance of Moses and Elijah, though it is not to them, but to the beloved Son, that the disciples must listen (9.7). Finally, it takes on markedly antitypical features in the passover meal with the sacrifice of the covenant, the judgment on the shepherds (14.27; cf. Num.27.17), the condemnation of Jesus by the high priest, his crucifixion and the cry of dereliction. Probably every Jew and Jewish Christian knew legends about the end of Moses, that either he was taken up into heaven without having to die or that God himself took his soul from his body without any of the pains of death, 'as with a kiss'. The contrast between the death of Jesus and that of the man of Sinai is evident.[96] In other words, the story of Jesus as the eschatological saving event, as gospel, stands in a relationship of tension with the story of Moses as 'saving event' for Israel, or with the Torah as 'saving' message. Jesus as messianic teacher on the one hand enforces the law even more strictly with the commandment to love (Mark 12.29-34), so that a scribe who has in fact to preserve the heritage of Moses (cf.Matt.23.2) agrees with him; indeed he bases the resurrection of the dead on the Torah – in a completely Pharisaic sense (cf. Mark 12.28: ὅτι καλῶς ἀπεκρίθη αὐτοῖς (12.18-27). On the other hand, however, he appears as the Lord over the Torah (2.28), who puts in question the sabbath commandment, the commandments about purity (7.15) or the permission for divorce, and who never again wants to pour the old wine into new skins (2.22). In other words, in the Gospel of Mark, the Pauline and Johannine contrast between Moses and Christ which the Prologue of John reduced to the impressive formula, 'The law was given by Moses, but grace and truth have come through Jesus Christ' (John 1.17), takes the form of the typological-antitypical contrast of two historical accounts. Matthew developed this dialectical relationship quite deliberately, stressing in particular Jesus as the messianic teacher. In his work it finds new expression in the antitheses of the Sermon on the Mount. It is astonishing to see how here one evangelist extends his hand to another as a theological teacher.

The liturgical consequence of what in the last resort is predominantly an antithetical parallel between Moses and Jesus is that the reading (and exposition) of the Gospels gradually takes the place of the reading (and interpretation) of the Torah as the climax of the ministry of the word,[97] while the Old Testament is subsumed totally under the prophetic promise which prepared for the gospel. The partly typological and partly antitypical relationship was also at work in Hebrews and then, in the second century, in I Clement, Barnabas, Justin, Melito of Sardis and Irenaeus. One of its roots may lie in the fact that in the Gospel of Mark the story of Jesus as gospel first becomes visible in a dialectical relationship to the story of Moses as the 'saving message' of the Torah. The subject matter itself is earlier and in the last resort goes back to Jesus.[98] Moreover, the contrast between law and gospel does not seem to have been so exclusively Pauline. Incidentally, it is grounded in a community tradition which thought even more strongly than Paul in terms of salvation history and typology, and which referred to the Jesus tradition; again we may ask whether it was not originally connected with the proclamation of Peter.

In that case, the Jesus story as gospel, which has been told to us above all by the Synoptics, i.e. in the first instance by Mark and – in a derivative form – by Luke and Matthew, who are dependent on him, would then also be influenced to some degree by Petrine tradition, making it the third significant corpus in the New Testament alongside the Pauline corpus and the Johannine corpus. The designation εὐαγγέλιον would then *perhaps* go back to this Petrine understanding of the gospel.

The Portrayal of Peter in the Synoptic Gospels

Reinhard Feldmeier

Mark[1] mentions Simon/Peter 25 times,[2] Matthew also mentions him 25 times, and Luke 30 times.[3] With a total number of 11078 words in Mark, 18298 in Matthew and 19448 in Luke, that gives a frequency in Mark of 1:443, in Luke of 1:648 and in Matthew of 1:722.[4] Given the approximate equivalence of Luke and Matthew, Peter is therefore mentioned most often in Mark (Mark:Matt. 1:1,65; Mark:Luke 1:1,46).

In the first instance this inequality is caused by Q, in which Peter is not mentioned anywhere,[5] just as in Q the disciples do not ever appear in an active role.[6]

1. In the Gospel of Mark Peter occupies a prominent position among the disciples. He is the first to be called (1.16), he receives the name 'Peter' as a mark of honour, and is mentioned first in the list of disciples, a clear indication of the importance attached to him. Next come the sons of Zebedee, and only then his brother Andrew (who was called when he was, 3.16ff.). His special position is also expressed in the phrase Σίμων καὶ οἱ μετ᾽αὐτοῦ (1.36). Simon always belongs to the most intimate circle around Jesus (5.37; 9.2; 13.3; 14.33), and apart from Mark 9.38ff. and 10.35-40 is the only disciple to appear as an individual over against Jesus (8.29,32f.; 9.5; 10.28; 11.21; 14.29ff.). His failure in Gethsemane is a particular cause of grief to Jesus: 'Simon, are you asleep (as well)?' (14.37). Moreover, Peter is the only one to follow Jesus after his arrest (14.54,66-72), and after the resurrection of Jesus the women receive the command to tell the news 'to his disciples and to Peter' (16.7).

There has been no lack of attempts to interpret this special position of Peter as a post-Easter interpolation. However, the very fact that some scholars want to see this as a confirmation of the position of the later leader of the church and others as a challenge to him shows the impossibility of explaining the position of prominence given to Peter in Mark on the basis of one particular aim. For Peter is a prominent counterpart to Jesus for good and for ill. His confession of Christ (8.29) is followed by his opposition to the way Jesus is to go and by Jesus' subsequent rebuke to him, 'Get behind me, Satan' (8.32f.); his readiness to unconditional discipleship (14.26-31) is matched by his fall, which is all the greater (14.37,66-72). A retrojection stemming from the later Peter would have had to depict him in a much more clearly positive or negative way – depending on attitudes towards him.

Another feature which tells against a subsequent interpolation is the fact that Peter has no leading position within the circle of the Twelve; this is partially already reflected in the picture of Peter in the synoptic parallels (with their strong post-Easter stamp).

Finally, it is impossible to explain why James the brother of the Lord, who was soon to play such a decisive role in Jerusalem, still has no significance in Mark.

While it is impossible to deny that Peter may have been typified as the spokesman of the disciples, the features in Mark's picture of Peter, some of which are very distinctive, may well in essence go back to historical reminiscence.

2. Matthew has omitted the name Peter/Simon 9 times as compared with the Marcan original (Mark 1.16b,30,36; 5.37; 11.21; 13.3; 14.37b, 67; 16.7); 3 times he has added it in clearly redactional passages (Matt.15.15; 18.21; 26.37) and 6 times the name appears in special material where it is impossible to make a clear distinction between tradition and redaction (Matt.14.28f.; 16.17f.; 17.24f.).

2.1 The omissions do not say very much. 3 times they are governed by stylistic considerations (Mark 1.16b, 29b; 14.67), 3 times the restriction of the participants in an event, a discourse or a question is removed in favour of all the disciples or all those involved (Mark 5.37; 11.21; 13.3). Mark 1.35-38 is missing from Matthew for reasons connected with the structure of his Gospel.[7] The omission of the reproach in Mark 14.37b which is addressed only to Peter is probably meant to spare him and share the responsibility with all the disciples. Like Luke, Matthew felt the strikingly lame 'and Peter' (Mark 16.7) to be disruptive.

2.2 In the additions, Peter is similarly shown as spokesman of the disciples (Matt.15.15; 18.21; 26.35). Matthew 18.21 already has him putting a question – of particular importance to a community already in existence; in contrast to Q he is thus introduced as a later authority in matters of community discipline.

2.3 In the special material, the sinking Peter (Matt.14.28ff.) is a legendary extension of Jesus' walking on the water (Mark 6.45-52).

The picture of Peter painted here – with 'willing spirit' and 'weak flesh' – corresponds to the picture of Peter as it is painted by Mark and others in the passion narrative. The picture of Peter which has been taken over has at this point moved further in the direction of anecdote and legend.

The tradition history of Matt.16.16b-19, in which Peter is praised for his messianic confession, and which contains the saying about the keys, is a matter of dispute. At all events, here the Marcan framework is abandoned with a view to the post-Easter position of Peter, as is especially clear from the term *ekklesia* (which the promise indicates as being permanently established).

The basic material in the passage on the question about the tax in Matt.17.24-27 certainly goes back to the time before the destruction of the temple; we can no longer discover what role Peter played in the original (if any at all).[8] The remarkable thing about the narrative in its present form is that those who want to know something about the 'teacher' turn to Peter, whereas Jesus (who already knows Peter's answer without being asked) simply instructs him. Here too there is probably already a reflection of the leading position of Peter after Easter; while he is instructed by Jesus, he does give authoritative answers to questions.

So in Matthew Peter – in the view of the third generation and beyond Mark – has become the man of the church. However, in the Gospel as a whole he has no greater importance than he does in Mark.

3. In comparison with Mark, Luke has omitted the name Simon/Peter 15 times (1.16a,16b,36; 8.32,33; 11.21; 13.3; 14.29,33,37a,37b,66, 67, 70; 16.7); he has added it 10 times (Luke 8.45; 9.32; 12.41; 22.8,34, 55,58,60,61a,61b); 9 times it occurs in his special material (Luke 5.3, 4,5,8,10a,10b; 22.31; 24.12,34). However, in these numbers it should be noted that Luke 5.1-11 was regarded as special material, although at the same time a relationship with Mark 1.16ff. is probable.

3.1 3 times the omissions are a matter of stylistic reshaping (Mark 14.66,67,70). The lame 'and to Peter' in Mark 16.7 may also have fallen victim to stylistic polishing. In Luke, the narrative of the attempt by 'Peter and those with him' to restrain Jesus (Mark 1.35-38),[9] which in Mark is presumably meant to be critical of the disciples, serves to stress Jesus' success: now it is the masses who look for Jesus and want to stay with him. The narrative of the withered fig tree is completely absent from Luke, and therefore so is Peter's question about it (Mark 11.21). Like Matthew, Luke too has done away with the restriction of the audience of the eschatological discourse to the four disciples who were first to be called (Mark 13.3). The name of

Peter from Mark 14.29 is indeed omitted, but it is introduced into the dialogue (Luke 22.34). A clear redactional intent underlies the omission of the saying about Satan directed against Peter in Mark 8.32f.: as elsewhere in the Gospel, this feature of the disciples' failure is toned down or deleted. This theme evidently also governs the rendering of the Lucan pericope about Gethsemane (Luke 22.39-46): Jesus finds all the disciples sleeping only once, and paradoxically ἀπὸ τῆς λύπης (Luke 22.45 end). Accordingly the reproach to Peter is also omitted (Mark 14.37ab).[10]

3.2 Of the additions, three are determined by stylistic consider-ations (Luke 22.55,58,60). Luke 22.61 (Jesus sees Peter after his denial) cannot be regarded as redactional, but it does represent a novellistic intensification of the event which is secondary in terms of the history of the tradition. In Luke 22.34, the name of Peter, which has been omitted, is supplied (see above). As the verbal agreements show, Peter's sleep at the Transfiguration (Luke 9.32) has probably been drawn from the Marcan Gethsemane scene, and in Luke has taken the place of the saying about Satan as a toned-down expression of his failure to understand. It can therefore be explained from Luke's tendency of Luke, already noted, to spare the disciples.[11] A deliberate stress on Peter and John indicates their identification with the two disciples who are anonymous in Mark (Luke 22.8); this is probably influenced by the later significance of the two apostles (cf. Acts 3.1,3ff.,11; 4.13,19; 8.14).[12]

3.3 Peter is mentioned 6 times in the narrative about the miraculous catch of fishes which belongs to the Lucan special material (Luke 5.3,4,5,8,10a,10b). This legend[13] has taken the place of the two brief Marcan narratives of the call (Mark 1.16-20). The concentration on Peter is striking; in contrast to the Marcan model, the saying about fishers of men is only applied to him. Here Peter is called in quite a special way as the later leader of the church and is given the missionary commission (this corresponds to his role as the decisive pioneer of the Pauline mission to the Gentiles in Acts). In remarkable parallelism to John (20.3), Luke 24.12 reports a journey of Peter to the tomb. The protophany of the Risen Jesus to Peter (Luke 24.34) is confirmed in I Cor.15.5.

Summary

It is a striking feature of the synoptic parallels that in their picture of Peter, on the one hand they are largely dependent on their Marcan model; on the other hand the contours of the image of Peter are smoothed down. Negative features are often deleted or toned down, while the usually hagiographical character of the additions already shows more or less clearly the later 'rock of the church'. Here, too, historical reminiscence cannot be completely excluded (cf. Matt.16.16ff.; Luke 22.31f.); however, for the most part the Marcan picture of Peter is simply retouched on the basis of the later significance of Peter. The notes in Luke 24.12, 34 show that Luke was familiar with a tradition corresponding to I Cor.15.3ff. It is striking that this post-Easter role of Peter otherwise plays no part in Matthew's and Luke's accounts of the resurrection appearances.

III

The Titles of the Gospels and the Gospel of Mark[1]

'That the church possesses *four* Gospels of equal value is a fact to which people have become so accustomed over the past 1700 years that it only rarely causes even the most thoughtful person to reflect on it. However, it is an extremely paradoxical fact... All the analogies in the history of religion to which we might want to refer for writings as significant as the Gospels suggest that people treasured *one* book and not several of the same kind, and that in worship they read from *one* book.' With these remarks Harnack introduced the discussion of the εὐαγγέλιον τετράμορφον, the 'fourfold Gospel', in his *Chronology of Early Christian Literature*. In so doing he was taking up a formula of Irenaeus, who round about 180 was the first to attempt to explain the 'paradoxical fact' that while there can be only one message of salvation – and accordingly the whole of the New Testament and the Apostolic Fathers have εὐαγγέλιον only in the singular - the church has four εὐαγγέλια.[2] The question of the one gospel and the four Gospels is quite certainly one of the central problems of the earliest church history down to the beginning of the second century. It is therefore much discussed, but at the same time it is obscure and a matter of controversy.

So it is strange that hitherto scholars should have neglected an essential element of this complex, although it sums up the problem in the shortest way: namely, the question of the significance, the age and the origin of the titles to the Gospels. Let me quote Rudolf Pesch, at the beginning of his large two-volume commentary on Mark, as a representative of numerous more recent commentaries: 'All the *inscriptiones* and *subscriptiones* in the Gospel manuscripts are late.'[3] The author thinks that this one sentence settles the matter – giving no further reasons for his view. It is a welcome exception to find even once a contrary judgment to the effect that the titles to the Gospels are 'old and presumably original designations' (this comment by von Campenhausen is tucked away in a footnote in his book *The Formation of the Christian Bible*).⁴ In this paper I shall give more detailed reasons for the latter view.

1. The form of the title

If we are looking for a real discussion of the problem, we must go back quite a long way, to those old masters Adolf von Harnack and Theodor Zahn.⁵ Both agreed that according to what were at that time the earliest parchment codices, Vaticanus and Sinaiticus, from the middle of the fourth century, the original titles did not follow the long form εὐαγγέλιον κατὰ Μαθθαῖον, Gospel according to Matthew, and so on, but read simply κατὰ Μαθθαῖον. The title εὐαγγέλιον referred, rather, to the *whole* canon of the four Gospels. Zahn observes: 'The title can have arisen only in the light of the fact that the four books belong together, i.e. at or soon after their being brought together.'⁶ Some difference is detectable only over the date at which this combination happened. In the interest of an early date for the canon of the four Gospels, Zahn, the conservative, supposes them to have been brought together between 100 and 120; Harnack puts this rather later, between 120 and 140, in Asia Minor.

Harnack also defines the significance of the title clearly, with explicit reference to Zahn: 'εὐαγγέλιον κατὰ Μάρκον etc. is not to be translated ... "the Gospel writing according to the tradition which derives from Mark", but *the* (namely the *one*) Gospel according to Mark's account.' He believes that the unknown figure who created the fourfold Gospel corpus had been led to do so by two concerns: first, 'to mark the unity of the Gospel', and second, 'to possess Gospel writings from the pens of apostles or their disciples'.⁷

First let us look at the interpretation of the titles. Compared with the usual title of a book in antiquity, εὐαγγέλιον κατὰ Μαθθαῖον sounds quite unusual. As a rule, the author would come first, in the genitive, followed by the title indicating the content: Πλουτάρχου βίοι παράλληλοι or Φιλοστράτου βίοι σοφιστῶν. The Christian authors took over this custom. I have found only a few very late instances of the designation of the author's name in book titles with κατά and the author's name.⁸ We cannot, therefore, see the preposition κατά with the accusative as a simple periphrasis for the *genetivus auctoris*, which is W.Bauer's view;⁹ the concern was in fact to avoid the genitive. Instead, the striking form of the title was used to express the fact that here the gospel was narrated in the particular version of the evangelist in question. The nearest parallel we have to this is that the Greek fathers often introduce the different versions of the Greek translation of the Old Testament with the formula κατὰ τοὺς ἑβδομήκοντα, κατὰ τὸν Ἀκύλον, κατὰ τὸν Σύμμαχον, which in an analogous way denotes the *one* 'Old Testament' in the particular version of the Greek translator or editor.[10]

We must therefore assent fully to the interpretation of the title in Harnack and Zahn. What is questionable, however, is their argument that the shorter form is original, and their association of the introduction of the title with a fixing of the canon of the four Gospels in the first half of the second century.

Granted, we still find the short versions κατὰ Μαθθαῖον, Μάρκον, etc., in the most recent, twenty-sixth, edition of Nestle-Aland, but the apparatus to the *inscriptio*, given for the first time, shows that this reading is based on weak evidence. Apart from Vaticanus and in part Sinaiticus, all the other normative manuscripts have the longer form εὐαγγέλιον κατὰ Μαθθαῖον, etc.[11]

In addition we have the evidence of the papyri, which Harnack and Zahn could not yet have known. We possess twenty papyri of canonical Gospels from the second and third centuries, some of them very fragmentary. In only three of them have the *inscriptiones* or *subscriptiones* been preserved:[12]

1. In P 66 from about 200 there is the *inscriptio* ΕΥΑΓΓΕΛΙΟΝ ΚΑΤΑ ΙΩΑΝΝΗΝ.[13]

2. In P.75, which is a little later, we have the *subscriptio* ΕΥΑΓΓΕΛΙΟΝ ΚΑΤΑ ΛΟΥΚΑΝ and, on the same page only a little further on, the *inscriptio* ΕΥΑΓΓΕΛΙΟΝ ΚΑΤΑ ΙΩΑΝΝΗΝ.[14]

3. On a page from P 4, 64 and 67, which belong together, with fragments from Matthew and Luke. This has the inscription ΕΥΑΓΓΕΛΙΟΝ ΚΑΤΑ ΜΑΘΘΑΙΟΝ.[15] Presumably this is the title page of a codex. Roberts dates this papyrus as early as the second century.[16] That means that the originals of these manuscripts at all events go back well into that century.

The long form is also supported by the Old Latin translation, which presumably came into being in the last quarter of the second century,[17] and by the Coptic versions. The procession of witnesses is brought up in the rear with the agreement in terminology between Irenaeus in Lyons and, a little later, Clement of Alexandria, the Muratorian Canon in Rome[18] and Tertullian in Carthage. What is striking here is the complete unanimity over the four titles of the Gospels in a distribution extending throughout the whole of the Roman Empire towards the end of the second century, from Lyons to Carthage and as far as the Egyptian Chora.

This unanimity of testimony to the titles of the Gospels, for which there are still no variants of any kind in this early period, rules out a late origin from the middle of the second century. It is extremely improbable that there is a connection with the fixing of the 'canon of the four Gospels', which can be clearly seen for the first time with the Gospel Harmony of Tatian the Syrian shortly after 170 and then a little later in Irenaeus, but can equally well be earlier. The canon of four Gospels really took *clear* shape only at a relatively late stage. Justin the Apologist, Tatian's teacher, living in Rome about 150, knows the Gospel of John but quotes it only once, in a rather free way.[19] Even at a later date, particularly in Rome, the Fourth Gospel had some opponents, as it was especially treasured by the Gnostics and also by the Montanists.[20]

Another argument against associating the establishment of the canon of four Gospels with the introduction of the titles is the fact that the *sequence* of the four Gospels in the early period, unlike the titles, was not always the same. In his history of the canon Zahn counts seven different possible orders for which there is evidence in early tradition – albeit with very different weight.[21] The most important variant, which has been preserved in Codex D, John, Matthew, Luke, Mark, is based on the estimation of the Gospels in the church. The order which then became established – Matthew, Mark, Luke, John – already appears in Irenaeus (*Adv.haer.* 3.1.1) and others after him as the chronological order of composition.

The explanation of this varying sequence in the early period is that at first, as a rule, only one Gospel was contained in a codex, and accordingly people could put the Gospels in any order they liked. We rarely find a collection of all four Gospels in the early papyri: such a large codex as P 45, with Matthew, Mark, Luke, John and Acts, extending to 220 pages, is exceptional.[22] This variability was a consequence of the fact that, depending on their popularity, the individual Gospels were used with very different frequency. Among the twenty papyri of the Gospels from Egypt from the time before Constantine, John comes first with eleven fragments, Matthew follows closely behind with nine, Luke has only four, and the only appearance of Mark is in the great Chester Beatty Codex. The gnosticizing apocryphal Gospel of Thomas, with three fragments in the Egyptian Chora, is represented more frequently than Mark.[23]

2. The attestation of the title in the second century

In comparison with the widespread attestation of the fourfold Gospel, its authors and its titles in about 180, it is striking that we have relatively few references from the early period and that some of them are only indirect. This is certainly connected with the fact that by far the greater part of the Christian literature from the second century, before Irenaeus, has been lost, and that with the exception of Justin, in the apologetic literature that remains the Gospels did not play a large part. At the same time, however, this indicates a certain lack of interest in the question of authorship – which is of particular interest to us – and in the distinguishing between different Gospel writings in the earlier period. The essential matter was not the authors, but the one Lord who stood behind his good news.

Nowhere before Irenaeus can we find any particular church-political activities aimed at disseminating the fourfold Gospel. Rather, Tatian's attempt to create a Gospel Harmony points to the fact that the plurality of the Gospels was felt to be a problem in the controversy with Marcion's counter-church and its one Gospel.

It accords with this that as far as I can see, the plural εὐαγγέλια appears only twice before Irenaeus. The earliest apologist, Aristides, speaks only in two places in general terms about the writings of the Christians and once of the εὐαγγελικὴ γραφὴ (or the Gospel in which the Emperor is to read).[24] We find the earliest instance of the plural in Justin, who is fond of mentioning the 'Reminiscences of the Apostles', ἀπομνημονεύματα τῶν ἀποστόλων - fifteen times in all. He probably takes over this designation from Xenophon's Reminiscences of Socrates.[25] Where he mentions these 'Reminiscences of the Apostles' for the first time, he adds by way of explanation, 'which are called Gospels' (ἅτινα καλεῖται εὐαγγέλια).[26] Whereas elsewhere he gives the impression that they were written collectively by the apostles, a fiction which we find often in the second century, at one point he makes his comments more precise and adds that 'the reminiscences were composed by apostles (of Jesus) and their followers'.[27] In other words, he knows that some of the Gospels are attributed to apostles, Matthew and John, and others to the disciples of apostles, Mark and Luke. In one single passage there could perhaps be a direct indication of an apostle as 'author' of a Gospel. In *Dialogue* 106,3 he reports that Peter received his name from Jesus and that this was written down in 'his (i.e. Peter's) reminiscences'. It emerges from the context that he is quoting Mark 3.16f., i.e. that he was evidently familiar with the tradition that Mark had been a disciple of Peter. Here, too, Justin is concerned not with the evangelists but with a reference to the reliability of the tradition, which can be traced back to those who were directly involved.

In complete contrast to us, Justin is not in any way interested in the individual theology or the personality of the evangelists, but only in the words and works of the Lord himself, credibly attested by the 'Reminiscences of the apostles', which for him appear as a unity and which, as he is fond of stressing, were carried by the apostles from

Jerusalem throughout the world and then written down.[28] In this way he presupposes knowledge of the Gospel titles, but unlike Irenaeus a generation later he does not yet reflect on the relationship between plurality and unity, but orientates himself almost naively only on the unity of the apostolic testimony which found expression in the 'Reminiscences of the Apostles'.

If we go back chronologically before Justin, we come to the Gospel of Marcion, which he presented about 144,[29] that rigorously bowdlerized version of the Gospel of Luke which he regarded as the one true Gospel and which, as Tertullian critically pointed out, he designated 'the Gospel', leaving out the author's name. For Tertullian, on the other hand, a work without a full title, including the name of the author, had no authority.[30] In the case of Marcion, too, we can presuppose that he knew several Gospels.[31] The best explanation of the fact that he chose the Gospel of Luke seems to me to be that its title and tradition already attributed it to a disciple of Paul. The Gospels of Matthew and John were ruled out, as they were attributed to original Judaizing apostles, and even more was that of Mark, since he was the disciple of Peter, the *legis homo*.[32] Since according to Marcion the Judaizers[32a] had falsified the gospel originally entrusted by Christ to Paul, and only Marcion could restore it to its pure, valid form, the removal of the false name Luke and the use of the true title 'The Gospel' (τὸ εὐαγγέλιον) seems to have been intrinsically necessary.

The best explanation of the much-disputed and basically critical double note about the origin of the Gospels of Mark and Matthew in the five-volume work of Papias of Hierapolis,[33] 'The Interpretation of the Words of the Lord', written about 120 or 130, also seems to be the presence of titles for the Gospels. Although the term εὐαγγέλιον itself does not appear in the two short quotations in Eusebius' *Church History*, since in them Papias merely speaks of Mark and Matthew as authors, Eusebius' two notes are only comprehensible to the reader if he knows of the attribution of the Gospels to the authors; in other words, Papias already presupposes this.[34]

According to Eusebius' quotation, the report about Mark goes back a generation further to the mysterious presbyter John, whom the Phrygian bishop often quotes as an informant,[35] which brings us to a time between 90 and 100. This rules out the derivation[36] of Papias' note about Mark from I Peter 5.13 ('The elect community in Babylon, and Mark, my son, greet you'), since I Peter, which Papias knew, is a pseudepigraphical writing from the time of Domitian and therefore is almost contemporaneous with the presbyter himself. Rather, both

I Peter and the presbyter have access to this earlier tradition. The beginning of the note about Mark runs:

> And the presbyter said this: Mark was the interpreter of Peter and wrote down carefully what he remembered of what had been said or done by the Lord, but not in the right order...

The even more mysterious note about Matthew, which Eusebius adds immediately afterwards, could also go back to the presbyter:

> Matthew composed the Logia in Hebrew, and each one translated them as best he could.

J.B.Lightfoot and Eduard Schwartz were probably right in conjecturing that the right order (τάξις) which Papias fails to find in the Second Gospel is that of the Fourth Gospel with its more comprehensive three-year chronology.[37] The devaluation of the Greek Gospel of Matthew, which established itself most rapidly in the church, is even more striking; at best it appears as a second-hand translation and not as directly apostolic. I would conclude from this that Papias – and even more his informant, the presbyter – were still aware of the problems of the writing of Gospels and the rival claims and traditions associated with it, which are evident from the different names of the authors. It is no coincidence that in the five-volume work he stresses his high opinion of the old, living oral tradition over against the written word:

> For I was convinced that what came to me from books was not as useful as what came from the living and abiding oral tradition.[38]

In other words, Papias is quite familiar with 'Gospel literature' (and other Christian writings), but rates oral tradition higher.

Papias' notes take our knowledge of the titles of the first two Gospels with some probability back to the end of the first century. That the titles are as old as this – a view which runs counter to prevailing opinion – is also confirmed by the titles of *apocryphal* Gospels known to us, the majority of which came into being as early as the first half of the second century, but later than the canonical Gospels. These titles had already been formed in analogy to those of the earlier Gospel writings – which later became canonical – including the Gospels according to Thomas, Peter, Philip, Matthias, Mary and so on.[39] The Gospels of particular groups received similar names: εὐαγγέλιον καθ᾽ Ἑβραίους or κατ᾽ Αἰγυπτίους.[40] In the Jewish-Christian or Gnostic groups where they belonged they may first have simply been called τὸ εὐαγγέλιον, but the tendency towards analogy was so strong that they too took on the designation with κατά and the accusative – against the original meaning.

It does not tell against this considerable age of the titles of the Gospels that the earliest references to the Gospels as writings, in the 'Teaching of the Twelve Apostles'[41] and so-called II Clement, from the first decades of the second century, simply quote 'the Gospel' in the singular without the mention of an author, e.g. in the formula, 'the Lord says in the Gospel'.[42] This singular form of expression is still widespread as late as the third century and arises from the fact that the Jesus tradition, i.e. the teaching of the Lord, was taken to be identical with 'the Gospel'; here the reference to the word of the Kyrios was still given pre-eminence throughout the second century.

It is significant for the earliest testimony to this terminology outside the New Testament, that of the martyr-bishop Ignatius, around 110, that we cannot always be completely certain whether he understands εὐαγγέλιον in terms of the *viva vox* of the proclamation of Christ, the Jesus tradition or the Gospel writings. The written character comes out most strongly in *Smyrn.*5.1:

Hitherto neither 'the prophetic predictions nor the law of Moses nor the gospel' have convinced his opponents.[43]

Similarly Smyrnaeans 7.2:

Therefore it is fitting ...to turn to the prophets and especially to the gospel, in which suffering is intimated to us and the resurrection accomplished.[44]

Ignatius certainly knows the Gospel of Matthew, and probably also that of John,[45] but for him the gospel as a message of salvation is still not firmly bound up with its written form; rather, it forms a living unity the centre of which lies in the passion of Jesus. He says nothing about the authors of the Gospels.

Probably contemporaneously with Papias, i.e. in the time of Hadrian, we find knowledge of the first three Gospels, Matthew, Luke and John, in Basilides, the first great Gnostic in Alexandria. He wrote a Gospel of his own – presumably eclectic – and in addition composed the first commentary on the Gospels that we know, in twenty-four volumes.[46]

Finally, the secondary conclusion to Mark, 16.9-20, points back to about the time of Ignatius or Papias: it works up material from Matthew, Luke and John along with apocryphal material, some of which was also known to Papias, into a mini-harmony of the resurrection appearances, and thus removed the offence of the original conclusion, with the flight of the women from the tomb.[47]

'Good news' could not really end with ἐφοβοῦντο γάρ, 'for they were afraid'.

The secondary conclusion to Mark and the *Epistula Apostolorum*,[48] which is likewise to be dated in the first half of the second century, are thus probably the earliest Christian texts to presuppose all the Gospels and Acts.

3. The four Gospels' own witness and the individuality of the author

The four Gospels themselves, with Mark the first and John the last,[49] composed between 69 and about 100, have no immediately evident reference in their texts to the names of their authors. Either the name of the author is absent, as in the case of Luke and John, or we find the name, but with no reference to authorship, as in the case of Matthew, or even – as in the case of Mark – we do not find either. Conversely, a distinguishing feature of the second and earliest Gospel known to us, that according to Mark, is that it is the only one in which the term εὐαγγέλιον has central theological significance. This is already evident from the introduction (Mark 1.1): ἀρχὴ τοῦ εὐαγγε-λίου Ἰησοῦ Χριστοῦ, which at the same time performs the function of a title. All in all, Mark uses the term seven times. The most interesting instance is the last one, at the beginning of the passion narrative (14.9), where Jesus says to the unknown woman who anoints him in Bethany: 'Truly I say to you, wherever the gospel is proclaimed (κηρυχθῇ) through the world, what she has done will also be told (λαληθήσεται) in memory of her.' In the first half of this statement Mark's Jesus talks in characteristically Pauline terms of the message of salvation being preached throughout the world; in the second half he presupposes that this preaching includes the narration of stories about Jesus and here once again the passion narrative in particular, in which the action of this woman has a place. For Mark, in contrast to what still seems to be the case with Paul, the 'historical' narrative account of the activity and passion of Jesus is an essential part of the proclamation of the gospel: for him, preaching and historical narrative are not opposites, but are indissolubly connected. For that very reason he can describe his work as εὐαγγέλιον Ἰησοῦ Χριστοῦ – to be understood in the ancient sense as a biography of Jesus.[50]

It is all the more striking that Luke completely avoids the term in the Gospel and removes it where he is dependent on Mark,[51] and also that Matthew, in his substantially larger work, limits it to four instances, three of them with the genitival attribute εὐαγγέλιον τῆς βασιλείας,[52] while the Johannine corpus does not use it at all.[53] In this sense one could say that really only Mark's work rightly bears the title εὐαγγέλιον. But in that case how did it come about that all four 'biographies of Jesus' received this one title?

In support of the predominant theory that the titles of the Gospels came into being very late and that the Gospels were originally presented anonymously or without titles, it is argued that in Judaism, in contrast to the Graeco-Roman world, writings were usually anonymous or pseudonymous. The correct insight here is that the problem of 'intellectual property' was discovered much later in Judaism than among the Greeks. The first Palestinian Jewish author to write under his own name is Ben Sira, about 180 BC; in other words, the discovery of the individuality of the author is an achievement of the Hellenistic period.[54] Later, in rabbinic Judaism, the knowledge of the names of teachers and those who handed down tradition was an important innovation. At the same time, underlying the name of the teacher and the tradent was his authority as a scholar.

This must also be noted in early Christianity. At the beginning we come across the towering authority of teachers like the pillars James, Cephas-Peter and John on one side and Saul-Paul and Barnabas on the other.[55] The earliest Christian writings – the letters of Paul – bear the name of a real author. This is a feature, if we want to put it that way, of the 'Hellenistic' character of earliest Christianity. The same is true of the book of Revelation, I Clement,[56] the letters of Ignatius, the Shepherd of Hermas and the letters of Polycarp and all the apologists. As a rule people no longer published (or had multiple copies made) anonymously,[57] and where they took refuge behind the pseudonym of an authority it was usually one of the great figures like the pillars Peter, James, John, Paul, or a well-known disciple from the group of Twelve like Andrew, Philip or Thomas. In other words, they looked for a significant name from the past; and that does not happen with the titles of the Gospels – with the exception of John,[58] over which there is dispute. We may not therefore assume *a priori* that in every case we have secondary, pseudepigraphical attribution of authorship. The question who added the title in individual cases may be left open here. The title could come from authors or from the editor or a scribe making a copy or a librarian. Irenaeus, whose main work, directed against Gnosticism, was written soon after AD 180 and is to be found on a papyrus fragment in Egypt even before the end of the second century, himself created the title of his work. At the same time it expressed a programme for him.[59]

It does not tell against this observation that the earliest Christian authors up to Ignatius, Polycarp and Hermas presented themselves as being borne by the Spirit. In fact the whole of the eschatological people of God of itself possessed the gift of the Spirit and precisely for that reason the Spirit had to become manifest in specific, apostolic and prophetic authorities (and authors), and be connected with distinct individual personalities.

4. The practical necessity of the titles

In order to understand the function of the titles of the Gospels, we must take a brief look at Greek literature.[60]

The first classical histories did not need any *inscriptio*. The author mentioned himself first: 'Hecataeus, the Milesian, narrates the following: I write this as it seems true to me, for the tales of the Greeks appear to me to be numerous and ridiculous.'[61] The title of a writing only became really necessary where there was a concern to *distinguish* between different works and authors, say in selling books,[62] in academic discussion and in public libraries,[63] especially in the Hellenistic period. 'The giving of titles is predominantly a matter of literary reception and communication, which is why it is often done by the public.'[64] In the libraries numerous earlier works had to be given secondary titles. Unless it was described more closely, a book was inaccessible and could not be quoted. In this connection we often find two (or even more) names. Thus the Dialogues of Plato were usually designated by the partners in the conversation, and in addition there was often a reference to the content, which sometimes took on a life of its own (Φαίδων = περὶ ψυχῆς; Φαῖδρος = περὶ καλοῦ).[65]

We find titles relating to content, to identify scriptural scrolls and indicate their content, in the great library of the Essenes of *Qumran*; there the names of authors are usually missing.[66]

About the beginning of the Christian era most books had already been given a title by their authors, especially if they were intended for the book trade. However, there were exceptions, since not everyone was ambitious enough to have the urge to appear before a literary public. Thus in his work 'On My Own Books', Galen stresses that he gave his works 'without a title to my friends or pupils', since he did not write 'with publication in mind, but for those who asked to have a record of what they had heard'. Because he thus presented his writings to his pupils without titles, when at a later date they nevertheless came into circulation, 'everyone gave them a different title'. The little importance Galen attached to titles is evident from the fact that he himself does not quote them consistently.[67] In the period of the Empire, in particular, there is especially frequent evidence of the editing of writings not by the author himself but by pupils, friends or even by a patron to whom the work was dedicated.[68] In the case of the Gospel of Luke we may therefore assume that the 'most excellent Theophilus'[69] to whom the work was dedicated was concerned for the wider circulation of the work, though not necessarily through the book trade, as Dibelius assumed;[70] Christian writings in the first and second centuries were still too much politically problematical 'underground literature' for that, and when Justin in the so-called *Second Apology* asks the Romans – presumably members of the Senate – to approve (προγράφειν) his work by public proclamation, so that he can 'make it accessible to all' (1,15; 15,2), this is the exception of a bold apologist which proves the rule.[71] However, Luke may have been interested in the fact that Theophilus could make the work known among like-minded friends, i.e. those sympathetic to Christianity in the educated upper classes.

The last editor of the Gospel of John, who added and inserted John 21 and other passages, and was concerned to introduce the work to the communities, was presumably a disciple of the author. It is improbable that both these figures, Theophilus and the unknown person(s) perhaps connected with the mysterious presbyter John of Ephesus, circulated works which had been entrusted to them anonymously and without titles.[72] The dedication to Theophilus also implies an author. People had a certain mistrust of anonymous works without any title,[73] so that pseudepigraphical writings had a better chance of being accepted in the communities. This attitude was exploited in the production of Christian literature, both among the Gnostics and in anti-Gnostic and popular writing.

(a) The reading of scripture in worship

Given the significance of the legitimacy of the tradition[74] and the authority of the teacher and those who handed down the tradition in earliest Christianity, it is evident that when a writing was circulated by means of copies sent to other communities, for practical reasons it was given either an appropriate short title to indicate its content or the name of an author or both. This is above all the case when writings were written and circulated not primarily for private edification but for the purpose of being read out at worship.

We find the reading of scripture, which along with preaching had long been a fixed custom in the synagogue,[75] in the first detailed account of organized early Christian worship, in Justin:

On the day which is called Sunday all those who live in cities or in the country gather together at one place and the *Reminiscences of the Apostles* or the writings of the prophets are read out while there is time. When the reader has finished, the president gives an admonition and an invitation to imitate these good things through a discourse.[76]

Here readings at worship seem to be an established institution which has grown directly out of synagogue worship. It is striking that the reading of the Gospels is mentioned before the prophets; to some extent it has taken over the significance of the Jewish reading of the Torah. Even if we no longer have any account of liturgical reading before Justin, we do at least have clear indications that it took place very much earlier. The literature which has come down to us often makes no mention at all of what was completely taken for granted as happening in early Christian communities, or mentions it only peripherally. Had there not been irregularities over the celebration of the eucharist in Corinth, we would assume that Paul did not celebrate it in his communities at all. Similarly, the reading of scripture in the earliest Christian worship remains an obscure matter, because it was not put in question. In his major letters Paul uses the Old Testament – or more exactly the LXX – in a way which presupposes that it was constantly read in worship and that its authority was completely taken for granted in an obvious way. We have a clear reference to the sequence of scripture reading and sermon some decades before Justin in II Clement 19.1.[77] Even earlier, round about 100, the invitation in I Tim.4.13, 'Attend to the public reading of scripture, admonition and teaching until I come', is to be understood as a sequence of scripture reading followed by a sermon,[78] and the blessing on the reader and the hearers in Rev.1.3 refers to worship; here we already have the reading of a writing of Christian revelation.[79]

The custom of reading letters in worship is attested by the earliest letter of Paul, in I Thess.5.27 (*c.* 50).[80] In his letter to Bishop Soter in Rome, Bishop Dionysius of Corinth stresses that the letter of his Roman colleague is still read in his community on the Lord's Day 'regularly for edification'; the same is also true of I Clement, which was written some seventy years earlier.[81] Now of course we may not simply identify liturgical *anagnosis* and 'canonization'. In the first place, reading merely indicated high esteem for a writing on the basis of its content or the authority of its author, both of which could be understood as the working of the Spirit. In addition, a distinction was made between individual writings in accordance with their dignity. From the beginning, particular books like the Prophets, the Psalms and the Pentateuch had a special status. As the communities usually had a variety of scriptures which could be read out, the title of the book and in some circumstances the name of the author must have been mentioned. Consequently the Paschal Homily of Melito of Sardes, about 170, begins with the observation: 'The scripture of the Hebrew exodus has been read'.[82] Luke already narrates that in the synagogue at Nazareth, Jesus was handed 'the scroll of the prophet *Isaiah*'.[83]

If anywhere, here in the reading is the Sitz im Leben for the use of the term εὐαγγέλιον: the story of Jesus is presented to the community as 'good news' in contrast to the Jewish reading of the Law or the Prophets. We could imagine that such a reading would be introduced with a formula as in the sermon II Clement 8.5: λέγει... ὁ κύριος ἐν τῷ εὐαγγελίῳ.[84] But if - as was certainly already the case round about 100 - communities had several books of Gospels, to distinguish one from another, κατά with the name of the author had to be added.

(b) Community libraries and book-chests

Now the institutionalized reading of a number of authoritative writings, 'composed under the influence of the Spirit', in worship – letters, the writings of the Old Testament understood as prophetic books, and Gospels – presupposed community libraries.[85] We have evidence of great church libraries only from the third century onwards, like the collection of books established by Bishop Alexander at the beginning of the third century in Aelia Capitolina.[86] However, Irenaeus in Lyons,[87] Justin in Rome,[88] the Catechetical School of Pantaenus and Clement in Alexandria and also the earliest Gnostic schools of Basilides or Valentinus must also have had learned libraries. Even travelling Christians could not be parted from their books,[89] and the satirist Lucian attributes an intensive preoccupation with books and his own production of books to the charlatan Peregrinus Proteus during his Christian phase in Palestine.[90]

Here, however, we are interested in the numerous smaller libraries of the communities made for practical use, which served both as community archives and as collections of books. In addition to the books for solemn liturgical reading and the study of scripture they also contained letters, which could also be read in services, lists and accounts. The seven letters of Ignatius[91] and the letter of Polycarp which goes with them (ch.13) – and not least the collections of the letters of Paul and later of Dionysius of Corinth – show that people made and circulated whole collections of letters. When Ignatius speaks in a quite unusual way in *Philad.* 8.2 of the prophetic books as ἀρχεῖα, literally 'title deeds' (preserved in an archive), this is perhaps also a reference to the 'community archive' in which the

writings of the Old Testament were kept.[92] We may not underestimate
the specifically Christian production of books in the first hundred
years of the new religion, even if relatively little of it is still preserved.
If we leave out of account the proliferations of Gnosticism, this served
not primarily for private edification but for the liturgical meetings of
the communities. The Bishop of Hierapolis's mistrust of books does
not derive from a lack of them in the church but from the over-
production of the 'many', though this did not prevent him from
writing five volumes himself; the few comments made by Eusebius
show that his community library was already well stocked.[93]

Tertullian's criticism of Marcion's newly produced Gospel,
Adv.Marc. 4.4.2, gives an appropriate picture of the historical situation in a rhetorical question: 'And in the end is that to be regarded
as more faithful to the truth which is later, even after so many and
significant works and testimonies to the Christian religion have been
produced for the world, which without the truth of the Gospel could
not have been published, i.e. for the truth of the Gospel?' But where
could those *tot ac tanta... opera atque documenta Christianae religionis
saeculo edita* be collected, if not in the libraries of the communities?

That means that Christian communities, which usually came
into being in the larger cities by splitting off from the synagogue
communities, would as a rule from the beginning have a 'book chest'
with the most important writings of the Old Testament, which were
then gradually supplemented by their own Christian writings.[94] That
even small communities had a 'Torah shrine' of this kind is clear from
the example of the Martyrs of Scilli, an otherwise unknown place in
North Africa, who when asked by the governor, 'What objects are in
your chest?' replied, 'Books and letters of Paul, a just man.' Here the
capsa corresponds to the Jewish *torah* shrine, and the books are
prophetic writings and Gospels.[95]

(c) Established patterns of writing in early Christianity

The work of Christian scribes[96] should be seen in the closest
connection with these community libraries for the reading of scripture
and teaching in worship. This work takes on a clear profile on the
basis of papyri from the second and third centuries and indicates
quite fixed patterns of writing which are in marked contrast to the
Jewish scribal rules and also to literary book production for the book
trade.

1. From the beginning – in contrast to contemporary book
production elsewhere – these scribes write on codices rather than, as
was originally still quite usual, on scrolls, whether copying Old
Testament texts or the Gospels. Presumably from the beginning the

specifically *Christian* texts were written on codices. As a volume, the codex was easier to handle, cheaper to produce, and could more easily be taken on journeys by Christian missionaries. In my view for practical reasons the letters of Paul would already have been produced as codices. This form was probably introduced for longer letters by Caesar for his reports to the Senate. Suetonius, who as Hadrian's secretary had access to state archives, gives his expert view on this: 'Moreover, the senate also received letters from him. It seems that he was the first to write on individual pages in the form of a notebook (*quas primum uidetur ad paginas et formam memorialis libelli conuertisse*), whereas previously the consuls and generals had sent them only on sheets of papyrus written crosswise.'[97] So the new form came about, specifically in connection with letters, for quite practical reasons.

2. Terms like God, Lord, Jesus and Christ are always written as *nomina sacra*, i.e. only in abbreviated form with the first and last letters, and emphasized for the reader with a stroke over them.[98]

3. The scribes were no calligraphers, but simply document scribes who worked in their spare time for the needs of the community.[99]

In all these three points the work of scribes differs from literary production elsewhere, and also from the customs of the synagogue, and we have good reason to suppose that these striking early Christian scribal customs are directly connected with the separation from Judaism: the place of the artistically written Torah scroll which is still used today in Jewish worship was taken by the codex, which in the first and second centuries was otherwise very rare, while the special writing of the Tetragrammaton, the secret name of God, in Hebrew letters in the Jewish manuscripts of the Septuagint was replaced in the Christian codices by the *nomina sacra*, which stress for liturgical reading not only the divine names, but also Christ and his titles. This development of a distinctive Christian scribal tradition which presumably goes back to the beginnings of Christian literature in the first century 'seems to indicate a degree of organization, of conscious planning and uniformity of practice among the Christian communities which we have hitherto had little reason to suspect, and which throws a new light on the early history of the church'.[100] The circumstances and customs in the church in the second half of the first century and the first half of the second century do not seem to me to have been as diffuse and chaotic as people like to represent them today.

One could understand this deliberate demarcation from Jewish scribal usage, with a pinch of salt, as a consequence of the replacement of sabbath worship by the assembly on the κυριακὴ ἡμέρα and the deliberate use of the term ἐκκλησία (θεοῦ) for the new eschatological people of God and the liturgical meetings which took the place of the συναγωγή.[101] Earlier conjectures which sought to connect the introduction of the *nomina sacra* and the codex with the formation of the canon of the four Gospels are by contrast to be rejected as firmly as the connection between the titles of the Gospels and the canon of the four Gospels: codex, *nomina sacra* and titles of the Gospels must be earlier.

It now seems to me that the surprising constancy and unity of the titles of the Gospels goes back to this strikingly strict early Christian scribal discipline. From the beginning people retained the traditional titles given to works without varying them. Fundamentally, here the gospel as *the* message of salvation, whether it was presented orally (as evidenced in Mark 14.9) or later in written form, replaced the previous message of salvation contained in the Law, i.e. the Pentateuch, so that the latter was from now on understood as the work of the prophet Moses, i.e. as the first prophetic writing.[102] It is therefore only consistent that Justin should put the reading of the Gospels before the reading of the prophets.

We already find a first reference to such Christian scribes as early as Rom.16.22: 'I greet you, I Tertius, who have written this letter, in the Lord.' Here we can already see something of the self-awareness of those in this position: a second, strange 'I' suddenly appears in the letter of an apostle.[103] As I have already said, by profession they were mostly document scribes; they looked after the community libraries, copying and sending out liturgical writings, letters, and other documents which were connected with the life of the community, and in so doing worked hand in hand with travelling teachers and messengers who went from community to community.[104] This abundant travelling, from the beginning associated with a constant exchange of books and letters, was one of the foundations of the unity of the church. We come across lively scribal activity in connection with the exchange of letters and messengers in the letters of Ignatius and in ch.13 of the Epistle of Polycarp, which is in fact an independent covering letter;[105] indeed the letters of Paul and the apostle's travel plans already presuppose a very active exchange of messengers.[106] There are later scribal notes by editors at the end of the Martyrdom of Polycarp, which was originally a letter from the community in Smyrna to that in Philomelium, 'the church of God and all the "sojourners" (παροικίαι) of the holy catholic church in all places', i.e. a circular letter, later worked over and given legendary embellishment.[107] This custom of exchanging and circulating letters also already goes back to the time of the Pauline mission.[108] Here a relatively uniform formula for a letter points on the one hand to the reading of these letters in worship and also in turn to the established scribal custom through which, among other factors, the unity of the Christian communities was expressed. The external form of the inspired word which was read out in worship was not completely a matter of indifference. C. Andresen will be right in his view that this intensive traffic in messengers with the exchange of letters and other writings and the reading of them in worship goes back to customs among the Jewish diaspora communities.[109]

In the Shepherd of Hermas the seer receives a commission to make two copies of the heavenly letter which is revealed to him and to give one of them to Clement, who is to 'send it to the cities abroad, for that is his task'.[110] Here in my view we come upon the historical origin of the titles of the Gospels which we find so mysterious. I can put what follows only as a hypothesis, but there seem to me to be good grounds for it and it explains the phenomenon better than previous suggestions. The titles of the Gospels could have been added by those early Christian scribes who saw to the dissemination of the first Gospel writings by copying them and sending them out to other important communities in those parts of the Roman empire where the Christian mission had been successful. The titles were necessary for arranging the Gospels in community libraries and for liturgical reading. This is the only explanation for their great age and the complete unanimity in them towards the end of the second century.

5. Summary and conclusions

1. It is extremely improbable that the Gospels were circulated in the communities and used in worship as writings without titles. Particularly if a new work was read in worship, there had to be an announcement of the kind of writing it was. This was made, as the titles of the Gospels show with the use of the term 'Gospel', by a reference to the author.

2. At the latest when communities had two different copies of the Gospels, titles had to be used to distinguish them, in order to avoid confusion. Where the author was well known to the community, a verbal reference would have been enough, but as soon as his work was copied, sent to other communities and put in an archive there, a title was absolutely necessary to distinguish it from other works. We may assume that at least the larger communities got hold of the newly composed Gospels relatively quickly because of the lively interchange between the communities. Probably, too – as in the case

of the Shepherd of Hermas – these works were even sent unasked. The sending of letters and other writings was always also an act of 'church politics'. Even the reading in worship of documents sent by other communities could also be a matter of 'church politics'.

3. If, as is usually argued today, the earliest Gospels were anonymous or lacked titles, because of the pressing need to distinguish them in community libraries a variation of titles would have inevitably arisen, whereas in the case of the canonical Gospels (in contrast to that of countless apocryphal writings)[111] we can detect nothing of this. Circulation of anonymous works without a title would of necessity have led to a multiplicity of titles.

4. It is improbable that the unity among the titles of the Gospels towards the end of the second century came about through some central redaction of the Gospels a few decades earlier, i.e. through an authoritative pronouncement within the church. In this obscure period, which was at the same time relatively free, there was no authority which could have carried through such unification with such far-reaching success in all communities. Rather, we must go back to the time of the final redaction and first circulation of the Gospels themselves.

5. More recent investigations have shown that the canon of the four Gospels was not forged into a unity at an early stage by a church-political act but rather that it came together in a slow process in which the Gospels were esteemed differently in different areas of the church. In other words, the Gospels took on their titles before they were combined in the canon of the four Gospels. In Rome people hesitated over the Fourth Gospel for a long time, while in Egypt it was particularly popular. The Gospel of Mark quickly lost significance once it had been almost completely worked over by Matthew. It is almost a miracle that it did not disappear altogether: it owes its preservation to its connection with the authority of Peter. Only the Gospel of Matthew enjoyed a high reputation almost everywhere very soon after it was introduced. Nevertheless, in Asia Minor, the province of the most theological importance in the second century, John's chronology and dating of Easter was preferred to that of Matthew.

6. On the other hand, the origin of the title εὐαγγέλιον can only have been the second Gospel, which was neglected so soon afterwards. By making his work begin with the statement ἀρχὴ τοῦ εὐαγγελίου Ἰησοῦ Χριστοῦ, Mark already presupposes that the story of Jesus which he tells is 'good news of Jesus Christ'. His use of the word εὐαγγέλιον is thus substantially different from that of Paul, for whom the story of Jesus does not as yet perform an essential function. We might ask

whether this understanding of εὐαγγέλιον, which differs somewhat from that of Paul and is indissolubly connected with the narration of stories about Jesus, could not perhaps go back to Petrine roots and stand in some degree of opposition to the Jewish saving event of Exodus and Lawgiving, which was similarly narrated as a historical account. For that very reason the Old Testament reading in worship needed an oral comment and later the reading of the story of Jesus as a supplement to refer to the fulfilment.[112]

7. At the same time Mark thus laid the foundation for the literary genre of the Gospel, which is a special instance belonging within the very wide range of ancient biographies. As the εὐαγγέλιον Ἰησοῦ Χριστοῦ expressed in writing, his work represented a revolutionary innovation for the communities who hitherto had had to rely predominantly on oral tradition about Jesus. Therefore particularly in his case it is questionable whether it was first circulated anonymously. The recipients in the other communities would have wanted to know whether it came from a reliable authority, especially if it differed from their own local oral tradition. So it seems that we should take seriously the possibility that the authority which copied the Gospel, presumably composed in Rome in the crisis year of 69,[113] and sent it to other communities – the note in the Shepherd of Hermas shows that this need not have been identical with the author – described it to the recipients as εὐαγγέλιον κατὰ Μᾶρκον.

8. Only as a result of the Gospel of Mark was it possible for the title 'Gospel' to establish itself for a 'biography of Jesus', for only there was the story of Jesus described as εὐαγγέλιον, and only there did the term have a basic theological significance which supports the whole work. In the Gospel of Luke this is quite remote (see n.51 above), in the Johannine corpus it is completely absent, and in Matthew it is used only in a markedly reduced sense. The transference of this title, quite unusual in ancient literature, to the later Gospels including the numerous apocryphal Gospels in the second century can only meaningfully be explained in the light of the earliest Gospel, that of Mark. We may therefore assume that the title was transferred to the later Gospels, Luke, Matthew and John (not to mention the later apocryphal works), on the model of the Gospel of Mark at the time when these works were to be circulated in the Great Church by being copied. In the case of Luke one could think in terms of an initiative by his patron Theophilus, in the case of John of the final editor(s) who can be heard in 21.24 in the reference to the author and put the authority of the beloved disciple above that of Peter, which was generally recognized in the church. Might perhaps the superiority of the new work over the Synoptic tradition founded by Peter's

disciple Mark be expressed in the superiority of the beloved disciple to Peter? Certainly, all this remains hypothetical. But it is not entirely unfounded. Anyone who wants to reject it outright must try to find an explanation with a better historical basis for the origin of those titles, which are completely novel and unusual in the ancient world, and the astonishing agreement between them.

9. Independently of these hypotheses it must be asserted that in the present state of our knowledge the titles of the Gospels are by no means late products from the second century but must be very old. With a considerable degree of probablility they can be traced back to the time of the origin of the four Gospels between 69 and 100 and are connected with their circulation in the communities. Their ultimate root lies in the terminology of Mark, who was the first to call a writing εὐαγγέλιον.

Wolfgang Schadewaldt

Wolfgang Schadewaldt (1900-1974) was a classical philologist. His years of study in Berlin in the period after the First World War brought him many privations, but his teachers still included the great philologists from the turn of the century: Wilamowitz, Diels, and Eduard Norden. In addition to them, he also encountered younger men who were indebted to the old style: the Latin scholar Eduard Fraenkel and the textual critic Paul Maas. As Schadewaldt himself once said at a later date, all his life he felt that he was a philologist of the old school. But the teacher who had by far the greatest influence on him was to be Werner Jaeger. Jaeger opened his eyes to the binding fundamental values of the culture of ancient Greece and to the unity of its forms, though their significance changed with history. Jaeger also included the great church fathers of the fourth century in this culture. As Schadewaldt bore personal witness, from that point on Plato and Aristotle were his constant intimate companions; he communicated his thoughts on them in seminars and discussions to his own pupils, who by then were pursuing their own completely independent research.

Schadewaldt's published works were on the three great tragedians: Sophocles, Aeschylus and Euripides; on lyric poetry: Pindar, Solon and Sappho; and also on Terence and Virgil; on early Greek historiography: Thucydides and Herodotus; on the rise of the Greek historical consciousness; and on the pre-Socratics and the awakening of early Greek philosophical awareness. He made an intensive attempt, in his own quiet manner of observation, to understand the basic shape of each individual work, what he used to call its inner 'structures', and in so doing sought to bring to life again the creator of the work, his unique character and the factors and circumstances which conditioned him. Much as he relied here on his own natural gifts of observation, his instinct, at the same time he always worked through the relevant scholarly literature on the subject. In other words, he took so seriously the most important things that were said about the matter in hand, above all anything that led to contemporary viewpoints, that he tried to understand the reasons for what he thought to be the errors or the contrary opinions of others; this understanding formed the starting point for his own productive new reflection on a subject. This is true above all of his research into Homer, which went on for decades, right down to the end of his life.

I had gradually studied my way to Homer, the interpretation of whom had increasingly developed over the previous century and a half into a distinctive discipline incorporating almost all branches of the study of antiquity and extended to the sphere of the study of epic generally. My first concern was to come to terms with the consequences of the scholarly consensus: while there was had a keen sense of Homer's worth, scholars had had a guilty conscience about admiring him and enjoying him. I saw that I would have to begin again from the beginning with Homer and first of all see what was there and how it had been composed; at the same time I conscientiously studied the history of our most recent Homeric research with the aim of discovering its innermost sense of direction, recognizing its errors and the reason why these errors could come about... I found the old dispute over the unity of Homer easier to solve on the basis of an approach which... sought to understand the special character of the Iliad from the living forms of its inner structure. From this perspective, as opposed to that of Wilamowitz's individual poem theory, the Iliad proved to be something like an independent creation with a long past to look back on, and Homer again emerged from behind its splendour and wholeness as a man and poet with a distinctive character of his own and a truly great creative skill (from W.Schadewaldt's Inaugural Lecture to the Berlin Academy of Sciences, 1943; see also: W.Schadewaldt, *Iliasstudien*, Leipzig 1938, Darmstadt [4]1983; *Von Homers Welt und Werk*, [4]1965; *Legende von Homer, dem fahrenden Sänger*, 1942-1959. Also the work which brought together all his understanding of Homer, a translation of the Odyssey into rhythmic prose aimed at reproducing the original wording; the translation of the Iliad into free verse; and the supplement *Der Aufbau der Ilias*, which summed up his research into Homer, published posthumously).

Wolfgang Schadewaldt was familiar with the Bible from his childhood. He owed this familiarity to his sister Hildegard Schadewaldt, who was eighteen years his senior. Unhappy circumstances meant that she remained unmarried, and in later years, up to her death, she was a somewhat sad, withdrawn person in the Schadewaldt home in the Riesengebirge. Nevertheless, thanks to her steadfast biblical faith and her religious experience, she radiated a strange restless tranquillity over the whole family, which seemed to point to something inexplicably more inward and at a higher level. She was mainly instrumental in educating her youngest brother Wolfgang, who was born after the death of his father; in addition to teaching him to read and write, she introduced him to all the parts of the Bible. He was allowed to go with her, too, when she visited the manses of her friends in the suburbs of Berlin and the Riesengebirge in Silesia; these visits made such a vivid impression on Wolfgang Schadewaldt that he often told his own family and friends of them later. In addition, Hilde would quote verses from the Bible on every occasion. Her brother had such an accurate ear for them, even in his later years, that when experts from the Württembergische Bibelanstalt came to visit him, in his sixties, to ask his advice about the new revision of the Bible (he was in fact regarded as an expert on the translation of ancient texts) he quoted whole verses to them with the stresses with which his sister had pronounced them. He then spoke out quite firmly against the planned revisions (his comments are preserved in the records of the Württembergische Bibelanstalt).

Later, after excellent religious instruction in the Fichte Gymnasium in Berlin, Schadewaldt's apparently very rationalistic confirmation instruction so disappointed him that subsequently he failed to find any middle way between his knowledge of the Bible (he constantly kept consulting it) and the practice of the church, especially since, having direct access to the 'cultic-sacramental' rites, he tended to over- or under-estimate preaching in accordance with the Protestant manner of the time. His attitude to the Bible as the 'book of books' remained unaffected by this. His researches into Goethe, Winckelmann and Hölderlin led him to read the Bible again: he could not understand why some theologians rejected Goethe, and he pointed out how many of Winckelmann's extracts from ancient writers were influenced by the devotional daily Bible readings of the Herrnhuter brethren. He was again prompted to turn to biblical criticism as a result of conversations with a liberal theologian of the older school, Arnold Meyer of Zurich, his father-in-law. Meyer in turn was fond of recalling how someone else who had joined in such a conversation was defending a view which still enjoyed a good deal of respect at the end of the 1920s, namely that Jesus never lived. Anticipating his father-in-law, the theologian, Schadewaldt vigorously and indignantly affirmed and demonstrated the historicity of Jesus.

Later still, it was his increasingly profound study of Homer and Heraclitus which made the classical philologist approach the text of the Gospels again, until he finally felt obliged to do some research here too: to reflect thoroughly, to observe, and to have his say.

The lecture included here is one which Wolfgang Schadewaldt gave in November 1966 to the theological faculty in Hamburg; it was preceded by a number of colloquia in Tübingen. A tape recording was made of this lecture, impressive in its immediacy and vividness, and there is also a text which does not always coincide exactly with the spoken word because of this liveliness and speed of delivery. After this lecture Wolfgang Schadewaldt gave others on the same theme: since in the first lecture he had skipped many of his preliminary observations, he added a good deal in subsequent lectures. In addition, he also had seminars in his home, to which a number of theologians came, above all on the Gospel of Mark and its structure. It may perhaps one day be possible to publish outlines of them. Wolfgang Schadewaldt hoped that after completing his translation of the Iliad and his account of the 'Structure of the Iliad' which summed up all his Homer studies, he would be able to turn all his energies to the criticism and the new recognition of the historical truth of the Gospels. However, he died before that proved possible.

As to this publication, I am very much aware of the fact that Wolfgang Schadewaldt, who would usually plough eight or ten times through anything that was to be printed, would hardly have allowed what follows to appear in this form. But then again, as far as the New Testament was concerned, he had no opportunity to work over his material, and many people keep asking what he said on that occasion. So here is a sketch of what he thought, as it is available to us. At the same time, with the greatest of care, I have inserted into the transcription of the tape the notes that we have and which he skipped in the lecture because of lack of time and the obvious passion with which he spoke. The same goes for the comments which he wrote in the margin for later lectures, along with those which he made for the more thorough colloquia which followed. So with due respect to the philologist who was unable to make further corrections and to theologians who are well versed in these matters, I feel justified in offering this sketch as a stimulus to further thought.

Maria Schadewaldt

The Reliability of the Synoptic Tradition

Wolfgang Schadewaldt

The subject on which I shall be talking here is one on which I have so far been very restrained. Even now, I am venturing on it with considerable hesitation and certainly not on an impulse of my own; what I shall be saying to you, you owe to the compelling verbal powers of persuasion of my friend Helmut Thielicke, which we all know very well. He has managed to overcome the hesitations which at first made me very reluctant, and so it is that today, as an outsider, I am speaking of things about which I can really talk only with fear and trembling. I would also like to stress that I do not really see this paper as a 'lecture', but as a basis for the discussion which I hope will follow. And although I am speaking here from a *cathedra*, I would ask you not to regard what I say as an *ex cathedra* pronouncement, but simply as a report of the attempts of one individual to clarify for himself the views of others on particular matters which have been dear and valuable to him from his childhood.

So I am speaking here, if I may put it that way, in two capacities: first as a classical philologist, and especially as a Homer scholar who has come to certain conclusions about matters of tradition and form in connection with Homer; and secondly also as a Christian layman. I should tell you that some time ago in my colloquium in Tübingen, where I used to discuss other issues than classical philology with a small group of students, our attention came to be focussed on the parables of Jesus. Several of my Tübingen theological colleagues were also there – I felt that this was very important because it provided a theological control. I was primarily interested in the parables of Jesus from a philological point of view, in connection with Homer and his parables, but also in connection with the very important parables of Heraclitus and Plato. Moving to a later period, we could say that parables are also very important in Dante, in Shakespeare and indeed also in Goethe. And so it came about that I told myself that I had to investigate the question where parables became supremely relevant, in the parables of Jesus. I must confess that at one time – please don't be shocked - I toyed with the idea of writing a book with the title

'Jesus as Poet'. To provide some theological justification for that as well, I might point out that since antiquity David has always been celebrated as a poet, and that an English theologian, C.F.Burney, wrote a book which bears the title *The Poetry of Our Lord* (Oxford 1925, a comparison of the form of his words with Hebrew poetry).

My concern was not to treat the parables of Jesus as poetry and to make Jesus a poet in the usual sense of the word. On the contrary, I was concerned to use an understanding of the parables of Jesus to penetrate into the deeper nature of poetry. I simply mention that in passing. In my book on Goethe (*Goethe-Studien*, 1963) I included a lecture (given at the Bavarian Academy of Fine Arts in Munich, 14 July 1960), entitled 'The Word of Poetry', which indicates something of what I understand by 'poetry'. Poetry seems to me to be somehow different from what is usually understood by 'poetry', whether in theory or in practice.

To continue this historical and biographical account, in a meeting of the two theological faculties in Tübingen, which in this instance was under the chairmanship of Herr Käsemann, I next attempted to say something about the parables of Jesus and the reliability of the synoptic tradition, matters which lay very close to my heart both as a theological layman and as a specialist in ancient philology. Both the personalities involved and the subject-matter made it an extremely lively session, in which there was some 'sharp shooting'. Herr Käsemann had already warned us of that, and it was congenial to both his temperament and mine. I myself was grateful for the clarity achieved in these discussions, and I would have no objections at all if later there were to be some 'sharp shooting' at me here, too.

Now when I studied the parables of Jesus, it was obvious that I was not starting from scratch, and that I had to take into account what people had said after working for years on such matters. So I took pains to study the works of New Testament scholars on the parables, the great works of Adolf Jülicher and Joachim Jeremias, W.Michaelis, Eta Linnemann, C.H.Dodd and so on. Of course, in order to understand the wider context, I also made a thorough study of Bultmann's significant and basic work *The History of the Synoptic Tradition*.

Let me make it quite clear – I must stress that I also have very close personal connections with Bultmann, but, as they say, *Platon amicus, magis amica veritas* – let me make it quite clear: I was bitterly disappointed, indeed in despair. After reading this book I felt somehow bereft. That was one thing. The other was that when I read Bultmann and noticed the means he used in his criticism, I was constantly reminded of the Iliad scholarship that I had once learned, say, from

Wilamowitz and others of the earlier analysts, the Iliad scholarship which dogged me for many years of my life. At that time I tried to counter this hyper-criticism which tore the Iliad completely to pieces and negated the person of the poet. I became progressively clearer about it, until finally I was quite sure that it did not do justice to its subject matter. As I have said, the Bultmann business reminded me of my detailed studies in another area, and it seemed to me that the similarities between Homer scholarship on the one hand and this scholarly trend in studying the Synoptic tradition on the other were perhaps more than coincidental. However, I must stress that I do not in any way wish to hold out my experiences in the study of Homer, Thucydides and Plato as a norm for New Testament scholarship. I do not want to present you with a norm, but simply with the perspective from which a classical philologist, concerned with the problems of literary criticism, of written and oral tradition, and especially with questions of authenticity, regards and has to regard New Testament criticism – especially as it was founded by Bultmann, and also already by his predecessors.

I think that my best course here is to be quite direct and specific. When we looked at the parables of Jesus, we began with the parable which Mark himself relates as a basic parable, so to speak as the basis of the meaning of the parables generally, i.e. the parable of the sower. I looked at what Bultmann says about this astonishing parable. In his book we read, for example: 'The original meaning of many similitudes has become irrecoverable in the course of the tradition...! And as for the Parable of the Sower in Mark 4.3-9, is it a consolation for every man when his labour does not all bear fruit? Is it in this sense a monologue by Jesus, half of resignation, half of thankfulness? Is it an exhortation to the hearers of the divine Word? Of Jesus' preaching? Or of the message of the community? Or was there originally no meditation at all on the Word, and have we to understand it as akin to IV Ezra 8.41: "For just as the husbandman sows much seed upon the ground and plants a multitude of plants, and yet not all which were sown shall be saved in due season, nor shall all that were planted take root; so also they that are sown in the world shall not all be saved..."' (pp.199f.) On the same pages we read about other parables: 'The original point of the similitudes of the mustard seed and the leaven (Matt.13.31-33) is quite irrecoverable now. The intro-ductory formula merely asserts – apart from any question as to its originality – that it is concerned with some truth pertaining to the kingdom of God. Since, in my view, the kingdom of God was not thought of, either by Jesus or the early Church, as an human community, there can be no talk of its "growth": and that is even more true of the results of the preaching of Jesus or the Church. Or has it to be interpreted in relation to the individual: do not despair if there seems to be little result from your labour (or from your striving after righteousness)? But no one is able to say whether the meaning is just the reverse, viz. a warning against the evil that poisons the heart or the fellowship.' That is the kind of thing we find in Bultmann. I need not expound it in detail now.

The most remarkable thing about these interpretations – and these are indeed interpretations which underlie the whole matter, for how can one draw any conclusions about anything without having interpreted it – is the categories in which the parables, and especially the parable of the sower, are interpreted. Consolation for every man? Is a parable meant to bring 'consolation'? That is a remarkably moralistic, 'liberal' interpretation! Or is it a half-resigned, half-grateful monologue on the part of Jesus? Jesus giving a monologue? Is it an admonition to the audience? Is it not a reflection on the word at all, but on those who are sown in the world and then are so to speak lost? And when it comes to other parables, the leaven and the mustard seed (Mark 4.31f.; Luke 13.18ff.; Matt.13.31ff.) – is the 'growing' quite unrelated to the kingdom of God, though that is expressly mentioned in the introduction to these parables? Shortly beforehand, Bultmann says: 'Thus it can remain undecided whether or not the birds that come and nest in the branches of the mustard tree are an allegorical representation of the Gentiles who are converted', etc. So with his often all-too-considered interpretation, Bultmann attempts to find a way to the basic category which is decisive for him, his predecessors and his successors: the reformulation of the words and actions of Jesus by the community, the so-called 'community tendency'. This is a criticism which culminates in what one might call an annihilation of whole parts of the Gospels. In other words, an effort is made to understand much of what the Gospels affirm that Jesus said and did as an innovation made by the Christian communities which developed only after Easter. It is a reconstruction of what really happened, but at best it *is* a reconstruction: kerygma, the proclamation at Easter or after Easter of what Jesus was, by the community. Granted, this new knowledge, new experience, after Easter is important enough in itself. Something else must also be said about the post-Easter community: what would we now know about what Jesus said and did had not this community or, to put things more accurately than is usually the case in New Testament criticism, its prominent figures, the apostles, like Peter, handed information down to us and preserved it for us? However, while the significance of the post-Easter event is not to be over-estimated, in my view we must once again attempt, with great care, to extract the 'historical' kernel from the community tradition, which in many places was certainly newly formed. In other words, we must discover what in all probability Jesus himself said and did. For such important critics as Bultmann and others the difficulty in doing this may lie in the fact that this criticism does not draw a clear enough distinction between the first apostles, like Peter, who were still direct witnesses, and the communities which had already been formed. For this criticism does not accept that even what the latter reported has been handed down to us correctly, although it is clear that there is such a tradition of witnesses even behind Paul.

We now come to the history of this critical consideration of the synoptic tradition: in terms of academic theology it goes back to form criticism. Form criticism made its main contribution in the Old Testament; the approach was then used to establish Jewish traditions in the New Testament, traditions which understandably continued to have an influence in the early Christian communities. In addition, as far as the tradition preserved in the New Testament is concerned, there is the newly-observed fact of oral tradition. Oral transmission can be an indication of a particular kind of living tradition in which, in some circumstances, the productive aspect of transmission and existential concern, in this instance the interest of faith, is stronger than mere preservation. In the works of Bultmann and others the word 'legend' keeps cropping up in this sense in connection with the synoptic tradition. What is meant is a non-historical narrative current in the community, often based on old models. Alternatively, we find the term 'legendary', in the sense of telling fictitious stories related to faith. However, oral transmission can also be a very accurate, fixed tradition, a clear reproduction of the original – and I could say a good deal about this from my experience of ancient philology.

We now turn specifically to the parables. The criticism of them which I have mentioned is based on an idea of what a parable is that can no longer be sustained today. In connection with this I want to begin by saying just one thing: in the conversations in Tübingen I was horrified to find myself confronted with a view of the meaning of parables which I regard as being completely out of date. And yet it still lives on, and not only in Bultmann. Suppose we take Jülicher. For him, the parable is part-imagery and part-substance, and in addition there is a *tertium comparationis*. This represents similarities between two logical judgments, and the whole parable is a means of overcoming doubt. Others have seen the parable as an illustration and yet others have attached pedagogical significance to it: something is to be explained which is intrinsically difficult to understand. Then of course there is the famous view – built on the fateful verses Mark 4.10-12 – that the parables are deliberate forms of concealment in the furtherance of the theory of the hardening of people's hearts.

Now I would like to point out – and not out of arrogance – that in the nineteenth century the Homeric parable was interpreted in very much the same way as it is interpreted here by Jülicher, Bultmann and others. However, in Homeric scholarship this view of the nature of the parable was already refuted in the early 1920s, above all by Hermann Fränkel in a fine book (*Die homerischen Gleichnisse*, 1921), and the parable was understood in quite a different way. Fränkel went against all that was being said about the parables in contemporary criticism – it could also be found in Jülicher – against this utterly rational and ultimately rhetorical way of looking at parables. I would also like to point out that to my extraordinary delight Eberhard Jüngel, in his excellent book *Paulus und Jesus* (Tübingen ²1964), has dealt admirably with these issues, especially on pp.94f., where he refutes Jülicher, and then again on pp.129ff., where (in connection with the unforgettable hermeneutical investigations of Ernst Fuchs) he implicitly observes that in speaking of the parables, Bultmann, too, has basically kept to Jülicher's standpoint. I shall come back later to the remarkable ambiguity in Bultmann's position. However, at this point I am referring in particular to Jüngel, for in very many respects I agree with him whole-heartedly. At any rate in the sphere of ancient philology, to return to that, in the wake of Hermann Fränkel a considerable literature has grown up around the parables in Homer. I myself have made some not completely unimportant contributions to it. Among other works I would refer to the significant book by Bruno Snell, *Entdeckung des Geistes* (Studien zur Entstehung des europäischen Denkens bei den Griechen, Hamburg ³1955). Jüngel knows all this and quotes it. To put things briefly:

When, say, the fall of Hector is compared with the fall of an oak, or when a hero is compared with a lion going out after prey - the Homeric parable, too, is not intended to make understandable something that otherwise would be incomprehensible. The fall of a hero is completely understandable and not open to misunderstanding. When he is hit, he falls and bites the dust: everyone knows that. Yet he is said to fall like an oak, which... What new element is added here? The parables open up two aspects, first the aspect of the real event, Hector falling, and then the aspect of another event, in this case a natural occurrence, the fall of an oak. This puts us in mind of the oak as a mighty and powerful tree. Opening up a perspective in both directions reveals the third feature in the two aspects, what they have in common – not as a *tertium comparationis*, but as their basic substance, their foundation. Homer's parables disclose the heart of the matter. In the parable in which Hector falls like an oak we have not only a characterization of his violent fall – what does fall like an oak? – but also a characterization of what Hector is: he is a man like an oak. All this is a complex totality. And that is always the case. Animals are truer to nature than human beings; human beings are odd, they have many aspects, presenting now one and now another. If I can say that someone seemed like a lion, then I am attributing the lionlikeness to him as a quality, an essential characteristic. If I say that he came like a wolf, I am saying something different. Both are beasts of prey, both are violent animals, but being like a lion is not like being like a wolf. I could go on further in this direction, but we are already getting too far afield.

You will understand what I mean when I say that the decisive feature of these parables is the way in which they disclose being: by looking elsewhere they make as it were transparent the conceptual world with which we are directly confronted so that we really look into the depths that support it all. This is not the only function of the parable; it also has other functions. However, it is a quite essential one. It is also essential for us continually to be shown that the present character of a person - the fact that he behaves in such and such a way – appears in the context of the parable in terms of what is always the case. The parable contains the universal, in the case of the human being we have the contingent; the contingent in human beings is always derived from the universal, i.e. the fundamental element.

First of all, I would like to say that of course the parables of Jesus cannot simply be compared with the Homeric parables. However, one thing is quite clear. As has been long realized and indeed stressed, the parables of Jesus are related above all to something, one thing, of which they speak, namely the gospel, the coming of the kingdom of God. Almost all the parables, and at any rate the original parables, are connected with the coming of the kingdom of God. Jesus himself calls the realization of the kingdom of God a mystery in Mark 4.11 (and Matt.13.11). In these mysterious verses, to which serious objections have already been made, he says that this mystery is given to those near to him, but to others outside everything 'happens' through parables – so it has been thought that he 'conceals' his real purpose. There is certainly also a concealment; of course the parable conceals. But what we have here is what I would want to call a 'revelatory concealment'. Revelation can conceal and concealment can reveal. It was Goethe above all who explained this conceptuality very clearly, because he kept stressing the nature of being as a manifest mystery. There are circumstances which can only be expressed adequately in the form of a revelation which conceals, and I believe that the 'mysteries' of Jesus are such situations. Not because the one who talks about such circumstances wants to be mysterious, wants to make a mystery out of something or surround it with mystery, but because the nature of these circumstances does not allow any other kind of language as an adequate expression. Jesus cannot speak adequately about the coming of the kingdom of God unless he primarily uses the form of parable as a revelation which conceals.

However, there is another factor here if I am right, something of a 'challenge', an invitation to try to understand. You know the Gospel well enough; we find that all these passages are constantly accompanied with phrases like 'You do not hear with your ears or see with your eyes'; people are constantly being told, 'Listen, listen', ἀκούετε: 'He who has ears to hear, let him hear!' συνίετε, we are told, 'You must understand'; νοεῖτε. Again and again what happens nearby is accompanied by suchlike invitations to hear, to perceive, to use the ears which one has and generally fails to use, to use the eyes which one has and generally fails to use.

This is probably the place, again very briefly, but now in the light of the new understanding of the character of the parable which I have just explained, to embark on an interpretation of the parable of the Sower. Bultmann says that its original meaning has become incomprehensible, like that of many other parables. You know the parable: there are the various 'successes' of the seed which is scattered from the hand of the sower, depending on the ground on which the seed falls. It does not take root on the path, which has been well trodden down, and the birds eat it; it grows quickly in the very shallow crust of soil on stony ground, but the sun comes, it withers and is burnt up. Where thistles and thorns grow nearby, it grows up with them, but is then smothered by the vegetation which grows more quickly. Finally, where it falls on good ground, the seed brings forth fruit: it grows and bears a crop, from thirtyfold to a hundredfold. I believe that the decisive factor here is the receiving, the hearing, the perception. The path does not accept the seed at all. The thin crust receives it, but too quickly, and it is soon gone. And then, the earth receives it, but at the same time it has other seeds, seeds of thorns and thistles, weeds, and these seeds grow more quickly. In the 'interpretation' (Mark 4.18f.; Matt.13.22), which is usually contested, these thorns and thistles are the various human passions, the emotions, the cares of this world, the concern for riches. Perhaps an excessively moralistic interpretation has found its way into the sayings of Jesus here from another side; but that is by no means certainly the case. At all events, the parable itself shows that this is what Jesus meant: the very nature of the thorns, a fact of human conditioning, human conduct leads to the seed being choked. And in the 'good earth', the fruitful earth, the seed is accepted - indeed not only accepted, but *received*.

It is attractive to see how at only this point in the Gospels, i.e. Mark 4.20, in Jesus' interpretation of the parable of the Sower, which I take to be an authentic historical interpretation by Jesus because of the weight of its pronouncement, do we find the word παραδέχομαι: 'Those who hear the word (τὸν λόγον) and receive it (παραδέχονται).' The important thing is not just for the word to be somehow received (or to be received but with some remaining disruptive element), but for it to be accepted, received, perceived.

And now – and here I begin to speak simply as a layman – I hope that you will allow me also to say, albeit with some hesitation, that I believe that the decisive question is how the first basic act of faith came about in those who heard the parables of Jesus, without their becoming pedagogical (they have nothing to do with pedagogy, which is quite a different matter). This seems to me to be amazingly clear in that story about the Greek woman from Syro-Phoenicia, the Canaanite woman (Mark 7.24-30; Matt.15.21-28), who asks the Lord to cast the δαιμόνιον (the unclean spirit, the 'devil') out of her daughter. Thereupon Jesus says: 'First let the children be fed', almost, 'Let them stuff themselves' (χορτασθῆναι): 'It is not right to take the children's bread and throw it to the dogs.' But she answered and said to him, 'Yes, Lord, but the dogs eat the scraps which the children drop under the table.' And at that moment he says, 'Because of this word go your way. The devil has departed from your daughter.' And she went back home and found her daughter lying in bed, and the demon had gone from her.

What has happened here? The woman has taken in the parable in the sense which I have just explained; she has taken it deep into herself, has understood it, and in understanding it has entered into the parable and answers in terms of it, developing the parable further: 'But the dogs eat the scraps which the children drop under the table.' And by doing this, by performing this act, by allowing herself to be taken up into the parable, by completely entering into the parable as Jesus has presented it to her – for this is not an act of understanding;

it is nothing pedagogical – the demon has already departed from her daughter. Jesus says, 'The demon has departed (ἐξελήλυθεν)'; she goes home and sees her daughter lying there peacefully, free (Matthew paraphrases it somewhat: 'Great is your faith, be it to you as you will. And her daughter was made whole in that same hour'). In both Gospels the situation of the parable and the event of faith are retained so specifically that there can be no dispute: this is an event of faith in parable, an event of faith and fulfilment. There are other events of faith in the Gospels, different and yet similar, which do not remain in the sphere of parable and which must nevertheless be perceived. For example, we have Luke 18.3ff., where the unjust, or at any rate unyielding, judge, dispenses justice to the widow who insists on her rights, because she incessantly asks for them: 'And the Lord said, Hear what the unjust judge says... will not God soon pronounce judgment?' Faith compels, it must be 'heard', even in an apparently paradoxical parable.

We see from all this the unprecedented significance of the parable in the New Testament for the primal phenomenon of faith. It does not in fact awaken faith in the sense of some aura of 'faith', but reveals by concealing, and in revealing only by concealing draws into its orbit the person who has ears to hear. We thus see how this person who hears performs a first act of deep commitment, commitment to the parable and to faith. This is also expressed by the parable of the sower, and I would say that almost all the other parables have the same meaning. So they are not tests which Jesus imposes on people – i.e., 'I am testing whether...'; they are forms of occurrence. It really is the case, as Jüngel puts it, that when Jesus tells the parables of the kingdom of God and these parables are perceived, the coming of the kingdom of God takes place.

Where the parables are subjected to a moralizing, trivial or allegorical explanation, by whatever kind of late-dating, a piece of holy scripture is destroyed, just as noble passages in Homer are destroyed by a merely rationalizing trivial explanation.

We move on to the parables of the mustard seed, the leaven, the seed growing secretly, the parable of the thief in the night and so on. Bultmann says, e.g. of the parable of the mustard seed, that there is 'growth' here, but the kingdom of God cannot grow, as it is not a plurality of human beings. Only a plurality of human beings can grow, and that means the communities. Accordingly this parable must derive from the community; it must be an allegorical representation of the primitive community from which further communities grew. And there is a marvellously specific possibility to be taken into consideration in such an allegory: the birds who come and nest in the branches of the shrub would be the Gentiles who are converted - so this is a post-Pauline parable and an allegory. I would dearly like to know what is so Gentile about birds, birds who come and nest where something has grown. As with the Homeric parable, this is the simple poetic development of an image. And would there be no growth of the kingdom of God? This is a serious matter! For that is the remarkable feature, which we continually come up against here, in the way in which Jesus depicts the coming of the kingdom of God: he cannot say how it happens, or can only say metaphorically that it happens mysteriously and silently. Human beings cannot perceive it; they sleep and the seed grows; the thief comes in the night, and is not expected; the grain of mustard is very small and becomes large by growing. There is in fact no more wonderful process – as our own experience will confirm – than the process of growth. This mysterious fact of something coming about imperceptibly before our eyes with unprecedented power – there is indeed no greater power than that which is regularly exercised in the spring, when everything comes back again: it is an inexorable power, but one which is silent, still, gentle, incomprehensible. So there is hardly a better image for the mystery of the coming of the kingdom of God than that of growth. Growth has nothing to do with accumulation. It is a miraculous process, and the parables of Jesus depict it. The parables are in fact often about nature – or about everyday human events which for Jesus also have something of 'nature' in them – they may not be rationalized, for otherwise we would end up with rationalistic rejections, or with the revision of sayings of Jesus to match trends in the community. The parables which I have mentioned here certainly do not derive from community tendencies, but all belong in the teaching of Jesus as we know it also from elsewhere, the teaching of the coming of the kingdom of God.

Now with these comments I have moved from the limited sphere of the parables of Jesus to the problems which have developed in the course of the last two centuries in connection with the question of the 'historical' Jesus. After a number of previous attempts, since Bultmann a particularly clear distinction has been made between the 'historical' Jesus and the Jesus of the post-Easter kerygma. Käsemann makes a very fine statement in his article about the historical Jesus ('The Problem of the Historical Jesus', in *Essays on New Testament Themes*, London 1964, 15-47): looking back on Bultmann, he points out that the stress on the kerygma in the synoptic tradition has bracketted off the 'historical' Jesus. Thus in connection with the credibility of the synoptic tradition it is asserted that the post-Easter community had no interest in the 'historical'. The community would have consisted of passionate believers whose faith would have led them to be interested only in the kerygma and the interpretation of the kerygma, i.e. the proclamation of the Easter experiences, the epiphany of Jesus at Easter after his resurrection and the pouring out of the Holy Spirit at Pentecost, the proclamation to and through the communities which were coming into being. I believe that there is a very important, indeed 'historical' insight here. We can hardly imagine vividly enough the unparalleled passion of a completely new, intensified rapture of faith during this marvellous time after what seemed to have been a collapse. However, I find it quite incomprehensible that anyone should affirm that those who produced the three Synoptic Gospels could have had no interest in the concrete, real and historical facts of Jesus and his circumstances. Look at other books of revelation – and there are quite a number of them over the broad area of the history of religion. As far as I know, the Gospels are quite unique. And what makes them so? The fact that they bring before our eyes this unprecedented, specific, experiential richness, that they do not speak of miracle workers, of wonders and the like. Of course we can also find such things in the Gospels; that is an aspect of their richness. Jesus did miracles, but not like other miracle workers. He always refused to make his miracles his credentials. Rather, everything in the Gospels, including the miraculous, is quite specific and at the same time somehow significant beyond the individual healing, the individual miracle.

These 'miracles' convey something: the lame walk, the blind see, the deaf hear, the old promise is fulfilled. That means that the kingdom of God is on the way, is somehow already there. Thus the miracles are somehow like the parables – concealing yet revealing, i.e. specific and concealing at the same time. In most passages in the Synoptic Gospels the miracles of Jesus are amazingly specific, in accord with the time, so that even a reasonably liberal theology at the end of the nineteenth and beginning of the twentieth centuries recognized them as real historical occurrences – as for example when Jesus puts his fingers in the ears of a man who is deaf and dumb, spits on him, touches his tongue and cries to heaven 'Be opened'; 'and his tongue was loosened and he spoke properly and heard' (Mark 7.33). In another instance Jesus spits on a blind man, lays his hands on him, and the one who was once blind slowly recovers his sight – 'I see men like trees walking' – until he can see everything clearly again (Mark 8.23). However, it is no accident that Jesus does not want these miracles to be talked about, since in his view there is more to them than the magic of miracles at the time. However, with his miracles he did not cut himself off from his time. As a person, he was 'historical'. There is certainly room for disagreement over some of the miracles narrated in the Gospels – as a non-theologian I am not competent to discuss this at length. But at all events I would venture to say that very many apparently 'impossible' miracles which are narrated in the Synoptic Gospels are hardly inventions, or the visions of community pluralities. As far as I can judge, they are experiences of those who still had personal knowledge of Jesus and had experienced all these things with him. It seems to me that such specific experiences also extend to the Gospel of John, as even 'liberal' theologians have conceded to me.

I would now like to discuss, in connection with the miracles, the feeding of the multitudes, which is narrated twice: first five thousand people are fed with five loaves and two fishes after spending a long time listening to Jesus preaching in the wilderness (Mark 6.32ff.; Matt.14.15ff.; Luke 9.12ff.); then four thousand are filled by seven loaves and a few fishes (Mark 8.1ff.; Matt.15.32ff.).

First of all, we can assume here that the story of the miraculous feeding was already being circulated in a duplicate form from the time of Jesus and the apostles onwards. Secondly, it seemed so significant that it was told twice. In epics from the time of Homer onwards, and also elsewhere, we often find the artistic device of *iterata*, repetitions. These repetitions are not insertions into a totality which exists without them; they support the whole structure, prompting remembrance by their repetition and thus holding the work together. In effect, healings by Jesus are also 'repeated' in the course of the Gospel narratives: they give a harmony to the career of Jesus, albeit a harmony which corresponds to reality. The same thing happens often enough in poetry which corresponds to actual truth. That is also true of the miracle of the loaves. And as to eating after or before a long period of listening, waiting or activity, we know all about that not only from everyday experience but also, say, from Homer. For instance, he reports a long conversation over breakfast before the decisive battle with the Greeks. Moreover, theological commentators demonstrated long ago that the miracle of the loaves is at the same time an important pointer to worship – long before the New Testament and long after it – with its sharing of the bread and being filled at a bite. In the Christian sphere this feeding has a quite special significance as a result of the historical Last Supper in which Jesus shared and which he held 'in remembrance'. At this point I do not want to embark on detailed criticism of New Testament passages, because for a long time I have been particularly interested in cultic patterns in ancient Greece and even more in the sphere of the

Christian church. I am not competent in specialist New Testament criticism. I would, though, like to tell a story, in passing, to demonstrate the concreteness of the situations depicted in the Gospel, and indeed their similarity to other occurrences. This story, from a personal source, is set in the present-day Near East, specifically in Upper Egypt. After strenuous excavation work in the desert, and perhaps also to celebrate the end of Ramadan, the period of fasting, the European leaders of the excavation wanted to share a roast sheep with the workers in a meal together. Thirty were invited, but three hundred came, because all the families and friends wanted to join in. And the servant asked the 'mistress' how all these would be fed. However, and this is the point, they *were* all fed, and went away delighted, and the servants gathered up the remnants in baskets. That kind of thing still happens, as it did then.

As a philologist, someone who has acquired some knowledge of 'literature', I am particularly concerned here to note that when we read the Synoptic Gospels, we cannot be other than captivated by the experiential vividness with which we are confronted. The conditions of their time stand before us: nature, the landscape of Palestine, the Sea of Galilee, places from the coast to the far side of the Jordan, and Nazareth with its sheer cliff. If only we read the text simply enough, we can imagine Jesus travelling here and there – a situation which we misunderstand if we see the repeated 'on the way' – the most important words are spoken and actions performed 'on the way' - as no more than literary decoration. Jesus' whole life was made up of travelling; he journeyed through Galilee and beyond, until he finally set out on the way to which everything had been leading up and which he did not want to escape, from Jericho to Jerusalem. I know of no other area of history-writing, biography or poetry where I encounter so great a wealth of material in such a small space. Think of all the landscapes; think of all the personalities, especially in the parables but also elsewhere; think of all the situations: the whole world is to be found in those few pages. People praise the wealth of imagery in Homer as a poet, and rightly so; and this wealth of imagery has a basis in reality. There can be no question that he simply invented it. We can also observe such riches, say, in Plato; although at the same time he is a philosopher, it can be found in his Dialogues. We also find such riches in Shakespeare, and also in Dante and Goethe. Elsewhere, however, it is very rare, and the works I have just mentioned are on the whole large-scale works, whereas here we have only a few pages. I would say that this wealth of imagery is a problem. It has certainly found its way into the Gospels, but how has it got there, all this specific detail relating to individual circumstances? I would claim that this specific wealth of imagery in the Synoptic Gospels is a theological problem, but I must leave it to theologians to investigate more fully. However, there might be an indication of its origin in Acts, where the new call of Matthias to be an apostle has as its condition that a witness to the resurrection of the Lord, along with the other disciples, must be one of the men 'who accompanied us during all the time that the Lord Jesus went in and out among us, beginning from the baptism of John until the day when he was taken up from us' (Acts 1.22f.). That means that direct involvement in the life of the historical Jesus was the basic condition for the apostolate of the earliest apostles.

We must now go on to consider questions of method. I said right at the beginning that I know this kind of hyper-criticism, say from Homeric scholarship; I also know it from a variety of areas in classical philology, in Plato regularly from the nineteenth century on, when the letters, above all the seventh letter, were said to be inauthentic. It is still practised occasionally even today, but with little success. In the case of Aeschylus, the authenticity of *Prometheus* has been and still is questioned. Herodotus used to be regarded as a lovable gossip and liar; now, however, he is regarded as a real historian. In tragedy even Antigone could be rejected or at least afflicted with a redaction and vigorously criticized, and so it goes on. One could find this over the whole range of both Greek and Latin authors. However, apart from a few rearguard skirmishes, we have really now given this approach up on all fronts. Things have changed, above all in Homer, and I myself have played my part in the change. I do not want to go into the whole Homer question here; I shall simply say that I know arguments in Wilamowitz which I have found again, amazingly, in Bultmann. I would, however, like to be quite firm on one point. In reading the Synoptic Gospels we come across sayings of Jesus or situations whose character is, as Jüngel has also understood, that they contain theological and kerygmatic nuclei. These are the tiniest little nuclei, preformations. It would be natural to claim that here we have the germs of later things. But New Testament scholars seem to claim that the reverse must be the case. If I come up against these things in the sayings of Jesus, the sayings are thought to be late, secondary.

As a rule, we do not usually find the Zeus of justice in the *Iliad*, and it is in Hesiod that the notion of the *dike* of Zeus is developed with full force. From Hesiod, a *dike* speculation, what one might almost call a *dike* theology, pervades the whole Greek world. The next important figure is Solon, then Aeschylus, and it continues on to Plato. Plato's work in fact ends with a path by which the participants in the conversation on Crete go up to the grotto in which Zeus was born. That is how Plato's work ends. There is, it should be noted in passing, only one other Greek god who developed a theology of himself, and that is Apollo. Zeus developed the *dike* theology, which is not yet present in Homer – apart from one passage, *Iliad* 16, 384ff. There – also in a parable – we find: when floods and rain come, Zeus is giving this bad weather in the autumn to people with whom he is angry, because they have forced through bad laws in the assembly, and have not paid heed to the gods. Here *dike* is the same as in Hesiod:

> Zeus, when he deals harshly with men in his wrath, who give bad judgments in the market place, exploit the law, and are heedless of divine retribution.

At one time it was thought that this was obviously a passage dating from after Hesiod, which had crept into Homer. Nowadays, we would say – or at least I am saying – that here in a few, definitely authentic verses of Homer we have the nucleus of a Zeus-*dike* theology, as it was later developed in Hesiod. It used to be thought that the presence of something of this kind could be affirmed only where it was developed in some magnitude. Small germs of it in earlier passages were thought to be secondary. Here, we have an exact parallel to that hyper-critical New Testament scholarship. No notice is taken of the original nucleus, but such nuclei are thought to be the secondary traces of later developments.

As we have already arrived at Homer and Hesiod, what I have just said also applies to the catalogue poetry, which is so important in Hesiod. In Homer there are much shorter catalogues. But as Hesiod, in whom this feature was more prominent, was taken as a criterion, the analytic Homeric scholars regarded all these Homeric catalogues as post-Hesiod, as having crept into the original Homer. However – and you know the Old Testament and the writings of the Ancient Near East better than I do – everywhere we find catalogues and they specifically belong to earlier periods. So why should we say that there were none in Homer and regard them as secondary insertions?

Now for something completely different, connected with the larger-scale, self-contained narratives in the Synoptic Gospels. Here my view is different from that usual in New Testament criticism. First of all, let us look at Peter's messianic confession – again 'on the way' – which in Mark is the way to Caesarea Philippi. In all three Synoptic Gospels it contains the confession, transmitted in almost exactly the same way in each Gospel and in all three connected with the prediction of the coming suffering in Jerusalem (Mark 8.27ff.; cf. Matt.16.13ff.; Luke 9.20ff.). Here Bultmann (258) speaks of a 'legend of faith', though he claims that the narrative is fragmentary, since after Peter says 'You are the messiah', one would have expected an indication of Jesus' attitude towards the confession which he had evoked. As Jesus does not indicate his own attitude, the passage is said to be fragmentary. But it is grotesque to imagine in this great passage that Jesus would have expressed an 'attitude' of his own to it. Similarly, in Homer, when something was thought to be missing, the fact that something seemed to be missing was taken as proof that the account could not be right.

At this point I must now confess something which we could only substantiate by lengthy discussions in a seminar, namely that in long attempts to distinguish between true and false – philologists are in fact constantly faced with this question – I have gradually come to believe that the truth is self-authenticating. Goethe said that he always thought reality to be more brilliant than his own inspiration, and I too believe that. I have continually found things happening which one could never have thought up. Things have happened in my own life which I could never have dreamed of. And so I believe that, for example, in poetry the great primal material is usually not invented, but is a reflection of an actual event at one time. Of course this material is then reflected on, taken further, combined, reshaped. I believe – as I have said, this is primarily no more than a belief, and we would have to sit down for six months were we to try to prove it – that there is something which I would like to call the unmistakable aroma of truth. There is an unmistakable smell of truth. There is a way in which a situation or a saying can be shaped which shows that it does not come from a community, a collective, but is a situation which once happened, a word which was once spoken. Many people derive the story in the New Testament in which Jesus goes on to speak of the suffering which he faces, and then says to Peter, who wants to avert it, 'Get thee behind me, Satan', from an anti-Petrine tendency. I can only feel that here especially we have the smell of truth.

Mark's narrative is sketched out very briefly. (In Matthew it is of course not without significance that we find a beatitude addressed to Peter as an interpolation, 'You are blessed, Peter,' a saying which was to become the foundation of a whole church tradition, the significance of which I want neither to disparage nor to doubt; there seem to be possibilities, above all in the light of the Old Testament, for regarding this section, too, as being historically authentic.) Anyway, in Mark, Peter's 'confession' is followed by a sharp command by Jesus to the disciples to say no more about the matter. Then comes the so-called first prediction of the passion and resurrection, and then (only in Mark), 'And he said the word quite openly': καὶ παρρησίᾳ τὸν λόγον ἐλάλει. Thereupon Peter takes him aside – or better, 'as if to protect him' – and begins to rebuke him (ἤρξατο ἐπιτιμᾶν) in a rather sharp tone (like Jesus above). In Matthew, Peter also says some solicitous words. In Mark, Jesus immediately turns away from Peter and with a look at the other disciples rebukes Peter and says, 'Depart from me, Satan, for you do not think the things of God, but of man.'

We find the same thing in Matthew. Here Jesus also calls Peter a σκάνδαλον, a stumbling block, a scandal; the term may be an improvement on 'Satan', but taken seriously it also includes the possibility of coming to grief. In both Synoptic Gospels (here Luke puts things in more general terms) it is clear that the word 'Satan', tempter, as addressed to Peter, must have made a tremendous impression on the disciples, and above all on Peter. It was probably clear to both evangelists that here together with the first prophecy of the passion and exaltation there was also a repetition of the first temptation, or *vice versa* – I do not want to make a decision on that now. If it is permissible to speak of the literary construction of the Gospel here, I would call such assonances reflections: here, in the case of Peter's confession of the Messiah/Christ, in a very human sphere, involving a final human decision. We have a confrontation between Jesus and Peter, the disciple who seeks to restrain Jesus, and Jesus himself, who certainly did not find the way to Jerusalem easy, rebuking him as a 'tempter'. As I have attempted to show, the whole story has the smell of truth about it.

I am not concerned to establish priorities here. However, I must say that the short form in Mark, the sharp accents in the scene, and the fact that here Peter is not spared, together with the omission of the benediction – Peter is already a Satan, a tempter – this demonstrable shorter form of the narrative, which does not spare Peter, makes it hard for me to understand how this particular Gospel of Mark could be seen as being hostile to Peter. That is what Bultmann calls, 'a polemic against the Jewish-Christian point of view represented by Peter from the sphere of the Hellenistic Christianity of the Pauline circle' (*Synoptic Tradition*, 258).

Let me put it this way: it is precisely the fact that here we have a negative portrait of Peter, that the one who shortly beforehand had designated Jesus as the Christ and wanted to dissuade him from his fore-ordained course of suffering was vigorously repudiated by Jesus, which seems to me to show that here – if one likes to put it that way

– Peter himself is speaking. That means – and let me say this quite plainly – that I have never understood, nor can I understand now, why Protestant theologians try so hard to find a way round the famous note by Papias in Eusebius. Eusebius says that Mark was a 'hermeneut' of Peter: Μάρκος μὲν ἑρμηνευτὴς Πέτρου γενόμενος, ὅσα ἐμνημόνευσε, ἀκριβῶς ἔγραψεν, οὐ μέντοι τάξει... ('Mark, indeed, having been the hermeneut of Peter, wrote accurately, howbeit not in order...', Eusebius, HE 3,39, 15,16). Regardless of whether one wants to understand the word 'hermeneut' here to mean translator or interpreter, Papias apparently said clearly enough that Mark heard Peter and then put Peter's various sermons in order, i.e. arranged them. This 'order' in Mark as we now have it is a very well-planned composition, a history of Jesus as told by Peter; I hope on another occasion to be able to provide, as far as possible, my own interpretation of the structure. However, it is basically clear that Mark heard Peter, and arranged material (as did the other evangelists, with other sources, in their own way), in order to put the various sermons of Peter in order. That means that Mark was a hearer, translator and interpreter of Peter. Why should we doubt Papias here? Eusebius, who wrote his Church History between the end of the third and the beginning of the fourth century, and was a very conscientious historian and philologist, says of Papias, who lived about 130, that he still knew the immediate disciples of the Lord (and Eusebius did not make this kind of thing up himself!). Moreover, the characterizations of the various evangelists by Papias which have been handed on by Eusebius indicate this. So according to Papias, in the Gospel of Mark we have an account of what Peter had said about Jesus and his own role; granted, it has been arranged, but it is still an apparently accurate account. For precisely the character attributed to the Gospel of Mark, namely that it is post-Pauline and biassed against Peter, indicates to me that almost everything in the Gospel of Mark comes quite directly from Peter. At all events, I see the greatness and power of the Gospel of Mark precisely in this fact. Only Peter himself can have told how directly after his own confession he sought to keep his Lord from suffering, and the same is true of the account of the denial. Any other members of the early communities would be horrified to tell something of this kind about Peter. Mark hands down the account in Peter's simple way, and the same is true of the story of the denial (Mark 14.66ff.; Matt.26.69ff.). We are told how Jesus had to appear before the Sanhedrin and how it was already clear that he would be condemned, and all the people around suddenly turned against him. Peter, who had somehow slipped into the forecourt and listened to the hearing, denied that he was one of Jesus' followers when a maid recognized him as a Galilean. Indeed he did so three times, until the cock crowed the second time, just as the Lord, who had a good knowledge of human nature, had predicted. And when the cock crew, Peter thought of the earlier words of the Lord and began to weep (καὶ ἐπιβαλὼν ἔκλαιεν, Mark 14.72). Bultmann says that the story should have told us what Peter did next, how he fled to Galilee, and so on. Thank God that the narrator did nothing of the sort. He is concerned with the collapse, and here it is before our eyes. The coming greatness of a person – or, from Peter's perspective, his coming task – lies in the fact that he once collapsed in this way, that he failed as a human being and a believer in such an incredible way, that he denied the Lord. We have the same situation as when, in an earlier indication of his nature, after his messianic confession he wanted to save his Lord from the suffering to come. This basic human fact of commitment followed by failure and then revival indicates Peter's greatness and power and thus at the same time lends truth to what is said of him, and of Jesus. Matthew and Luke have heightened the scene further, so that we now usually quote them: 'and he wept bitterly'. Mark simply says, 'and he began to weep.'

I am glad to be able to note that Hans Lietzmann, whom I revere as a teacher, in his great study of the trial of Jesus, also derives the tradition of the passion of Jesus from the apostle Peter.

Certainly, in the narratives which have been preserved for us in the Synoptic Gospels, there have been further combinations and further reshapings, just as Matthew and Luke reshaped the basic narrative of Mark and other sources. However, the basic content of the stories about Peter, which are authentic history, is also preserved in the other Synoptic Gospels. Mark too arranged his material, as we know, but it seems to me that the important thing is the basic content of what he arranged.

We now return once again, methodically, to the problem of tradition – which I earlier left in the background. I propose to discuss the doubt cast on the veracity of oral tradition, the problem of oral tradition. I have in fact made a thorough study of oral tradition; the Homeric legends, about which I have also written a short book, gave me occasion for this. There is a very fine book by a Dane called Liestøl (*The Origin of the Icelandic Family Saga*). In it he investigates some very interesting examples, e.g. where the history of a farm is still extant in farm records. These can be used to test the purely oral tradition; it proves to be very accurate. Liestøl further demonstrates how the tradition often goes from grandfather to grandson and always skips a generation, so that centuries are quickly bridged. We also know from Homer the kind of memory that these narrators had (see now T.Boman, *Die Jesus-Überlieferung im Lichte der neueren Volkskunde*, Göttingen 1967). Liestøl also points out what strict control the audiences always exerted over the singers and how they immediately noticed if something was presented in a different form. Children behave in the same way. We always have to tell them a story just as we did the previous time. We have a similar example from the early Christian communities (it may be that here things were fixed in writing, but in that case the word handed down by written tradition stuck as firmly in their heads as if it were oral tradition). A sermon was preached on the story of the paralysed man who was let down through the roof on a bed or a couch. Jesus healed him and said, 'Take up your bed and walk' (Mark 2.4-9). Instead of using the word κράββατος for bed or couch, the preacher chose a more refined one (σκίμπους). One of his congregation immediately called out, 'Are you better than the one who said κράββατος?' (Sozomen I 11, PG LXVII, col.889).

At all events, the congregations exercised very strong control over the sayings of Jesus, and must have done from a very early stage. We must add another concept or, better, fact to that of oral tradition: memory. That is particularly important in the case of the Gospel of Mark, where Peter's recollection has provided the framework of the narrative. Particularly from Homer, as from other Greek literature, e.g. from Plato, we have learned the significance of μνήμη, memory: a fixed, but not rigid, living presence of what happened, what was once perceived and lives on faithfully in a person's brain and heart. Perhaps you will allow me a personal reminiscence. As I have gradually become older, I have myself become the source for some things. In 1962 I had to make a speech about Werner Jaeger. So I had occasion to recall the time when I made his acquaintance, in 1921. At that time I had been invited to the Berlin house where he was living and we had the experience of a common occurrence in Berlin houses: at eleven o'clock at night, the cockroaches began to emerge from every corner. So Jaeger said, 'It's no good, let's go out.' Then we went into one of the most modern cafés – tables lit from below, soft music, and so on, and Jaeger sat there, seeing and hearing nothing. He just talked and talked and I sat as it were at his feet and listened. I have a vivid picture of the scene, which happened now fifty-five years ago, and I can remember what he said down to the last word. That was fifty-five years ago, and Jaeger was a wise man of whom I was very fond, but he did not speak 'with authority', ὡς ἐξουσίαν ἔχων. And people keep acting as though the perhaps forty years which had elapsed between the death of the Lord and the Gospels was a period of three hundred years. I keep hearing the words, 'in the course of tradition'. A human brain can bridge that, as I have learned in my own life.

And now another personal experience. My grandfather came to Berlin as an itinerant journeyman (a plumber) at the beginning of the nineteenth century – I didn't know him, nor did I know my father, who was quite elderly and died before I was born. This plumber must have been quite a character; his pithy sayings were passed on to me by his daughter, my aunt. They included the saying, 'I light a three-branch light for the Lord God and three for the devil' – very interesting theologically, and probably apotropaic. Whether he got it from elsewhere is irrelevant; it was told to me as his saying. I have passed it on, e.g. to my son, who was born more than 150 years after my grandfather, and he will in turn pass it on to his children. That is a stereotyped saying. It will change a bit; instead of 'three-branch light' we now say 'candle', but the basic structure has been retained for well over two hundred years: light candles, God, devil. This is just one example of well-founded oral tradition.

We can also see the opposite error in the history of tradition. That also happened in Homeric scholarship! People have always acted as though it took years for the Ionian epic to cross to the mother country. In Homer himself Achilles said, 'The day after tomorrow I will be at home in Phthia, on the third day!' I have checked this out with old ships' logs, and it is true: ships went as fast as that. But according to earlier Homeric criticism the epic took centuries to find its way round gradually. It is always a good thing for scholars – I put this quite generally – to use common sense as well as their methods.

So much for oral tradition. Another matter is community tradition in connection with form criticism. I shall deal with this briefly. I believe that collective compositions are always pallid, that they betray themselves by their lack of creative power, that they are general, whereas images with a clear character are usually individual and not just thought up afterwards. The plurality of a community is not really productive. Moreover, although I respect form criticism – I learned it where it was first used, in the Old Testament, and it has become very important to me – we can often see it used on a mistaken assumption: people always act as though what is expressed in a form is less real. That is quite wrong. Something can be moulded into a form a hundred times and still be quite real. Indeed, even today we put everything in forms. If someone writes a biography of Bismarck today it will be quite definitely expressed in forms. Whether it is unreal or not depends on quite different circumstances, and not on the 'wicked' form. So the form has no connotations of deficient reality. Generally speaking, we should be careful with means of thinking. All these are certainly means of thinking. We have to use our means of thinking one way or another, and it is right that we should. But my view is that we must always be aware that these *are* means of thinking, because people are constantly tempted – as I have been often enough myself – as it were to project means of thinking on to the subject-matter. The means of thinking become a label stuck on a good wine, and in the end they take over and usurp the subject. That is wrong. So we must take care to keep our means of thinking pure and allow any form of criticism which is used to be controlled by a special, higher self-criticism. It is quite clear that the whole Gospel is not to be accepted lock, stock and barrel as authentic tradition. But what does have to be accepted as tradition in this sense? Historical works? How then do we criticize historical works? It is quite clear that in fact we can detect a tendency towards shaping, theological shaping; we can see that quite clearly when we compare Matthew with Mark and then again with Luke; we can see how the tendencies develop increasingly strongly and in different ways; we can establish that directly. That is clear, and I would not deny it. The only question is how far we go in this direction.

It is clear that arrangements were made; Papias himself says that. And it is clear that there were interpretations, new compositions of a legendary kind, as the beginning of the Gospel of Luke demonstrates. But I would assert that while all this is true, in essence things are different. As to the substance of the narratives and sayings, I would say that if, as often in philology, we make a comparison in terms of good tradition, bad tradition, and very good tradition, on this scale of values we would say that the Synoptic Gospels, are very good tradition.

One last thing. If we look at these Bultmannian things and investigate their origin, remarkably enough we have to conclude that this very man who represented in so magnificent a way a completely new theological starting point, simply remained in the nineteenth-century in his methodology. That is true both in respect of his kind of criticism, which I compared with e.g. Wilamowitz, and also in his concept of history. The concept of the historical Jesus, which is discussed anew over and over again, is basically nothing but a historicist conception of the historical Jesus. If we note that, e.g. in Käsemann's articles, then we can see that this concept of the historical Jesus is governed first by facticity, positive facticity; secondly by causality; thirdly by compensating plausibility; fourthly by psychologizing; and fifthly by inner development. These are all concepts according to which someone like Plutarch was not a biographer. For in a marvellous and clear way antiquity did not base its biographies on causality, plausibility and inner development (this was only a nineteenth-century development) but on two things, πράγματα and λόγοι, τὰ πραχθέντα καὶ τὰ λεχθέντα. And I think that that, too, is right. If we have a correct understanding of the events, above all the situation, i.e. the pattern of events, and the λόγοι, then we have the best that one can say about a historical phenomenon. The way in which we understand a figure from the πράγματα and λόγοι is a particular approach of the noble biographer; this is the way the noble biographer acts. I think it must also be said that with Bultmann and others all these things are rationalized in a nineteenth-century way, are understood moralistically in terms of liberalism – and then refuted. However, they are not refuted by a rejection of the method, but by a rejection of the word of scripture. What is destroyed here with the destruction of the Jesus of history is none other than what lives on indomitably in the Gospel, the figure of the Lord. The way in which this has been constructed for us from actions, sayings and suffering is untouchable, and cannot in any way be set aside.

I could now go more deeply into the way in which this whole concept of history has had its day and how we should put another in its place, but I must stop. The only other thing I want to say is that the time, the world, in which Jesus appeared was one in which people really lived, lived vigorously, lived boldly, lived to the full, where life was intensified – and life is not always like that. Time and again we can see how in some periods – and there are also other, different periods in the history of the world – great deeds are done and great words are spoken. Then there are periods in which no great word is spoken and no great event takes place. In the former case situations and sayings are concentrated, they have a special intensity and power in the way in which they are shaped. Käsemann wants to put the brute facts, as he calls them, on one side and says that these brute facts make sense only through a new understanding and a new decision. I beg to differ. My view is that these so-called brute facts have the character that Goethe once attributed to a Dutch painting: their truth hits us in the eye. The brute facts have an energy, a concentration, a form which gives them a concentrated, alarming, evocative power just as they stand, as facts, words and situations in the Gospel. They affect us, they call us, they require an answer of us, demand it no matter what. What is historical is the unprecedented energy of these brute facts, the creative power of these sayings and situations. Why? Because it is itself the basis of history. That cannot be brushed aside as 'the merely historical'. The concept of history must be altered.

But I must break off here. In conclusion I would only say that it seems to be improper in criticism to offend against the word of the Lord who ultimately said that while heaven and earth would pass away, his words would not pass away. I believe that his sayings are safeguarded against all criticism. Secondly, though, it also seems to me important to point to what Luke says to Theophilus at the beginning of his Gospel, in the prologue, where he explains why he has followed his predecessors in writing a connected account: 'That you may recognize in respect of the words, the teaching, in which you have been instructed, τὴν ἀσφάλειαν.' Luther translates this 'sure ground', ἀσφάλεια, that which cannot be shaken. And Luke locates that which cannot be shaken in the Gospel.

Abbreviations

AAMz	Abhandlungen der Akademie der Wissenschaften, Mainz
AGG	Abhandlungen der Gesellschaft der Wissenschaften, Göttingen
AGLB	Aus der Geschichte der lateinischen Bibel
AGSU	Arbeiten zur Geschichte des Spätjudentums und des Urchristentums
AnBib	Analecta Biblica
AncB	Anchor Bible
ANRW	*Aufstieg und Niedergang der römischen Welt*, ed. H. Temporini and W. Haase, Berlin and New York
ANTT	Arbeiten zur neutestamentlichen Textforschung
BBB	Bonner biblische Beiträge
BETL	Bibliotheca ephemeridum theologicarum Lovaniensium
BEvTh	Beiträge zur Evangelischen Theologie
Bibl	*Biblica*
BTAVO	Beihefte zum Tübinger Atlas des Vorderen Orients
BZ	*Biblische Zeitschrift*
BZNW	Beiheft zur Zeitschrift für die neutestamentliche Wissenschaft
CAH	*Cambridge Ancient History*
CB.NT	Coniectanea Biblica. Novum Testamentum
CC	Corpus Christianorum
CIJ	Corpus Inscriptionum Judaicarum
CIL	Corpus Inscriptionum Latinarum
CSEL	Corpus Scriptorum Ecclesiasticorum Latinorum
CW	*Die christliche Welt*
DACL	*Dictionnaire d'archéologie chrétienne et liturgie*
DJD(J)	Discoveries in the Judaean Desert (of Jordan)

DLZ	*Deutsche Literaturzeitung*
EKK	Evangelisch-Kritischer Kommentar
ET	English translation
EVV	English versions
FRLANT	Forschungen zur Religion und Literatur des Alten und Neuen Testaments
GCS	Griechische Christliche Schriftsteller
HM	Hallische Monographien
HNT	Handbuch zum Neuen Testament
HSCP	Harvard Studies in Classical Philology
HTK	Herders theologischer Kommentar zum Neuen Testament
HTR	*Harvard Theological Review*
ICC	International Critical Commentary
JAC	*Jahrbuch für Antike und Christentum*
JBL	*Journal of Biblical Literature*
JSHRZ	Jüdische Schriften aus hellenistisch-römischer Zeit
JSS	*Journal of Semitic Studies*
JTS	*Journal of Theological Studies*
KAT	Kommentar zum Alten Testament
KEK	Kritisch-Exegetischer Kommentar (Meyer Kommentar)
KP	*Der Kleine Pauly*
LCL	Loeb Classical Library
LWQF	Liturgiewissenschaftliche Quellen und Forschungen
LXX	Septuagint
NF(NS)	Neue Folge (New Series)
NTS	*New Testament Studies*
OECT	Oxford Early Christian Texts
ÖTK	Oekumenischer Taschenbuch Kommentar
PG	Patrologia Graeca
PRE	*Paulys Realencyclopädie der classischen Altertumswissenschaft*
PTS	Patristische Texte und Studien
QD	Quaestiones Disputatae
RAC	*Reallexicon für Antike und Christentum*
RB	*Revue Biblique*
RBen	*Revue Bénédictine*
RdQ	*Revue de Qumrân*
RE	*Realencyclopädie für protestantische Theologie und Kirche*

RGG	*Die Religion in Geschichte und Gegenwart*
RHR	*Revue de l'Histoire des Religions*
RNT	Regensburger Neues Testament
SAW	Sitzungsberischte der Österreichischen Akademie der Wissenschaften in Wien
SBL.DS	Society of Biblical Literature. Dissertation Series
SBS	Stuttgarter Bibelstudien
SC	Sources chrétiennes
SHAW.PH	Sitzungsberichte der Heidelberger Akademie der Wissenschaften. Philosophisch-historische Klasse
SHG	*Subsidia Hagiographica*
SNTS.MS	*Studiorum Novi Testamenti Societas. Monograph Series*
SPAW	*Sitzungsberichte der preussischen Akademie der Wissenschaften*
TDNT	*Theological Dictionary of the New Testament*, ed. G.Kittel
ThB	Theologische Bücherei
ThBeitr	Theologische Beiträge
TPAPA	Transactions and Proceedings of the American Philological Association
TRE	*Theologische Realencyclopädie*
TU	Texte und Untersuchungen
VC	*Vigiliae Christianae*
VNAW	Verhandelingen der koninklijk nederlandse akademie von wetenschappen
WUNT	Wissenschaftliche Untersuchungen zum Alten und Neuen Testament
ZDPV	*Zeitschrift des deutschen Palästina-Vereins*
ZNW	*Zeitschrift für die neutestamentliche Wissenschaft*
ZTK	*Zeitschrift für Theologie und Kirche*

Notes

I. The Gospel of Mark: Time of Origin and Situation

1. Tacitus, *Dial.de orat.* 17.3; Plutarch, *Numa* 1.4.

2. *Lycurgus* 1.1. Cf. *Solon* 27.1; *Themistocles* 27.1; *Camillus* 22.1f. etc.

3. Unfortunately the Heracles biography is lost, see K.Ziegler, *PRE* 21,1, 1951, cols. 895, 697 (Lamprias catalogue no.34). Cf. also *Theseus* 6,6.

4. F.Overbeck, *Christentum und Kultur. Gedanken und Anmerkungen zur modernen Theologie*, ed. C.A.Bernoulli, 1919 (reprinted 1963), 20: 'Problems of primal history are in constant danger of being dealt with in the light in which all cats are grey. They are therefore permissible only to scholars who can see in this light, i.e. scholars with "cats' eyes", which can see in the dark.' A bold remark: it is not far from the scholar's 'cat's eyes' to Matt.15.14.

5. See my 'Literary, Theological and Historical Problems in the Gospel of Mark', below 31–63.

6. K.Niederwimmer, 'Johannes Markus und die Frage nach dem Verfasser des zweiten Evangeliums', *ZNW* 58, 1967, 172-88, is a typical example; cf. H.-M.Schenke/K.M.Fischer, *Einleitung in die Schriften des Neuen Testaments II. Die Evangelien und die anderen neutestamentlichen Schriften*, 1979, 79ff., 90ff.; P.Vielhauer, *Geschichte der urchristlichen Literatur*, 1975, 346f.: composed by an otherwise unknown Mark in Greek-speaking Syria. The simple title of the Gospel suggests that this Mark was by no means unknown in the communities of his time, see below, 28ff. For the Syria hypothesis see below, 28f.

7. Op.cit. (n.5), 47–50.

8. See the survey below, 7ff., 127 n.86.

9. John A.T.Robinson, *Redating the New Testament*, 1976, 95, 107ff., 352f. Mark accompanied Peter to Rome in AD 42 as interpreter and catechist. After his departure, 'he acceded to the reiterated request for a record of the apostle's preaching, perhaps about AD 45'; in AD 46 or 47 he was again in Jerusalem, cf. Acts 12.25 (114). Here Robinson closely follows the quotation from Clement of Alexandria, *Hypotyposeis* 6, which is contained in Eusebius, *HE* 2,1,3f. He refers to W.C.Allen, *St Mark*, 1915, 5f., who conjectures a similar date without giving a place. Putting Mark in this period to some degree matches the *Chronicon Hieronymi*, which is dependent on Eusebius, *Eusebius Werke* VII, GCS 47, *Die Chronik des Hieronymus*, ed. R.Helm, ²1956, 179: second year of Claudius = AD 42: *Petrus Apostolus cum primus Antiochenam ecclesiam fundasset, Romam mittitur, ubi euangelium praedicans XXV annis eiusdem urbis episcopus perseuerat*. Third year = AD 43: *Marcus euangelista interpres Petri. Aegypto et Alexandriae X̄P̄m adnuntiat*. Earlier Catholic exegesis still tended to follow this information: see the collection of authors in H.J.Holtzmann, *Lehrbuch der*

historisch-kritischen Einleitung in das Neue Testament, ³1892 (first edition 1885), 373; his brief but full collection of authors and views shows how little we have advanced here beyond the results towards the end of the nineteenth century. The readings of José O'Callaghan, 'Papiros neotestamentarios en la cueva 7 de Qumran?', *Bibl* 53, 1972, 91-100, who also sought to identify fragments of the Gospel of Mark among the Greek papyrus fragments from Cave 7Q and would thus have arrived at a very early date of composition, were all rejected as erroneous by P.Benoit, *RB* 79, 1972, 321-4; 80, 1973, 5-12. For further literature see J.A.Fitzmyer, *The Dead Sea Scrolls,* 1975, 119ff. Among the introductions and commentaries published after the Second World War I have found a tendency to put forward an early dating, before the Neronian persecution and the death of Peter, only in D.Guthrie, *New Testament Introduction* I, ¹1965 (³1970), 72ff. He considers various possibilities of harmonizing the contradictory information in Clement of Alexandria and Irenaeus. Guthrie also wants to take seriously A. von Harnack, *Beiträge zur Einleitung in das Neue Testament* IV, *Neue Untersuchungen zur Apostelgeschichte und zur Abfassungszeit der synoptischen Evangelien,* 1911, 88-93 = *The Date of Acts and the Synoptic Gospels,* 1911, 126ff. In the interest of an early date for his beloved Luke, Harnack has to date Luke's source Mark even earlier, and arrives at the time before AD 60 ('at the latest in the sixties', 93). Thus like W.C.Allen, op.cit., 5f., he arrives at the conjecture of a date of origin before 50. A situation of persecution and hatred of the Christians in Rome is already to be presupposed at the time of the expulsion of the Jews under Claudius. I also found an early dating of Mark in H.Staudinger, *Die historische Glaubwür-digkeit der Evangelien,* ³1974, 20, 'in the fifties', and in B.Reicke, 'Synoptic Prophecies on the Destruction of Jerusalem', in *Studies in New Testament and Early Christian Literature = Essays in Honor of Allen P.Wikgren,* ed. D.E.Aune, 1972, 121-34: if Matthew, Mark and Luke are earlier than Acts, 'they were also written before 62'(134). Only after preparing this study did I receive the volume edited by R.Wegner, *Die Datierung der Evangelien,* Symposium Paderborn 20-23.5.1982, printed as manuscript (Deutsches Institut für wissen-schaftliche Bildung). Here the early dating is discussed at length, though with unsatisfactory results. The problem can only be solved by thorough historical and exegetical work.

10. C.C.Torrey, *The Four Gospels: A New Translation,* 1933, ²1947, 261f., conjectured an origin connected with the uproar caused by Caligula. B.W.Bacon, *The Gospel of Mark. Its Composition and Date,* 1925, 53-63, carries on a detailed discussion with Torrey. However, here Torrey began from the questionable hypothesis of an Aramaic Gospel of Mark.

11. See below 14ff.

12. See the survey of commentaries by W.Werbeck, *RGG*³ II, 1958, col. 768. The hypothesis on the Gospel of Mark attributed to Cyril of Alexandria, which appears in *Catenae Graecorum Patrum in Novum Testamentum, Tomus I in Evangelia S.Matthaei et S.Marci,* ed. J.A.Cramer, 1844 (reprinted 1967), 263, stresses that many people had written about the Gospels according to Matthew and John, few about the Gospel of Luke, οὐδενὸς δὲ ὅλως, ὡς οἶμαι, εἰς τὸ κατὰ Μάρκον εὐαγγέλιον ἐξηγησαμένου. For the Prologue attributed to

Cyril see R.A.Lipsius, *Die apokryphen Apostelgeschichten und Apostellegenden* II, 2, 1884, 324f., n.5.

13. *Irénée de Lyon, Contre les hérésies* 3,1,1, ed. A.Rousseau and L.Doutreleau, SC 211, II, 1974, 522ff. = Eusebius, HE 5,8,2-4, GCS 9,1 ed. E.Schwartz 1903 = Kurt Aland, *Synopsis quattuor evangeliorum...*, [7]1971, 533.

14. Quoted by Eusebius, HE 3,39,15-16. For its part Papias' note on the Gospel of Mark goes back to the presbyter John, see my analysis, 47f. below, and G.Zuntz, *Markusphilologie*, ed. H. Cancik, WUNT 33, 1984, 47–71, 69ff.: 'Papias und kein Ende'. Here we cannot rule out the possibility that these notes are not just based on Papias but also reflect a more widespread consensus. Cf. I Peter 5.13 and Justin, below n.41.

15. Clement of Alexandria, *Hypotyposeis* 6 = Eusebius, HE 6,14,5-7 (see n.23), cf. 2,15,1f. Tertullian, *Adv.Marcionem* 4,5,3: *licet et Marcus quod*(= evangelium) *edidit Petri adfirmetur, cuius interpres Marcus.*

16. *Sancti Irenaei episcopi Lugdunensis libros quinque adversus haereses*, ed. W.W.Harvey 1857 (reprinted 1965) II, 5 n.2. Cf. also T.W.Manson, *Studies in the Gospels and Epistles*, ed. M.Black, 1962, 38ff. D. Guthrie, op.cit.(n.9), 73. Against this A.Rousseau/L.Doutreleau, op.cit. (n.13), SC 210, I, 1974, 217, p.23 n.3.

17. W.Bauer/W.F.Arndt/F.W.Gingrich, *Lexicon*, [2]1979, p.276: Wisdom 3.2; 7.6; TestNapht 1.1; Luke 9.31; II Peter 1.15; Justin, *Dialogue with Trypho* 105.3,5; *Epistola fratrum Lugdunensium*, quoted in Eusebius, HE 5,1,36,55, see also G.W.H.Lampe, *A Patristic Greek Lexicon*, 1961, col.498 s.v.

18. Cf. H.Lietzmann, *Petrus und Paulus in Rom*, [2]1927, 232ff.; id., *History of the Early Church* I, ET 1937, 254f.; R.Pesch, *Simon-Petrus, Geschichte und geschichtliche Bedeutung des ersten Jüngers Jesu Christi*, 1980, 109-34.

19. D.de Bruyne, 'Les plus anciens prologues latins des Évangiles', *RBen* 40, 1928, 193-214; A.von Harnack, *Die ältesten Evangelienprologe und die Bildung des Neuen Testaments*, SPAW, Ph.-h.Klasse 1928, 24, 324, 326 (reprinted in id., *Kleine Schriften zur Alten Kirche* II, *Berliner Akademieschriften 1908-1930*, 1980, 803-22). The most recent critical edition is in J.Regul, *Die Antimarcionitischen Evangelienprologe*, AGLB 6, 1969, 29f. (Der Markusprolog I), 35, 75f., 84f., 95ff.

20. *Refutatio omnium haeresium* 7,30,1 (GCS 26, ed. P.Wendland, 1916, 215 line 16): further very late instances in R.A.Lipsius, op.cit. (n.12), II, 2, 327ff. The reason given in the prologue for these unusual nicknames (*ideo quod ad ceteram corporis proceritatem digitos minores habuisset*) sounds more neutral and therefore more original than that in the later detailed so-called Monarchian arguments on Mark (J.Regul, op.cit. [n.19], 47f., lines 20f.): *Denique amputasse sibi post fidem pollicem dicitur, ut sacerdotio reprobus haberetur.* The arguments put forward by Regul (96) do not take us further. It cannot be proved that the attempts of the prologue at explanation are a 'mixture of rationalization and legend' any more than that 'it rests on genuine reminiscences'). In the case of the nickname itself, de Bruyne is to be accounted right (*RBen* 40, 1928, 201); he is followed by Harnack (op.cit. [n.19], 326/reprint 807): 'Marc a été colobodactylus de naissance ou par accident; ce sont des choses qui ne s'inventent pas.' The information certainly comes from one of the countless lost sources of the second century. Cf. now J.L.North, 'Μάρκος ὁ κολοβοδάκ-

τυλος: Hippolytus, *Elenchus* VII, 30', *JTS* 28, 1977, 498-507, with new evidence; North seeks to derive the name from a word-play *murcus*, 'the mutilated one' = Marcus, which is said to have been occasioned by Mark's refusal in Acts 13.13. A learned but unconvincing attempt.

21. *Partes* can, of course, also mean 'region' in isolated instances in Latin. However, here it seems to me that we have biblical language from LXX and NT: LXX I.Reg.30.14: ἐπὶ τὰ τῆς Ἰουδαίας μέρη (Vulgate, Josh.9.1); Tobit 8.3 Sin; Matt.2.22: εἰς τὰ μέρη τῆς Γαλιλαίας (Vulg: *in partes Galilaeae*); cf. 15.21; 16.13; Mark 8.10; John 6.1 D; Acts 7.43 D. Cf. Josephus, *Antt.* 8.154; 12.234; 13.357; 15.410: ἐν δὲ τοῖς ἑσπερίοις μέρεσιν τοῦ περιβόλου; id., *contra Apionem* I, 75. See already Thucydides 2,96,1; 4,98,4. Cf. Bauer/Arndt/Gingrich, *Lexicon*, p.506, s.v.1 βγ. The meaning 'part of an area' or 'area' occurs often for the plural in the papyri: see F.Preisigke, *Wörterbuch der griechischen Papyrusurkunden* II, 1927, 73. The other prologues and arguments only have *in Italia*, cf. Heb.13.24. This does not rule out Rome. The prologues are also fond elsewhere of speaking of provinces (J.Regul, op.cit. [n.19], 30ff.): *in Boeotia, in Achaiae partibus, in Bithynia, in Asia, in Ponto*.

Gregory of Nazianzus also says in a general way that Mark preached 'in Italy' (*Oratio* 33 [88] *contra Arianos*, PG 36, col.228). Cf.R.A.Lipsius, op.cit. (n.12) II, 2,322: for the late legends about Mark in Aquileia and Venice see 346ff.

22. See below, 47–50.

23. Preserved by Eusebius, HE 6,14,5-7 (GCS 9,2, ed. E.Schwartz, 1908, 550) = Aland, *Synopsis*, 539. See the *Adumbrationes Clementis Alexandrini in epistolas canonicas* (GCS 17, ed. O.Stählin, ³1930, 206), ad I Petr.5.13 = Aland, *Synopsis*, 539.

24. HE 2,15,2 = Aland, *Synopsis*, 539. See Morton Smith, *Clement of Alexandria and a Secret Gospel of Mark*, 1973, 19-33. The fragment of a letter he discovered similarly reports that the Gospel (τὰς πράξεις τοῦ κυρίου) was composed by Mark in Rome in Peter's lifetime. After Peter's martyrdom Mark brought his and Peter's notes to Egypt and with their aid expanded the original work for those advanced in Gnosticism, thus making a 'more spiritual gospel'. If the fragment of the letter is really genuine – and I am not quite sure about that – it is the earliest information about Mark's stay in Alexandria, which only appears again in Eusebius, HE 2,16,1: is this tradition also intended to express the superiority of the 'Alexandrian' gospel (see n.32 below) to the Roman gospel? See below nn.27,160. For 'the Alexandrian saga(s) of Mark' see R.A.Lipsius, op.cit (n.12) II, 2, 322-7; for the Acts of Mark, 329-46.

25. Cited in Eusebius, HE 6,25,5.

26. H.von Soden, *Die Schriften des Neuen Testaments* I, 1, ²1911, 305 (90): Μάρκος ὁ εὐαγγελιστὴς Ἀλεξανδρεῦσι... ἐκήρυξε τὸ εὐαγγέλιον, ὑπηγορεύθη δὲ ὑπὸ Πέτρου τοῦ ἀποστόλου ἐν Ῥώμῃ καὶ ἀπεδόθη αὐτῷ. Cf.311 (108); 312 (112): Πέτρος τὸ κατὰ Μάρκον ἐν Ῥώμῃ ὑπηγόρευσεν; 318 (122 = ε 1307 Smyrna, thirteenth century): Πέτρου ἐν Ῥώμῃ ἐντειλαμένου αὐτῷ Μάρκος συγγραψάμενος εὐαγγέλιον.

27. H.von Soden, op.cit (n.26), 312 (114 = ε 1314 EvgCod.Sinai thirteenth

century): τὸ δεύτερον εὐαγγέλιον τὸ κατὰ Μάρκον ἐγράφη ἐν ᾿Αλεξανδρείᾳ ὑπ᾿αὐτοῦ τοῦ Μάρκου ἐπιτρέψαντος αὐτοῦ τοῦ ἁγίου ἀποστόλου καὶ κορυφαίου Πέτρου. Cf. also n.24, the secret Gospel in Clement of Alexandria, and below n.160.

28. Eusebius, *Werke II, Die Kirchengeschichte*, 3.Teil, *Einleitungen, Übersichten und Register*, GCS 9,3, ed. E.Schwartz, 1909, CCXVf.:'According to Eusebius' own information (8.21) the Church History is an extension of his Χρονικοὶ κανόνες.'

29. HE 2,14-17; for the Chronicle see the quotation in n.9.

30. E.Schwartz, 'Eusebios', *PRE* 6,1,1907, cols. 1377ff.:'Africanus is without doubt heavily used by Eusebius, even where he does not say so' (col.1378). Cf. id., op.cit.(n.28), CCXXIf. The Chronicle extends to AD 217 or 221.

31. I.26.

32. HE 2,16,1 = Aland, *Synopsis*, 543.

33. HE 2,17,1.

34. See n.9 above (cf. n.27 and 24). Codex L puts the note about Peter and Mark in the first year of Claudius; Codices A and P put both together in the second. See also G.Zuntz, op.cit.(n.14), 66ff.; cf. also *Eusebii Chronicorum libri duo*, Vol.II, *Chronicorum Canonum*, ed. A.Schoene, 1846, 152; according to this Mark's arrival in Rome fell in the year 2057 from Abraham, i.e. in the first year of Claudius = AD 41.

35. H.von Soden, op.cit.(n.26), 312 (114, see above n.27); 313 (115 = ε 1115 and (?) ε 341 Oxford Christ Church): τὸ κατὰ Μάρκον εὐαγγέλιον συνεγράφη ὑπὸ Μάρκου μετὰ δέκα χρόνους. Cf. the Prologue by Theophylact, PG 123, 1864 (reprinted 1978), col.492: τὸ κατὰ Μάρκον εὐαγγέλιον, μετὰ δέκα ἔτη τῆς τοῦ Χριστοῦ ἀναλήψεως συνεγράφη ἐν ῾Ρώμῃ. See the prologue to Matthew, col.145D.

36. E.Hennecke/W.Schneemelcher/R.McL.Wilson, *New Testament Apocrypha* II, ET 1965, 18f. The Pseudo-Clementine Recognitions mention seven years, see my forthcoming article 'Jakobus der Herrenbruder – der erste "Papst"?', in the Festschrift for the 80th birthday of W.G.Kümmel, 1985. See also R.A.Lipsius, op.cit. (n.12) I, 1883, 13f., and A.Strobel, *Ursprung und Geschichte des frühchristlichen Osterkalenders*, TU 121, 1977, 115ff. For Mark and the twelve years see G.Zuntz, op.cit., 65ff.

37. *Stromateis* 1,21, 146,3 (GCS 15, Clemens Alexandrinus II), ed O.Stählin, 1906, 90 line 25.

38. See A.von Harnack, *Geschichte der altchristlichen Literatur bis Eusebius* II, 1, 1897, 243f.; A.Strobel, op.cit. (n.36), 117f. He goes on to refer to the chronicles of Cassiodorus, ed. T.Mommsen, *Chronica minora* II, 1894, 137, which puts the death of Jesus in 29 and Peter's journey to Rome twelve years later, in 41.

39. Eusebius, *Chronicle of Jerome*, op.cit (n.9), 183 (cf.404): in the eighth year of Nero (62): *post Marcum euangelistam primus Alexandriae ecclesiae ordinatur episcopus Annianus*, see also HE 2,24: Νέρωνος δὲ ὄγδοον ἄγοντος τῆς βασιλείας ἔτος, πρῶτος μετὰ Μάρκον τὸν εὐαγγελιστὴν τῆς ἐν ᾿Αλεξανδρείᾳ παροικίας ᾿Αννιανὸς τὴν λειτουργίαν διαδέχεται. Cf. also the life of Mark according to Sophronius in H.von Soden, op.cit. (n.26), 309. An obscure Life of Mark

'from the synopsis of Dorotheos, martyr and Bishop of Tyre', which itself in turn is dependent on the Acts of Mark composed in the fourth century, reports that Mark was burnt by idolaters under Trajan (307); cf. R.A.Lipsius, op.cit. (n.12), II, 2, 337ff., who conjectures that the Τραϊανοῦ is a corruption of Γαίου.

40. Op.cit. (n.35). Further instances in G.Zuntz, op.cit.

41. *Actus Petri cum Simone* 20, in R.A.Lipsius/M.Bonnet, *Acta Apostolorum Apocrypha* I, 1891, 66f. For the time of origin see *New Testament Apocrypha* (n.36), II, 187, before c. 190, presumably 180-190. For Peter as the alleged author of the Gospel of Mark see Justin, *Dialogue with Trypho*, 106,3, where in connection with a reference to Mark 3.16 it is said that this is written ἐν τοῖς ἀπομνημονεύμασιν αὐτοῦ (i.e. Πέτρου). There is no indication of the later apocryphal Gospel of Peter in the Acts of Peter or in Justin, even if Justin himself probably knew it.

42. A.Jülicher/E.Fascher, *Einleitung in das Neue Testament*, [7]1931, 304: 'We thus feel thrown back on the Gospel alone for defining its date.'

43. See the collection of the various datings in J.Moffatt, *An Introduction to the Literature of the New Testament*, [3]1918 (1911), 213: F.C.Baur, after 130; K.T.Keim, 115-120; K.R.Köstlin, 100-10. See also K.R.Köstlin, *Der Ursprung und die Komposition der synoptischen Evangelien*, 1853, 385, who dates the Gospel of Mark 'in the first decade of the second century'; F.C.Baur, *Kritische Untersuchungen über die kanonischen Evangelien*, 1847, 535-67. Cf. also F.Bleek, *Einleitung ins Neue Testament*, 1862, 243, 289f., who regards the Gospel of Mark as later than Matthew and Luke and presumably also than John, and assumes that it was composed by John Mark after the destruction of Jerusalem, probably for the Romans.

44. Augustine, *De consensu evangelistarum* 1,2,4 (CSEL 43, ed. F.Weihrich, 1904), 4 line 12f.: *Marcus eum* (sc. Matthaeum) *subsecutus tamquam pedisequus et breuiator eius uidetur*, see H.Merkel, *Die Widersprüche zwischen den Evangelien*, WUNT 13, 1971, 229f.

45. 'Marcus im NT', *RE* 12, 1903, col.294. The reference to 13.24 does not make much sense, since this point in time μετὰ τὴν θλῦψιν has not yet been reached. The time of distress is only beginning (see 20 below). A.Jülicher/ E.Fascher, op.cit. (n.42), 303ff. differ somewhat: 'we shall regard AD 70 as the *terminus a quo*; in our view the boundary can only be found through a comparison with Matthew and Luke; the lifetime of Mark would also be enough for a later dating' (304f.). Cf. S.G.F.Brandon, 'The Date of the Markan Gospel', *NTS* 7, 1960/61, 126-41: 'According to the general consensus of expert opinion Mark was composed some time between the years AD 65-75' (126). However, his own conjectures are not convincing: there is no trace in the second Gospel of the triumph of Vespasian and Titus in AD 71.

46. See B.H.Streeter, *The Four Gospels. A Study of Origins*, [9]1956, 295-331; F.Neirynck, *The Minor Agreements of Matthew and Luke against Mark*, BETL 37, 1974.

47. Op.cit. (n.45), col.294.

48. Ἀμὴν λέγω ὑμῖν ὅτι οὐ μὴ παρέλθῃ ἡ γενεὰ αὕτη μέχρις οὗ ταῦτα πάντα γένηται.

49. Matt.16.28; 24.30; cf. 10.23. For the author of Matthew, so aware of having been a scribe and now being a Christian teacher, the Gospel of Mark is already a determinative authority, in which he often even leaves untouched things which no longer correspond exactly to his own theological bias. In my view this is connected with the fact that the author of the first Gospel was aware that the authority of Peter stood behind the second.

50. Luke 9.27 omits the reference to the 'coming of the kingdom of God in power'. This 'de-eschatologizes' the verse. In Luke 21.32 the important ταῦτα is missing.

51. Cf. Mark 6.3: Jesus' mother, Mary, and his brothers are known to the community, but not his father Joseph, see Acts 1.14. A further example of such an identification of a son known in the present occurs in II Macc.4.11, where the ambassador John, who obtained royal concessions for the Jews from Antiochus III after 200 BC, is described as follows: διὰ Ἰωάννου τοῦ πατρὸς Εὐπολέμου τοῦ ποιησαμένου τὴν πρεσβείαν... πρὸς τοὺς Ῥωμαίους. This Eupolemos was known as a later contemporary of the author Jason of Cyrene and his contemporaries, cf. I Macc.8.17 and on it my Judaism and Hellenism, ET 1974, I, 64,92. For Simon of Cyrene and his sons see also Between Jesus and Paul, 148 n.117: the ossuary inscription 'Alexander son of Simon' with the addition in Hebrew qrnyt = 'from Cyrene'(?). Of course the feminine form is puzzling. A Rufus and his mother – who is probably much older than the apostle – who are well known to Paul do, however, appear in the list of greetings in Rom.16.13, which in my view is certainly addressed to Rome (see below, 180 n.103). It remains uncertain whether there are any connections here.

52. R.Pesch, Das Markusevangelium II, 1977, 477, conjectures 'that their names were first mentioned by the translators of the passion narrative'. The existence of an Aramaic source cannot, however, be demonstrated.

53. Mark 15.1: παρέδωκαν Πιλάτῳ; Luke 3.1: ἡγεμονεύοντος Ποντίου Πιλάτου. For the name see Acts 4.27; I Tim.6.13; Matt.27.2: παρέδωκαν Πιλάτῳ τῷ ἡγεμόνι. For ἀρχιερεύς see Mark 14.60ff.; Luke 3.2; Matt.26.3: εἰς τὴν αὐλὴν τοῦ ἀρχιερέως τοῦ λεγομένου Καϊάφα. Cf. also John 11.49; 18.13f. etc.

54. Pesch, Markus II, 21; id., Das Evangelium der Urgemeinde, 1979, 84.

55. For the kind of historian that Josephus is see his arrogant and pretentious prologues to the Bellum Judaicum, the Antiquitates and contra Apionem, and on them S.J.D.Cohen, Josephus in Galilee and Rome, 1979, 47,65,232ff.

56. Mark probably introduces them in order to heighten the tension: they appear for the first time in Mark 3.22: οἱ γραμματεῖς οἱ ἀπὸ Ἱεροσολύμων καταβάντες, 7.1: καὶ συνάγονται πρὸς αὐτὸν οἱ Φαρισαῖοι καί τινες τῶν γραμματέων ἐλθόντες ἀπὸ Ἱεροσολύμων. Before that they appear only in 2.6; 2.16 (see n.57). Note the clear distinction in contrast to the later unified terminology in Matthew.

57. Mark 2.16: οἱ γραμματεῖς τῶν Φαρισαίων.

58. The Pharisees appear twelve times in Mark 2-10: 2.18 (twice), 24; 3.6; 7.3; 8.11,5; 10.2 without and 2.16; 7.1,5; 9.11 (Sin, L, pc lat.) with the scribes (four times). In Jerusalem, by contrast they appear only once: 12.13. We meet the 'scribes' in Mark 1-9 eight times (ignoring the γραμματεῖς of the Sanhedrin

in the passion predictions of 8.31; 10.33, which refer to Jerusalem); in Mark 11-15, however, they appear ten times.

59. We meet them only once in the scene Mark 12.18ff., but cf. the schematic use of the term in Matt.3.7; 16.1,6,11, which shows that Matthew hardly knew anything about the Sadducees.

60. Mark 3.6 and Mark 12.13. In Luke they disappear completely; Matthew has them only in 22.16.

61. Mark 12.28,32. For Mark these are 'scribes of the Pharisees'. The scene shows that there were some groups in Judaism which stood nearer to Jesus than others.

62. ἀρχιερεῖς: Mark 8.31; 10.33; 11.18,27; 14.1,10,43,55; 15.1,3,10,11,31. They are also the real opponents of Jesus in the Sanhedrin. After AD 70 they were in fact exterminated and lost all significance. For the whole question see the relevant articles in *TDNT* and J.Jeremias, *Jerusalem in the Time of Jesus*, ET 1967, 147-270; E.Schürer, ed. G.Vermes/F.Millar/M.Black, *The History of the Jewish People in the Age of Jesus Christ (175 B.C. – A.D. 135)*, II, 1979, 199ff., 381ff.

63. Above all in Acts 4.5ff.; 5.33f.; 23.6ff.; 24.1f.

64. For Peter in Mark see below, 50–3, and the excursus by R.Feldmeier, 59ff. Mark does not yet show the hagiographical over-painting that we find in Matthew, Luke and John.

65. Mark 1.19,29; 3.17; 5.37; 9.2; 10.35,41; 13.3; 14.33: nine times.

66. Matt.4.21; 10.2; 17.1; Luke 5.10; 6.14; 8.51; 9.28,54.

67. Cf. the stress on John in Luke 9.49; 22.8; also Acts 1.13; 3.1,3f.; 4.13,19; 8.14; 12.2. For Luke, John has essentially greater significance than James, a sign that he was not killed with him (*pace* E.Schwartz), but continued to be active as an authority (cf. Gal.2.9). There is still no trace at all of this in Mark. Nevertheless he seems to know of his death (at a later date).

68. Mark 3.14,16; 4.10; 6.7; 9.35; 10.32; 11.11; 14.10,17,20,43: eleven times. Matthew eight times; Luke seven times; John 6.67, 70f.: three times. In going so far as to assert that 'the ominous process of early Catholicism begins with the Gospel of Mark', or that Mark is its 'first representative', S.Schulz, *Die Mitte der Schrift*, 1976, 201, is only demonstrating his inability to think in historical categories. Accordingly his picture of the second evangelist simply piles up one cliché on another.

68a. See my article 'Jakobus, der Herrenbruder – der erste "Papst"?' (121, n.36 above).

69. Loc.cit (n.45).

70. See e.g. the interpretation of the miracle of the sea in Pamphylia in Strabo 14,3,9 and Arrian, *Anabasis* 1,26,1f., and the interpretation by his historiographer Callisthenes, FGrHist 124 F.31, and W.W.Tarn, *Alexander the Great*, 1948/1950, II, 357ff.; the message of the priest in the oracle of Ammon that he is 'Son of Zeus': Strabo 17,1,43 = FGrHist 124 F.14; the prayer of Alexander for divine support before Gaugamela, 'if he stems from Zeus': Plutarch, *Alexander* 33 = FGrHist 124 F.36. For the whole question see also R.Merkelbach, *Die Quellen des griechischen Alexanderromans*, ² 1977, say on the theme of the alleged poisoning of Alexander by Antipater: 'One can see that

this is a real saga. It is impossible for it to have arisen centuries after the events. Saga emerges wherever we can observe it, contemporaneously with or directly after the events' (61). 'It is not surprising that the soldiers told themselves such stories. For them Alexander's expedition must have been an unheard-of adventure' (61). (One could also say the same sort of thing about the disciples' following of Jesus.) Cf. 92: 'Now even in his lifetime, for many of his contemporaries, and above all for his own soldiers, Alexander was a mythical figure. The accounts of the history of Alexander have largely concealed this. However, this mythical element is part of the authentic picture of the historical Alexander.' If we substitute Jesus for Alexander and critical research into Jesus for 'historians of Alexander', we have a misunderstood main problem in New Testament scholarship. Cf. also E.Mederer, *Die Alexanderlegenden bei den ältesten Alexanderhistorikern*, Würzburger Studien zur Altertumswissenschaft 8, 1936, and M.Reiser, 'Alexanderroman und Markusevangelium', in *Markus-Philologie*, ed. H.Cancik, WUNT 33, Tübingen 1984, 131ff.

71. Cf. Suetonius, *Augustus*, 94-99; 97.1: *Mors quoque eius... divinitasque post mortem evidentissimis ostentis praecognita est*. This was written by a scholar who as Hadrian's personal secretary had access to private lists and secret acts. Cf. 100.4: *Nec defuit vir praetorius, qui se effigiem cremati euntem in caelum vidisse iuraret*, and 6: the penal miracle which had recently happened (*sed et mox confirmata*, i.e. in the time of Suetonius) in the room in which Augustus was born.

72. *Peregrinus* 39-41 and *Philopseudes* 11ff.

73. See K.S.Frank, *Frühes Mönchtum im Abendland* II, *Lebensgeschichten*, 1975, 13ff.; cf. *Sulpicii Severi Vita Sancti Martini* 25 (CSEL 1, ed. C.Halm, 1866, 134f.); and op.cit., 171ff. The basic study is now C.Stancliffe, *St Martin and his Hagiographer*, 1983; Stancliffe also reports some unease among contemporaries towards the miracle-worker Martin of Tours (249-61). I recommend that all New Testament scholars should read this extremely interesting book. For contemporary eye-witnesses to miracles see also the Venerable Bede, *Historia ecclesiastica gentis Anglorum*, ed. G.Spitzbart, 1982, 5,12 (p.472): *qui adhuc superest*; 5,13 end (p.476); 5.18 (487ff.). People were hardly more critical in Galilee in the time of Jesus than in England in the time of Bede. The rejection of miracle in principle which we find in the mild Epicurean Horace (*Sat.* 1,5,97ff., cf. Pliny the Elder, *Nat.hist.* 2, 250; 7,173-9) and Lucian's *Philopseudes* was the rare exception in antiquity. Pliny the Younger, who accused the Christians of absurd superstition (*Ep.*10.96.6), gullibly believes in the reality of ghosts and tells some feeble stories, appealing to eye-witnesses (7.27). It is significant that Horace accused the Jews carrying on an active mission in Rome (cf. *Sat.*1,4,142f.) of especial credulity over miracles (1,5,100): *Credat Judaeus Apella*. The miracle was not a *specific* characteristic of the Hellenistic pagan world. Rather, it was part of primitive Christian proclamation from the beginning. For the problem see also E.Meyer, *Ursprung und Anfänge des Christentums* I, 1921 (reprinted 1962), 159 n.1, and his dissension from the theory of J. Wellhausen, *Einleitung in die ersten drei Evangelien*, ²1911, 155, that the Gospel of Mark has nothing to do with Peter or eye-witnesses: 'The

miracle stories in the form which they are given in Mark above all tell against a derivation from the most intimate disciples of Jesus. But nothing at all comes from eye-witnesses...' Contrast E.Meyer: 'Believing eye-witnesses at all times, not just in the Middle Ages and in the East but in the Greek world (...) and even in the present tell of miracles on pilgrimages, in visions and so on in just the same way as they are narrated in Mark.' See W.Schamoni, *Wunder sind Tatsachen*, ²1976, with abundant material collected from acts of canonization. Questionable though the apologetic tendency of this book is, the 'eye-witness reports' and phenomena which it records are very illuminating.

74. *Histories* 4,81,3: *utrumque* (the healing of a lame man and a blind man) *qui interfuere nunc quoque memorant, postquam nullum mendacio pretium*, i.e. even at the time of the composition of the *Histories*, about forty years after the events in Alexandria (69, or c. 110), eye-witnesses could report it at a time when there was no longer any point in flattering the Flavian imperial house with lies.

75. See my 'Christology and New Testament Chronology', in *Between Jesus and Paul*, 30-47; *The Son of God*, ET 1976. Cf. also G.Zuntz, op.cit. (n.14), 49f.

75a. See now R.Laufen, *Die Doppelüberlieferungen der Logienquelle und des Markusevangeliums*, 1978; he shows that the majority of the Marcan traditions have a later form.

76. See my 'The Origins of the Christian Mission', *Between Jesus and Paul*, 48-64; *Acts and the History of Earliest Christianity*, 1979, 92ff.

77. The basic study is M.Werner, *Der Einfluss paulinischer Theologie im Markusevangelium*, BZNW 1, 1923.

78. E.Preuschen, *Antilegomena*, ²1905, 94f., fr. 5, according to Philippus Sidetes, and fr.6 according to Cod.Coisl.305 of Georgius Monachus = F.X.Funk/K.Bihlmeyer, *Die apostolischen Väter*, 1924, 138f., fr.11,12.

79. 'Über den Tod der Söhne Zebedaei', in *Gesammelte Schriften zum Neuen Testament und zum frühen Christentum* V, 1963, 48-123 = Abhandlungen der Göttinger Gesellschaft der Wissenschaften, NF VII, 5, 1904. Against this, F.Spitta, *ZNW* 11, 1910, 39-58, and the reply by E.Schwartz, ibid., 89-104.

80. According to Josephus, *Antt.* 20,200, as well as James the brother of Jesus καὶ τινας ἑτέρους, ὡς παρανομησάντων were accused and stoned (AD 62).

81. The portrayal of the historical events and circumstances extend to 11.39; from 11.40 the apocalyptic utopia begins with the formula, 'in the time of the end', with which real political expectations are connected. The clash of the Seleucid with the 'king of the south', i.e. Ptolemy VI, did not take place. Rather, in 165 BC Antiochus set off for an expedition to Iran. His death was announced in Babylon between 20.11 and 18.12.164 BC. The author knows nothing of this. He only mentions the events after the desecration of the temple in 167 BC, with the persecution and the first beginnings of the Maccabeaen revolt in 166 BC (cf. 11.34). Thus the work should probably be dated in the first half of the year 165 BC. See O.Plöger, *Das Buch Daniel*, KAT, 1965, 164-7, cf. 29f.; M.Delcor, *Le livre de Daniel*, 1971, 15, 246ff.: 'De fait, les

premiers mots du début de la péricope *wb't qs* (v.40), "et au temps de la fin", montrent que la prophétie fictive, c'est-à-dire le rappel historique du passé, est terminée, et que maintenant commence la vraie prophétie'(247), following A.Bentzen. In Mark the shift comes in v.14, see 18ff. below.

82. M.Hengel, 'Das Gleichnis von den Weingärtnern Mk.12.1-12', *ZNW* 59, 1968, (1-39) 31,38.

83. Cf. Josephus, *BJ* 6, (288-315) 293ff.: the miraculous opening of the eastern gate in the temple; 299: the departure of the deity, see O.Michel and O.Bauernfeind, *De bello Judaico* II, 2, 1969, 179-90: 'There must have been a priestly tradition which expected a future destruction of the temple' (184); cf. Tacitus, *Histories* 5,13,1, and M.Stern, *Greek and Latin Authors on Jews and Judaism*, II, 1980, 60f. The Gospel of the Hebrews, fr.20, says that the enormous temple threshold, rather than the curtain, burst apart, but this account is certainly secondary. For the rabbinic 'predictions' of the destruction of the temple see P.Billerbeck I, 1045f. For Christian interpretations see loc.cit., the interpolations in T XII (T Levi 10 and TBenj.9) and R.Pesch, op.cit. (n.52), 498f. The rationalistic argument to the effect that the tradition of the rending of the curtain must have come about after 70, since before that it could have been verified, misses the point completely and misunderstands the over-abundance of ancient traditions and interpretations of omens. Moreover, what is meant is presumably the inner curtain, which was not visible from outside.

84. For the departure of the deity (the *evocatio* theme) see Jer.12.7; Ezek.8.12; 9.9; Ps.Philo LAB 19.2: *et irascetur Deus in vobis, et derelinquet vos, et discedet de terra vestra*. Further ancient examples in M.Stern, op.cit. (n.83), II, 60f., see W.Eisenhut, *KP* II, cols. 472f., s.v. *evocatio*.

85. M.Hengel, *The Atonement*, 1981, 42,45.

86. The majority of the more recent commentaries on Mark understand this verse as a *vaticinium ex eventu*, see R.Pesch, op.cit. (n.52) II, 271; W.Schmithals, *Das Evangelium nach Markus*, Ökumenischer Taschenbuch-kommentar zum Neuen Testament 2,2, 1979, 558: 'the *total* destruction of the temple... corresponds to the reaction of the Romans after the conquest of Jerusalem, which of course could not be foreseen in advance'. J.Ernst, *Das Evangelium nach Markus*, RNT, 1981, 369f., however, regards a *vaticinium ex eventu* as improbable. See also the discussion in R.Wegner (ed.), op.cit. (n.9), 63f., 72ff., etc.

87. *BJ* 7.1-4; cf. 5.391 (Nebuchadnezzar); 7, 379 (discourse of Eleazar): τὴν ἱερὰν... πόλιν... κατασκαπτομένην, ...τὸν ναὸν... ἐξορωρυγμένον; *Antiquitates* 5,248 (Abimelech and Shechem): καὶ κατασκάψας εἰς ἔδαφος τὴν πόλιν; 7,145 (David and Rabbath Ammon); 8,151 (Pharaoh and Gezer); 8,128; 10,80, 112,149,230; 11.1,6 (Jerusalem and the temple by Nebuchadnezzar); *BJ* 1,50,65 (the Acra and Samaria by the Hasmonaeans). See also II Chron.36.19 LXX. Cf. Taan 4.6: 'On the 9 Ab the temple was destroyed the first and the second time and the city (= Jerusalem) was ploughed over.' See the Senate decree on Carthage in Appian, *Historia Romana* VIII, 135: οἳ Καρχηδόνος μὲν εἴ τι περίλοιπον ἔτι ἦν, ἔκριναν κατασκάψαι Σκιπίωνα, καὶ οἴκειν αὐτὴν ἀπεῖπον ἅπασι. See the fate of Corinth, Strabo 8,6,23: αὐτή τε κατέσκαπτο.

The thorough destruction of a hostile city along with its sanctuaries was a very widespread practice in war. Thus already in the OT: Josh. 7.24,26; 8.28 (Jericho and Ai); Deut. 13.7: the apostate Israelite city. Cf. also Rev.18.2-8,19,21 and Sibyll.5,163,168-78: οὐκέτι σου σημεῖον ἔτ᾽ἔσσεται ἐν χθονὶ κείνη: complete annihilation by divine judgment.

88. We find the phrase ...λίθος ἐπὶ λίθον at the building of the temple in Hagg.2.15, but there are no earlier parallels for its use in connection with destruction. Against R.Pesch, loc.cit. (n.86), and J.Dupont, 'Il n'en sera pas laissé pierre sur pierre (Marc 13,2; Luc 19,44)', *Bibl* 52, 1971, 301-20, I think that the threat in Luke 19.44, καὶ ἐδαφιοῦσίν σε... καὶ οὐκ ἀφήσουσιν λίθον ἐπὶ λίθον ἐν σοί, which relates to the destruction of all Jerusalem, is dependent on Mark 13.2 and represents a real *vaticinium ex eventu* according better with the historical circumstances than Mark 13.2, which merely relates to the temple. At most we could find an analogy in II Sam.17.13 LXX, where Hushai advises Absalom to dismantle a rebellious city so thoroughly, ὅπως μὴ καταλειφθῇ ἐκεῖ μηδὲ λίθος.

88a. For the interpretation see Origen on Ps.73.5f., *Selecta in Psalmos*, PG 12, 1529, and Euthymius Zigabenus, *Commentarius in Psalmos*, which sums up patristic exegesis, on Ps.73, PG 128, 749-64.

89. Cf. Jer.7.12-14; 26.6,9,18 (cf. Micah 3.12): 'Zion is ploughed as a field, Jerusalem becomes a heap of ruins, the temple mountain becomes a wooded height.' This threat presupposes that 'no stone remains on another'. For the complete destruction of Jerusalem, the temple and the city, by Nebuchadnezzar see II Kings 25.9; II Chron. 36.19; Tobit 14.4b (BA). Eth. Enoch 90.28f. mentions only a radical transformation and purification of the temple: by contrast texts like Dan.8.11 ('It magnified itself, even up to the Prince of the Host; and the continual burnt offering was taken away from him, and the place of his sanctuary was overthrown' – *weḥušlak mekōn miqdāšō*, cf. LXX) could be interpreted later as a prophecy of a complete destruction of the temple. Cf. also Dan.9.26f.; 11.31.

90. II Macc.14.33: τόνδε τὸν τοῦ θεοῦ σηκὸν εἰς πεδίον ποιήσω καὶ τὸ θυσιαστήριον κατασκάψω καὶ ἱερὸν ἐνταῦθα τῷ Διονύσῳ ἐπιφανὲς ἀναστήσω. In this threat we have a formal parallel to the saying about the temple in Mark 14.58; John 2.19, which is similarly determined by the contrast between tearing down and rebuilding. Cf. II Macc.6.7 and my *Judaism and Hellenism* II, 296. The lamentation from 4Q 179 (ed. J.M.Allegro, *Qumran Cave 4*, DJDJ V, 1968, 75f.), col.1, lines 5ff. contains the description of a complete destruction of the temple by fire in the form of centos dependent on Old Testament texts (Lamentations, Zephaniah, Isaiah, Ezekiel, etc.). See J.Strugnell, *RdQ* 26, 7, 1970, 250: 'On se demandera à quelle destruction de Jérusalem l'auteur pensait.' For the reconstruction and interpretation see M.P.Horgan, *JSS* 17, 1972, 22-34. The origin of the manuscript is put at about 50 BC; the text may go back to the time of the Maccabees.

91. Diodore 34/35, 1,1-5; M.Stern, op.cit (n.83), I, 1974, 181f., and Josephus, *Antt.* 13,245f. See the report by Sulpicius Severus, *Chronica* II, 30 (CSEL 1, ed.C.Halm, 1866), which probably goes back to Tacitus = T.Reinach, *Textes d'auteurs grecs et romains relatifs au Judaïsme*, 1895 (reprinted 1963), 324f., on

Titus' council of war as to whether the temple should be destroyed or not. This is fundamentally different from the apologetic account by Josephus (*BJ* 6,236ff.) and probably accords with historical reality.

92. *Antiquitates* 17, 259-64; cf. *BJ* 2,49f.

93. Cf. the warning in the speech by Agrippa II, *BJ* 2,380: μηδὲ τὸ Καρχηδονίων τέλος σκοποῦντες, and 6,332, Titus' speech to the leaders of the revolt: ἀλλὰ μὴν ἤδειτε καὶ Καρχηδονίους ἁλόυντας.

94. This already begins with the transformation of Judaea into a Roman province in 6, when the high priest Joazar son of Boethus convinced the people to accept the taxation census and the attempt at rebellion by Judas the Galilean and the Pharisee Zadduk failed (*Antt.* 18.3f.). See M.Hengel, *Die Zeloten*, 336ff.

95. *BJ* 2, 400; φείσασθε τοῦ ἱεροῦ καὶ τὸν ναὸν ἑαυτοῖς μετὰ τῶν ἁγίων τηρήσατε. ἀφέξονται γὰρ οὐκέτι Ῥωμαῖοι τούτων κράτησαντες, ὧν φεισάμενοι πρότερον ἠχαρίστηνται.

96. *BJ* 6,300f. Cf. also 109f., 311; 5,412 and by contrast 6,99, 285; Dio Cassius 66,5f. See M.Hengel, *Die Zeloten*, ²1976, 246ff. Something of this kind may have influenced Rev.11.1,8.

97. See E.Lohmeyer, *Das Evangelium des Markus*, KEK, ¹²1953, 268: 'The saying seems to be "chopped up" and scattered in various forms through the Gospel tradition... The colourlessness of the form does not justify the verdict that the saying must be a *vaticinium ex eventu*. If it is based on apocalyptic thinking and Jesus shared in this thinking, as indeed the name Son of man shows, then the word is not only possible, but indeed probable, on his lips...' Cf. also G.Theissen, 'Die Tempelweissagung Jesu', in id., *Studien zur Soziologie des Urchristentums*, WUNT 19, 1979, 142-59.

98. See M.Smallwood, *The Jews under Roman Rule*, ²1981, 310ff., 316-51; E.Schürer, op.cit. (n.62), I, 1973, 496-513.

99. M.Smallwood, op.cit. (n.98), 328, 334ff.: Herodion surrendered probably late in 71. Masada probably fell in May of 73, but perhaps only a year later. Machaerus in Peraea, near to the Nabataean sphere, lies outside the perspective of this account (as does Pella in the north-east, in the Jordan rift, see below 18); it was probably conquered in summer 72 (*BJ* 7, 190ff.).

100. Cf. *BJ* 4,444: Vespasian settled subjugated Jews in Lydda and Jamnia. 6,115: Titus assigns Gophna as a place for those who come over to him: 'He will restore to each person his possessions as soon as the war is brought to an end.' By contrast, fugitive rebels tried to go abroad (Arabia, Babylonia or Egypt). 7,210-214 reports a skirmish with rebels who fled from Jerusalem and Machaerus in the 'forest of Jardes'; the Romans killed 3000 for the loss of only twelve of their men: a nonsensical exaggeration. The location is unclear, see C.Möller/G.Schmitt, *Siedlungen Palästinas nach Flavius Josephus*, BTAVO B14, 1976, 99. Presumably it is to be located in the Jordan valley (I Macc. 9.42,45) or east of it. According to *BJ* 7,409ff., other Sicarii fled to Egypt.

101. The flysheet hypothesis already appears in G.Volkmar, *Die Evangelien*, 1870, 542; see also R.Pesch, op.cit. (n.52), II, 264ff.; Lars Hartman, *Prophecy Interpreted*, CB.NT 1, 1966, shows very impressively the way in which this text is deeply permeated, in midrashic fashion, with linguistic material from

the Old Testament and apocalyptic. For 13.14-20 see 151ff., 162ff. Daniel above all was behind this.

102. For the events in Judaea between winter 39/40 and the murder of Caligula on 24.1.41 see M.Smallwood, op.cit. (n.98), 174-80. Thanks to the presence of mind of the legate Petronius, the conflict developed only relatively slowly. Moreover the reaction of the Jews in Palestine was not flight, but to threaten open rebellion. They would not have allowed Petronius in the city any more than Cestius Gallus at a later date. See W.Bousset, *Der Antichrist in der Überlieferung des Judentums, des neuen Testaments und der alten Kirche*, 1895, 14: 'A life and death struggle would probably have taken place before the statue was set up.' Cf. Zuntz, op.cit. (119 n.14), 47ff.

102a. For the theme of flight in I Macc.2.28 see J.A.Goldstein, *I Maccabees*, AncB 1976, 236ff.; M.Hengel, *Die Zeloten*, ²1976, 255ff. Cf. also *The Charismatic Leader and his Followers*, ET 1981, 19.

103. Cf. the Q apocalypse Luke 17.24ff. Luke has inserted Mark 13.15f. here in 17.31. See also I Cor.15.52.

104. Op.cit. (n.101), 152f.

105. G.Volkmar, loc.cit (n.101), conjectures that Mark found 'the abomination of desolation in the Roman army, which set itself up where it should not be, before Jerusalem, and thus at the same time announced the ἐρήμωσις of Jerusalem'. He wants to date the Gospel itself to the year 73, see p. VIII.

106. Josephus, *BJ* 6,316 (cf. already 6,226).

107. Verse 14: ὅταν δὲ ἴδητε... τότε φευγέτωσαν.

108. Cf. F.Blass/A.Debrunner/R.W.Funk, *NT Greek Grammar*, 1961, p.74.

109. *BJ* 6,415: camp for prisoners in the Court of the Women; cf. *Vita* 419; *BJ* 7,20, retreat to Caesarea in October. Titus wintered there and in the cities of Phoenicia and Syria; in Spring AD 71 he again visited the ruins (*BJ* 7,112–115) and then hastened back via Egypt to Rome, arriving in June AD 71. There he celebrated the triumph with his father. See Weinand, *PRE* 6, 2, 1909, cols. 2705f.

110. *BJ* 6,414-29: 1.1 million dead in the siege and capture, 97,000 prisoners, the majority of whom did not come from Jerusalem but from the country (6,420). The numbers are certainly exaggerated, but give some indication of the war of annihilation which Titus was waging against the Jews.

111. Eusebius, HE 3,5,3: οὐ μὴν ἀλλὰ καὶ τοῦ λαοῦ τῆς ἐν Ἱεροσολύμοις ἐκκλησίας κατά τινα χρησμὸν τοῖς αὐτόθι δοκίμοις δι'ἀποκαλύψεως ἐκδοθέντα πρὸ τοῦ πολέμου μεταναστῆναι τῆς πόλεως καί τινα τῆς Περαίας πόλιν οἰκεῖ κεκελευσμένου, Πέλλαν αὐτὴν ὀνομάζουσιν. Cf. Epiphanius, *Panarion* 29,7 (GCS 37, ed. K.Holl, 1933): *de mensuris* 15, etc. There are no tenable grounds for the historical depreciation of this note, which is popular today. It remains an unprovable hypothesis that it is to be attributed to Ariston of Pella and represents the aetiological legend of the origin of the community in Pella. Of course it has nothing to do with the φευγέτωσαν εἰς τὰ ὄρη of Mark 13.14b. Pella was not in the hills, but in the predominantly Gentile northern rift of the Jordan. There is now a detailed discussion of this problem in F.Neirynck, *Evangelica*, BETL 60, 1982, 566ff., 577ff., 597. In Josephus, *BJ* 2, 458 there is no mention of the capture of Pella, but as in the

case of the other Hellenistic cities, we do hear of the plundering of its territory by the Jewish rebels. The Jews were not able to capture any of the Hellenistic cities, cf. 459f., 466f., 478ff. Significantly, Josephus reports nothing of any pogrom against the Jews in Pella.

112. Luke is writing about 75-80: he is nearest to the catastrophe of 70: by contrast, Matthew presupposes the complete reorganization and consolidation of Palestinian Judaism after the war, about 85-90.

113.Cf. Dan.9.27; 11.31; 12.11. Above all 9.27 LXX (καὶ ἐπὶ τὸ ἱερὸν βδέλυγμα τῶν ἐρημώσεων ἔσται ἕως συντελείας, καὶ συντελεία δοθήσεται ἐπὶ τὴν ἐρήμωσιν) clearly points to an event at the temple which goes on until the end, i.e. the dawn of the kingdom of God (cf. Dan.12.1ff.).

114. Mark 13.19: ἔσονται γὰρ αἱ ἡμέραι ἐκεῖναι (i.e. the time of the events introduced by ὅταν δὲ ἴδητε in v.14) θλῖψις οἵα οὐ γέγονεν τοιαύτη ἀπ᾽ἀρχῆς κτίσεως. Cf. Dan.12.1b LXX and Th.

115. It is worth considering whether the pseudo-Pauline II Thess. does not also belong in that turbulent time between the martyr death of Paul c.62 and the destruction of the temple, when the expectation of an imminent end was bubbling over among Jews and Christians and the personal recollection of the apostles was still very much alive. After AD 70 the reference to the 'temple of God' would hardly have made sense any more. Evidently the letter was already part of the Pauline corpus edited towards the end of the first century. Marcion already took it over in this corpus. Polycarp 11.3f. also presupposes its recognition. Cf. A.von Harnack, Marcion, ²1924 (reprinted 1960), 50, 113*. In my view, the most recent commentary on II Thess., by W.Trilling, EKK XIV, 28 ('so wide a time span between 80 and the early second century'), puts the letter too late.

116. It is improbable that Mark, who certainly thought through every sentence that he wrote, here unthinkingly takes over from an 'apocalyptic flysheet' a marginal note that no longer makes any sense to him. Nor is it possible to demonstrate a secondary gloss in Mark himself, especially as Matthew's copy of Mark contains this note and the first evangelist also takes it over. H.Conzelmann, 'Geschichte und Eschaton nach Mc.13', ZNW 50, 1959, (210-221) 220 n.50 (= Theologie als Schriftauslegung, BEvTh 65, 1974, 72), is right here: 'not a remnant from a written source that he has taken over, but the evangelist's nod to his reader.'

117. Cf. Dan.8.11-13 (see above 128 n.89), 9.27; 11.31. One might also think of Ps.74 (LXX 73).3: ὁ ἐχθρός and 22, ἄφρων (see above 15).

118. Mark 11.15-18, 28; 12.12; 14.1f.; 14.57-65; 15.29ff.,38.

118a. See the analogous sudden annihilation of Babylon-Rome in Rev.18.8: ἐν μιᾷ ἡμέρᾳ; 18.17,19: μιᾷ ὥρᾳ. It too is brought about by the Antichrist – as a divine judgment; cf. 17.16.

119. Nor is the suffering of the crucified Jesus elaborated. The author is in no way interested in eschatological visionary paintings in the style of Rev.12-20, though in my view he is very familiar with apocalyptic conceptions of this kind. Like all the evangelists, he knows much more than he says. He does not want to say more.

120. M.Hengel, Die Zeloten, ²1976, 235ff., 296ff.

121. *Antt.* 20,97f.; cf. Acts 5.36.

122. *BJ* 7,437ff.

123. *Das Markusevangelium*, HNT, ³1950, 133 on Mark 13.6; cf. 136 on Mark 13.21: '*within* the tribulation false Messiahs will also emerge with the claim that they are bringing in the end.' Alongside and with the enemy of God Jewish pseudo-messiahs appear. Here the author may be thinking of the events in Judah after AD 66, where presumably Menahem and later Simon bar Giora made messianic claims, see below n.120. In addition to Simon Magus, Dositheus also emerged among the Samaritans with 'messianic' claims, see S.J.Isser, *The Dositheans*, 1976.

124. For the prophetic and apocalyptic background see L.Hartman, op.cit. (n.101), 80ff., 148ff., 159ff. Here too Daniel becomes particularly significant.

125. Tacitus, *Annals* 4,32, laments this state of peace because it robs him of the chance to write about great affairs in contrast to earlier ages: *nobis in arto et inglorius labor; immota quippe aut modice lacessita pax, maestae urbis res, et princeps proferendi imperi incuriosus erat.* There were frontier wars in Germany. Distant Britain was conquered and was a constant source of disorder. The Parthian wars, which constantly brought setbacks, produced some unrest under Nero from AD 54; they came to an end in AD 63 with the subjugation of Tiridates of Armenia, who three years later paid splendid homage to Nero in Rome.

126. Cf. A.Heuss, *Römische Geschichte*, ³1971, 328: 'A revolution broke out throughout the kingdom, in geographical extent only comparable to the death throes of the declining Republic. Troops were on the march from West and East, from the Rhine and from the Danube. The city of Rome changed masters four times; twice bitter battles were fought for it and for Italy; three emperors were raised and overthrown, cities were devastated, the civil population sometimes suffered bitter tribulation and in Rome the supreme sanctuary of the state, the temple of Jupiter Capitolinus, went up in flames.' Even the Druids in Gaul regarded this catastrophe as a *signum caelestis irae*; they expected the annihilation of the Roman armies and the transfer of the rule over the world to the peoples north of the Alps (Tacitus, *Histories*, 4.54). Cf. G.H.Stevenson/A.Momigliano, *CAH* X ²1952, 808-65; M.P. Charlesworth/R.Syme, *CAH* XI ² 1954, 3,145,151,168f.

127. Tacitus, *Histories* 1,2,1: *Opus adgredior opimum casibus, atrox proeliis, discors seditionibus, ipsa etiam pace saevom. quattuor principes ferro interempti; trina bella civilia, plura externa ac plerumque permixta.*

128. Op.cit. (n.123), 133. Earthquakes and famine also belong within this apocalyptic pattern, see G. Bornkamm, σείω, *TDNT* 7, 64, 197.

129. For the accounts of earthquakes in the first century see A.Hermann, 'Erdbeben', *RAC* 5, 1962, col.1104: AD 60; Laodicea in Phrygia, Achaea, Macedonia; AD 62/63, Pompeii; AD 68, Rome (Suetonius, *Galba*, 18.1): one is said to have announced Galba's death; in the same year in the area of the Marrucini on the east coast of Central Italy, Pliny the Elder, *Natural History* 2,199. Hermann overlooks Dio Cassius 63,28,1, the earthquake at the flight of Nero shortly before his death. Famine was a natural consequence of severe catastrophes in war, since the Civil War threatened the provision of grain for

Rome. For the unwillingness of the people see Suetonius, *Nero* 45.1, cf. also the limitation of the provision of grain in Dio Cassius 62,18,5. For the two oracles see 62,18,2-4, cf. E.M.Sanford, 'Nero and the East', *HSCP* 48, 1937, (75-103) 81, 84. Cf. H.Cancik, 'Die Gattung Evangelium', in id.(ed)., *Markus-Philologie*, WUNT 33, Tübingen 1984, 104ff., 'The historiographical tradition about the end of Nero.'

130. Cf. Acts 5.40f.; 22.19; cf. II Cor.11.24.

131. Cf. Acts 23.33-26.32; 18.12ff.

132. The plural βασιλεῖς may include the Jewish client kings Agrippa I and II (Acts 12.1ff.; 25.13ff.); however, the climax does not lie with them but with the emperor himself, cf. Acts 25.10 and for the title βασιλεύς for the emperor I Tim.2.2: the prayer ὑπὲρ βασιλέων; cf. I Peter 2.13,17; Rev. 17.9; I Clem.37.3; H.I.Bell/T.C.Skeat, *Fragments of an Unknown Gospel*, 1935, 11 line 48: cf W.Bauer/W.F.Arndt/F.W.Gingrich, *Lexicon*, p.136. The first acquaintance of Christians with imperial legislation in Rome may be connected with the disturbances which led to the edict of Claudius and the expulsion of the agitators from the city about 48 (Suetonius, *Claudius* 25.4; Orosius, *Historiae adversum paganos* 7,6,15; Acts 18.2). The decisive emperor is in that case Nero (AD 54-68). The first severe conflict took place under him.

133. Tacitus, *Annals* 15,44,2,4. I must reject out of hand the conjecture by E.Koestermann (Cornelius Tacitus, *Annals*, IV, books 14-16, 1968, 10f., 253f.) that these were followers of an otherwise unknown Jewish agitator Chrestus (according to Suetonius, *Claudius* 25,4), whose supporters were then called *Chrestianoi*. This would make the whole of Tacitus' text and its influence incomprehensible. For the *multitudo ingens* (*Annals* 15,44,4) cf. I Clem. 6.1 (πολὺ πλῆθος). This goes back to Livy's account of the Bacchanalia scandal, 39.13.14, and is to some degree exaggerated. Cf. G.Volkmar, op.cit. (n.101), 541: 'thus Mark expresses the fearful doom that the Christians inevitably incurred as the *odium generis humani...*' L.Hartman, op.cit. (n.101), 168, refers to Ps.106.41; 25.19; 69.5; 105.25 and Isa.66.5: hatred against the righteous and against the people of God. However, this *universal* hatred against the Christians, which the evangelist can only understand in eschatological terms, is at the same time the specific experience of the community, which sees itself exposed not only to the whim of the courts but also to the attacks of the crowd with its absurd accusations, some of which are derived from ancient antisemitism. Cf. already the charge of hatred against humanity in Tacitus, *Histories* 5,5,1, which he raises against the Jews: *adversus omnes alios hostile odium*. We later find the complaint about hatred of Christians in John 15.19,24; 17.14; in the prayer I Clement 60.3; and above all in the apologists: Justin, *Apology* I,1,1; 4.4f.; 20.3; 24.1: μισσούμεθα δι'ὀνόμα τοῦ Χριστοῦ; 57.1; II,8,1f.: *Dialogue with Trypho* 134,6; Tatian, *Oratio ad Graecos* 4.1; 9.4; 25.3. Both are writing in Rome. Cf. also Athenagoras, *Supplicatio* 2.4.

134. The position of this verse is determined by the conclusion of the complex of Mark 13.5-13 which describes the past and the present and resounds in the admonition: 'but whoever perseveres to the end, i.e. martyr death or the parousia, will be saved.' In that case, the saying about the coming Antichrist, who cast his shadow forwards, already begins with v.14. The

concluding γρηγορεῖτε in 13.37 points yet again to this critical situation in the evangelist's day.

135. Compare the *multitudo ingens* of Tacitus, see below n.133. However, reports of earlier martyrdoms are very rare in the early period. Granted that Acts 12.1 speaks of Herod's (Agrippa I's) κακῶσαί τινας τῶν ἀπὸ τῆς ἐκκλησίας. However, only James the son of Zebedee was executed. The death sentences of which Luke speaks in Paul's description of himself as persecutor are probably an exaggeration (but cf.8.3; 22.4). According to Josephus, *Antt.* 20,200, the high priest Annas son of Annas (the brother-in-law of Caiaphas) had James the brother of the Lord καί τινας ἑτέρους executed. The persecution of Nero, however, created a new situation. Pliny the Younger, *Ep.*.10,96,5, speaks of an anonymous accusation *multorum nomina continens*, cf. also 9: *multi... omnis ordinis*, and he proceeds against them all legally; according to Rev.17.6 the whore Rome is 'drunk with the blood of the saints and the blood of the witnesses of Jesus', cf.6.10; 16.6; 18.24; 19.2. Matthew 23.35,37 probably presupposes the execution of both James and the abomination of the Jewish War. Cf. also John 16.2: these are all later texts. For the Neronian persecution cf. also I Clem.6.1: συνηθροίσθη (i.e. to Peter and Paul as martyrs) πολὺ πλῆθος ἐκλεκτῶν, οἵτινες πολλὰς αἰκίας καὶ βασανοὺς διὰ ζῆλος παθόντες ὑπόδειγμα κάλλιστον ἐγένοντο ἐν ἡμῖν. Probably composed more than twenty-five years after Mark, this is certainly to be connected with this persecution, see 6.2 and n.133.

136. Mark 4.17: persecution and apostasy; cf. 10.30, the immediate μετὰ διωγμῶν. 14.31,37f.,69,72 becomes even more vivid if the community knows of the past martyrdom of Peter; cf. later also John 21.18. Discipleship of the cross: Mark 8.34-38.

137. Tertullian, *Ad nationes* I, 7,9; cf. *Apologeticum* 5,3; 21,25.

138. Cf. L.Hartman, op.cit. (n.101), 168f.

139. The close family connection is in fact radically broken in Mark: Mark 3.31-35; 10.29ff.; cf. also I Peter 5.13; I Tim.1.2; II Tim.1.2; Matt.23.8, etc.

140. Pliny the Younger, *Ep.*10.96.8: *per tormenta quaerere*.

141. *Annals* 15,44,4; cf. the extension of the accusations in Pliny the Younger, *Ep.*10,96,2,4: *diffundente se crimine plures species inciderunt*; 9: *propter periclitantium numerum*. This extension came about not least as a result of denunciations in the interrogation of Christians.

142. Cf. Mark 12.12,17,40 etc.

143. Against H. von Campenhausen, *Die Idee des Martyriums in der alten Kirche*, ²1964, 25, I do not believe that we can understand Mark 13.10, bracketed as it is by Mark 13.9 and 13.11, which are texts about persecution, without looking at the effect of the Gospel. Mark 13.9–11 cannot be understood without reference to the paradigmatic significance of the death of Jesus (Mark 15.39). Like the suffering of Jesus, so too that of his community has the character of witness. Campenhausen therefore (148 n.1) rightly cites Mark 15.39 in connection with the missionary effect of martyrdom, which is expressed most clearly in Tertullian, *Apologeticum* 50,12f.: *semen est sanguis Christianorum*. In Mark, though, ch.13 has a christological foundation and is interpreted in terms of the approaching parousia.

144. In my opinion, the interpretation of the 'abomination of desolation' in the synoptic apocalypse Mark 13.14 in terms of the Antichrist is taken over in Matt.24.15 and continued in Irenaeus, *Adv.haer.* 5,30,2 (5,2, p.378, ed. A.Rousseau). Here he combines Rev.13.18; I Thess. 5.3 and Jer.8.16. Cf. also 5,30,4 (5,2, p.386): *Cum autem devastaverit Antichristus hic omnia in hoc mundo, regnaverit annis tribus et mensibus sex et sederit in templo Hierosolymis, tunc veniet Dominus de caelis...* Matthew 24.15ff.; II Thess.2; Dan.9 are also combined in Hippolytus I, 2 *Antichr.* 62-64, GCS, ed. Achelis, 1897, 42ff., and referred to the Antichrist. Irenaeus and Hippolytus are already dependent on earlier second-century exegetes, Melito or even Papias. Cf. also W. Bousset, op.cit.(n.102), 104ff. In his *Commentary on Matthew*, Origen juxtaposes the interpretation by Josephus in terms of contemporary history with that in terms of the Antichrist; he reinterprets the Antichrist allegorically as ἑτερόδοξος λόγος καὶ ἀσεβὲς δόγμα (Lat: *Antichristus, quod est falsum verbum*) and 'the holy place' in terms of the holy scriptures of Old and New Testaments, see Origen XI, *Matth.* II, GCS 38, ed.Klostermann, ²1976, 83. Theodore of Heraclea (c. 355), in J.Reuss, *Matthäus-Kommentare aus der griechischen Kirche*, TU 61, 1957, 90f., fr. 121,122, attributes the interpretation of the desecration of the temple by an idol in terms of contemporary history to the Jews, and offers the alternative interpretation: βδέλυγμα ἐρημώσεως καθολικῶς ὁ ἀντιχριστός (fr.122). By contrast, the Mark *catena* in J.A.Cramer, op.cit. (n.12), I, 410-12, is completely orientated on the contemporary interpretations of the desecration of the temple by the Romans under Pilate down to the capture of the city according to the account in Josephus, which confirmed the truth of the prophecy; similarly also Theophylact, op.cit. (n.35), col.637, cf. col. 409 on Matt.24.15. However, Jerome, *Commentariorum in Mattheum libri* IV,24,15 (CC 77 I, 7, 1969, pp.225ff.) puts first among his possible interpretations the Antichrist, who is also mentioned in II Thess.2. See B.Rigaux, *L'Antéchrist*, 1932, 245f. There is no doubt that the reference to the Antichrist in Mark 13.14; Matt.24.15 is the more original. In my view, here, beginning with Mark, there is a continuous tradition of interpretation which was later made into one in terms of contemporary history by the introduction of Josephus.

145. See on this J.J.Collins, *The Sibylline Oracles of Egyptian Judaism*, SBL.DS 13, 1974, 188 n.47; P.A.Gallivan, 'The False Nero: A Re-examination', *Historia* 22, 1973, 364f.; A.E.Pappano, 'The False Nero', *CJ* 37, 1937, 385-92; M.Hengel, 'Messianische Hoffnungen und politischer "Radikalismus" in der Diaspora', in D.Hellholm (ed.), *Apocalypticism in the Mediterranean World and the Near East*, Tübingen 1983, (655-86) 669ff.

146. Suetonius, *Nero* 57.2: *Et tamen non defuerunt qui... modo imagines praetextatas in rostris proferrent, modo edicta quasi viventis et brevi magno inimicorum malo reversuri.* Cf. H.Cancik, 'Die Gattung Evangelium', in id. (ed.), *Markus-Philologie*, WUNT 33, Tübingen 1984, 105f.

147. Tacitus, *Histories*, 2,8,1: *Sub idem tempus* (he has just been describing the situation in the East after the murder of Nero) *Achaia atque Asia falso exterritae, velut Nero adventaret, vario super exitu eius rumore eoque pluribus vivere eum confingentibus credentibusque.*

148. Op.cit (n.147), 2,8,2: *inde late terror: multi ad celebritatem nominis erecti rerum novarum cupidine et odio praesentium.*

149. Op. cit. (n.147), 2,9,2: *is in maestitiam compositus et fidem suorum quondam militum invocans, ut eum in Syria aut Aegypto sisterent, orabat.*

150. 64,9,3 (ed. Boissevain, 1955, III, 108): ἑάλω δέ τις καὶ Νέρω εἶναι πλασάμενος... καὶ τὸ τέλος καὶ δίκην ἔδωκεν (Xiphilin). - ἐν τούτοις δέ τις πλασάμενος Νέρων εἶναι ἐκ τῆς πρὸς τὸν Νέρωνα οὔσης ἐμφερείας αὐτῷ, τὴν Ἑλλάδα ὀλίγου πᾶσαν ἐτάραξε, καὶ χεῖρα κακούργων ἀνδρῶν ἀθροίσας πρὸς τὰ ἐν τῇ Συρίᾳ στρατόπεδα ὥρμησεν. ἐν Κύθνῳ δὲ περαιούμενον αὐτὸν ὁ Καλπούρνιος συνέλαβε καὶ ἀπέκτεινεν (Zonaras).

151. See also the clear account by Josephus (*BJ* 6,312), Suetonius (*Vespasian* 4,5; cf. *Titus* 5,3) and Tacitus (*Histories* 5,13,2) about that old – messianic – prophecy that the ruler(s) of the world would emerge from the East, or more exactly from Judaea: *ut valesceret Oriens profectique Iudaea rerum potirentur* (in Tacitus' version). Here there was a mixture of Jewish and Eastern-Zoroastrian expectations of salvation; it was also eagerly taken up by non-Jews and later used to legitimate the claims of the Flavian house, which of itself had no tradition. See H.Windisch, *Die Orakel des Hystaspes*, VNAW 28, 3, 1929, 65ff., and the quotation from it in Lactantius, *Institutiones* 7,15,11 ...*et imperium in Asiam revertetur ac rursus Oriens dominabitur et Occidens serviet.* See also the commentary on the *Histories* of Tacitus by H.Heubner and W.Fauth, V, 1982, 151ff.

152. Dio Cassius 66,19,3b, c (ed. Boissevain III, 154f.): πολλοὺς γοῦν ἔκ τε τῆς κάτω Ἀσίας... ἀπατήσας... τέλος πρὸς Παρθαίους... κατέφυγεν (Joannes Antiochenus, fr. 104 Muell). Cf. Tacitus, *Histories* 1,2,1: *mota prope etiam Parthorum arma falsi Neronis ludibrio.*

153. See my 'Messianische Hoffnungen' (n.145), 669ff. Cf. Rev. 16.12-18.24; cf. 11.1-10; 12 and 13; Sib.5,52ff., 143ff., 218ff., 361ff.

154. Suetonius, *Nero* 56: *Religionum usque quaque contemptor, praeter unius Deae Syriae.* For his plans for flight see 47.2; Dio Cassius 63,27,2: he planned to kill all the senators, burn Rome to the ground and sail to Alexandria.

155. Suetonius, *Nero*, 40,2: *Spoponderant tamen quidam (a mathematicis) destituto Orientis dominationem, nonnulli nominatim regnum Hierosolymorum, plures omnis pristinae fortunae restitutionem.* See E.M.Sanford, op.cit (n.129), 84ff., who refers to the imitation of Alexander by Nero.

156. b.Gittin 56a: 'He sent against them the emperor Nero... He said: The Holy One, blessed be He, wills to destroy his house and to wash his hands of me. Then he escaped and became a proselyte. R.Meir descended from him.' See G.Stemberger, 'Die Beurteilung Roms in der rabbinischen Literatur', *ANRW* II, 19.2, 1979, 338-96, on Nero, 346-9.

157. The Roman authorities regarded this perseverance of Christians as *pertinacia* and *obstinatio*, see Pliny the Younger, *Ep.* 10,96,3: *pertinaciam certe et inflexibilem obstinationem debere puniri.* Cf. Tertullian, *Apologeticum* 50.15: *Ipsa illa obstinatio, quam exprobratis, magistra est.* Cf. Tacitus, *Histories*, 5.13,3, on the Jews in the Jewish war: *obstinatio viris feminisque par... maior vitae metus quam mortis.* This is a resolution which death can no longer terrify: cf. *Histories* 2,46,3 on the soldiers of Otho.

158. See below, 45ff., 50–53.

159. Paulus, *Sent.* 5,21,3 (ed.P.Krüger); cf. the addition, 4: *non tantum divinatione quis, sed ipsa scientia eiusque libris melius fecerit abstinere.* Cf. also Justin, *Apology* I, 44, 12; cf. W.Speyer, *Büchervernichtung und Zensur des Geistes bei Heiden, Juden und Christen*, Bibliothek des Buchwesens 7, 1981, 55. For censorship from Augustus to Nero see ibid., 56-69.

160. It is remarkable that no one these days has taken up the theory put forward by John Chrysostom (*In Matthaeum Homiliae* I,3, PG 57, 17) and by C.R.Gregory, *Einleitung in das NT*, 1909, 760f., that the Gospel was written in Egypt. The theory also appears on occasion in the *Hypotheseis* of later manuscripts (see above, and G.Zuntz, op.cit.[119, n.14], 68f.). Chrysostom's view probably goes back to a wrong interpretation of Eusebius, HE 2,16,1; see B.H.M.G.M.Standaert, *L'Evangile selon Marc. Composition et genre littéraire*, 1978, 468 n.4, and H.B.Swete, *The Gospel according to Mark*, [3]1927, XXXIX.

161. See the fine survey in F.Blass/A.Debrunner/R.W.Funk, *Grammar* (n.108), 4-6. The large number of instances from Mark is striking. Second comes the two-volume work by Luke, which is very much longer and the content of which is much more closely related to the Roman world. See also my short study of the problem of Latinisms in *ZNW* 60, 1969, (182-98) 197f., and B.H.M.G.M.Standaert, op.cit. (n.160), 465-91. Of course we must not go so far as P.L.Couchoud and, following Ephraem, some *Hypotheseis* of minuscule manuscripts and the Peshitta, assume that Mark was originally written in Latin: that view is based on a crude misunderstanding of accounts since Papias and Clement of Alexandria. However, the linguistic and textual-critical material that Couchoud has collected is not uninteresting: 'L'Evangile de Marc. A-t-il écrit en Latin?', *RHR* 94, 1926, 161-92. For the Shepherd of Hermas see A.Hilhorst, *Sémitismes et latinismes dans le Pasteur d'Hermas*, 1976.

162. Plutarch, *Cicero* 29.5. See Bauer/Arndt/Gingrich, *Lexicon*, 437. The three rabbinic examples for the *quadrans*, which depend on each other, in Billerbeck I, 292, on Matt.5.26, are all comparative tables of coinage.

163. See H.P.Rüger, 'Die lexikalischen Aramaismen im Markusevange-lium', in *Markus-Philologie*, ed. H.Cancik, WUNT 33, Tübingen 1984, 73ff., for the numerous lexical Aramaisms in Mark, which in linguistic terms are amazingly exact. To mix elements from different languages, e.g. Greek and Latin, was regarded as a sign of semi-education and bad style: see the scorn of Cicero, *De officiis* 1,111; Horace, *Sat.* 2,10, 20-30; Lucian, *Hist.conscr.* 15.

164. See B.H.M.G.M.Standaert, op.cit. (n.160), 473ff. In the Greek sphere the term is very rare and late. The earliest example outside Mark appears in Lucian (late second century), *Deorum Concilium* 4: the base origin of the god Dionysus (on his mother's side) from the 'Syro-Phoenician' Cadmus. Cf. even later Eunapius (fourth century) on the origin of Libanius, *vitae Sophistarum* 496 (LCL, ed. W.C.Wright, 522f.), cf. also Bauer/Arndt/Gingrich, *Lexicon*, p.794. Details of the change in the name of the province are also there. *Phoinix* alone sounded much better to Greek ears. So this name was given to true Syrians (Philustratus, *Vit. Soph* 2.33: Apsines of Gadara (LCL, 314). Diodorus Siculus (who came from Agyrion in Sicily and later lived in Rome) 19,93,7, reckoned Ake (Acco) as a place τῆς Φοινίκης Συρίας, Joppa, Samaria and Gaza as

belonging to Syria, in contrast to 20.55.3, Φοίνικες μὲν οἱ τὴν Καρχηδόνα τότε κατοικοῦντες, Λιβυφοίνικες δὲ πολλὰς ἔχοντες πόλεις. Cf. also Strabo 17.19 (835), Polybius 3,33,15. The name Συροφοινίκη appears for the first time, again in Rome, in Justin, *Dialogue with Trypho* 78. E.Honigmann, *PRE*, 2.R 4, 1932, cols.1788f., conjectures an interpolation, as he thinks that the name is only conceivable after the formation of the double province of Syria and Phoenicia in 194. Perhaps, however, here the Palestinian Justin, like Mark, is dependent on special Roman terminology. I have seen subsequently that J.M.Lassèrre, *Ubique Populus. Peuplement et mouvements de population dans l'Afrique Romaine de la chute de Carthage à la fin de la dynastie des Sévères*, Paris 1977, 398f., in listing all the inhabitants of Roman North Africa who come from Syria, gives three out of about sixty names with the addition *Syrophoenix*, and one with *Syraphoenix*, in contrast to only five examples of *Syrus/Syra* (at the same time a frequent slave's name), a priestess *Sidonia* and two Palmyrenes. It is striking here that *Syrophoenix* is never a proper name, but only a designation of origin. Cf. H.Solin, 'Juden und Syrer im westlichen Teil der römischen Welt', *ANRW* II 29,3, 1983, 587-1249: '*Syrophoenix*, which... was probably used to distinguish the person from *Libyophoenix* in North Africa' (602). Over against the very much more frequent *Syrus/Surus*, Solin nevertheless notes a *Syrophoenix* in Italy (736): Beneventum, CIL IX, 1718...*nepos Syrophoenix vivos fecit*, and also a *Phoinix* (676, CIL 27,868). Cf. also the *Syrus nation(e) Arabus* (CIL X 3546) or the *Iudaeus Syrus* or *Palaestinus Syrus* in Ovid *ars amatoria* I, 76, 416 (602). By contrast, *Syrophoenix* does not appear in Egyptian papyri, as opposed to *Syros*, which is frequent as a name and designation of origin, see F.Preisigke, *Namenbuch*, 1922, 398 (there also 467, on *Phoenix*), and id, *Wörterbuch der griechischen Papyrusurkunden* III, 1931, 273f. Thus in my view the Marcan terminology points clearly to the West.

II. Literary, Theological and Historical Problems in the Gospel of Mark

1. R.Pesch, *Das Markusevangelium*, HTK II/1, ³1980; II/2, ²1980. See the extended critical reviews by F.Neirynck, *Evangelica, Gospel Studies - Études d'évangile*, BETL 60, 1982, 491-564.

2. Op.cit., 1,2: 'Because Mark is guided by catechetical and missionary interests, because the conservative redactor is compiling traditional material and is hardly producing literature ...'

3. W.Schmithals, *Das Evangelium nach Markus*, two vols., ÖTK 2/1,2, 1979, and here above all the Introduction, 1, 21-70. See the review by Neirynck (above n.1, 613-17): 'Malgré le caractère fantaisiste de certaines positions de S., son commentaire rendra certainement service à l'exégèse marcienne' (617). Quite certainly, the author shows all that can be done with Mark today. He has now put forward his imaginatively constructed theories in the article 'Evangelien', *TRE* 10, 1982, 570-626 (above all 600-12), as the summary of about two hundred years of critical study of the Gospels. Here he refers above all to the investigations made by Gustav Volkmar, of which he has had a study made in a dissertation: B.Wildemann, *Das Evangelium als Lehrpoesie. Leben und Werk Gustav Volkmars*, Berlin theological dissertation 1982. Here

one is reminded of the scene between Faust and Wagner: Forgive, it is a great amusement\to put oneself in the spirit of the times\to see how a wise man thought before us\and how we have then recently developed things so splendidly.

4. Cf. W.Schmithals, 'Kritik der Formkritik', *ZTK* 77, 1980, 149-85.

5. J.Gnilka, *Das Evangelium nach Markus*, EKK II/1, 1978; II/2, 1979 (on this cf. the review by Neirynck, op.cit., 609-31) and J.Ernst, *Das Evangelium nach Markus*, RNT, Regensburg 1981.

6. *Metamorphoses* 2,137.

7. A typical example of such investigations is the article by T.J.Weeden, 'The Heresy that Necessitated Mark's Gospel', *ZNW* 59, 1968, 145-58, and his subsequent study, *Mark: Traditions in Conflict*, Philadelphia 1971; cf. his preface to the 1979 paperback edition, VIIf.

8. A possible connection between the Gospels, and above all the earliest Gospel, and ancient biographies was resolutely challenged by the fathers of form criticism. Granted, R.Bultmann, *History of the Synoptic Tradition* (1931), ET ²1968, 370, concedes the decisive fact that 'it seems but natural that the tradition which had an historical person at its centre should have been conceived in the form of a coherent, historical, biographical story' (it is certainly not that; we could also have had a fabricated myth with heavenly journeys and revelations in the style of Enoch or the Ascension of Isaiah, in which above all the risen and glorified Jesus was portrayed), and even says that Mark 'was the first to try to write ... *a presentation of the life of Jesus*' (348, my italics). Then, however, he largely withdraws these insights by rejecting 'Hellenistic biography' as a possible '(analogy) for explaining the form of the Gospel' with the often-quoted statement (cf. e.g. R.Pesch, op.cit., I, 2), 'There is no historical and biographical interest in the Gospels; that is why they have nothing to say about Jesus' human personality, his appearance and character, his origin, education and development' (372). The work does not have 'a biographical unity, but an unity based upon the myth of the kerygma' (371). Here Bultmann is not only concerned with a modern scientific understanding of the 'historical-biographical interest' which he fails to find in Mark; he also misunderstands completely the literary variety of 'Hellenistic biography', which is not always interested in 'appearance, character, origin, education and development' in the same way. The amazing thing about ancient biography is its varied form. Not only the ancient biographies of Heracles, Achilles, Theseus, Romulus and many other figures from the primal period but also those of Pythagoras, Alexander and Augustus show that myth and biography are not exclusive (cf. C.H.Talbert, *What is a Gospel*, 1977, 25ff.). Plutarch wrote biographies both of heroes from the mythical period (Heracles – this has not survived – Theseus and Romulus) and contemporaries (Otho, Galba). His forty-eight biographical portraits which have survived are very different in content, though they have the same basic tendency. Although they are divided from the Gospels by a great gulf in terms of aim and style, they do contain numerous parallels: delight in miracle and anecdote, the focal point in the 'passion narrative' (e.g. in Cato Minor and Eumenes), the scant chronological interest, the lack of a deeper psychology and a real

development, the characterization through 'words and actions', and so on. In some of them, the youth and education of the subjects are narrated extremely briefly (for example, Sertorius and Eumenes or Lucian's Demonax). I hope that I shall have the opportunity to develop this theme at more length. In literary terms, Mark and Matthew seem to me to be better and more 'dramatically' arranged than many of Plutarch's *Lives*, see 34–7 below. For the problem see also A.Dihle, 'Das Evangelium und die griechische Biographie', in *Das Evangelium und die Evangelien*, ed. P.Stuhlmacher, WUNT 28, 1983, 383ff.; G.N.Stanton, *Jesus of Nazareth in New Testament Preaching*, SNTS.MS 27, 1974, 117ff.; M.Hengel, *Acts and the History of Earliest Christianity*, ET 1979, 18ff. H.Cancik, 'Die Gattung Evangelium. Markus im Rahmen der antiken Historiographie', and 'Bios und Logos. Formen geschichtliche Untersuchungen in Lukians "Leben des Demonax"', in *Markus-Philologie*, WUNT 33, 1984, 85ff., 110ff. Moreover, scholars tend to overlook the fact that we have a biographical tradition from the Old Testament and Judaism which extends from the patriarchal narratives in Genesis, through the life of Moses from Exodus to Deuteronomy (see below, 56ff.), to Tobit, Judith and Esther and which has links with 'Hellenistic biography' in II Macc., Philo and Josephus, and especially in Philo's *Vita Mosis*. Old Testament scholars have so far taken too little notice of these 'biographical' features of the narrative texts, or of the prophetic books. There are the beginnings of this in K.Baltzer, *Die Biographie der Propheten*, 1975, cf. especially 38f. The salvation-historical narrative tradition about men of God must have had biographical features. The special character of the Gospel lies in the fact that here we have the narrative of a 'biographical' saving event in Jesus of Nazareth the Son of God, culminating in his death, which is unique and valid for all.

9. That is true both of the exposition by W.Schmithals and of the investigations by W.Schreiber, *Theologie des Vertrauens*, 1967; *Die Markuspassion*, 1969, and his article 'Die Bestattung Jesu', ZNW 72, 1981, 141-77, which is quite untested by historical insights. For a criticism of this method cf. E.Grässer, 'Text und Situation', *Gesammelte Aufsätze zum NT*, 1973, 15 n.9, 29f. n.91. In this way Mark simply becomes a cryptogram the key to which has to be guessed at. Here we are at the threshold of a new epoch of exegetical whim, and may expect a good deal more of it.

10. M.Dibelius, *From Tradition to Gospel*, ET reissued 1971, 3.

11. R.Bultmann, *History of the Synoptic Tradition*, 350.

12. A.Jülicher and E.Fascher, *Einleitung in das Neue Testament*, [7]1931, 297. Cf. his article 'Marcus im NT', *RE*[3] XII, 1903, 288-97. The remarks by Jülicher on Mark are among the best that have been written on the second Gospel. Cf. e.g. 294: 'He is a master of the "gospel" material; from the wealth of what has been handed down about Jesus Christ he selects and groups material as seems appropriate to win new faith and strengthen old faith in the Son of God despite his apparent defeat. He writes not as a historian but as a religious agitator, but perhaps his greatest achievement was the insight that the most effective way of carrying out this agitation was to write a history of Christ, a continuous narrative of the life of Jesus. He did not practise historical criticism on his material... but similarly, he was not a didactic poet, nor did he try

to preserve another's work exactly even down to the wording.' Jülicher anticipated much of what I shall be going on to say.

13. See above all the extremely stimulating dissertation by B.H.M.G.M.Standaert, *L'évangile selon Marc. Composition et genre littéraire*, Nijmegen 1978, and before him the article by F.G.Lang, 'Kompositionsanalyse des Markusevangeliums', *ZTK* 74, 1977, 1-24, of which too little notice is still taken.

14. Op.cit., 18ff. For the different attempts at division see R.Pesch, op.cit. (n.1), 1, 32ff.; id., *Naherwartungen*, 1968, 50ff. Of course there is no 'absolutely valid' solution here. We cannot reconstruct exactly the plan which Mark made for himself before writing the Gospel. Therefore the discussion of details will be endless.

15. Cf. Aristotle, *Poetics* 11,5 = 1452a, 32: καλλίστη δὲ ἀναγνώρισις, ὅταν ἅμα περιπέτεια γένηται.

16. Op.cit., 20f. Here Lang refers to H.Lausberg, *Handbuch der literarischen Rhetorik*, 1960, 1, 585 sec. 1213: 'A sudden piece of knowledge which introduces a change of direction (μεταβολή) in the action'. It presupposes an error, 'tension in information between the person who is not informed and reality'(586). For the basic role of 'recognition' in Mark cf. also Standaert (n.13), 89ff.

17. Aristotle, *Poetics*, 11.1 = 1452a, 22ff.: ἔστι δὲ περιπέτεια μὲν ἡ εἰς τὸ ἐναντίον τῶν πραττομένων μεταβολή... καὶ τοῦτο δὲ... κατὰ τὸ εἰκὸς ἢ ἀναγκαῖον. Cf. H.Lausberg, op.cit., 1, 584f., sec. 1212.

18. S.H.Lausberg, op.cit., 1, 568, sec. 1194,3, quotes Scaliger: *catastrophe (est) conversio negotii exagitati in tranquillitatem non expectatam*, cf. 1, 569f., sec.1197.

19. Cf. op.cit., 1,583, sec. 1207 and Aristotle, *Poetics* 11.10 = 1452b, 9ff.: alongside περιπέτεια and αναγνώρισις, πάθος is the third important ingredient of the dramatic narrative (μῦθος = *fabula*): πάθος δέ ἐστι πρᾶξις φθαρτικὴ ἢ ὀδυνηρά, οἷον οἵ τε ἐν τῷ φανερῷ θάνατοι καὶ αἱ περιωδυνίαι καὶ τρώσεις καὶ ὅσα τοιαῦτα.

20. Cf. Standaert, op.cit. (n.13)., 99ff.

21. Cf. H.Lausberg, op.cit. (n.16), 1,568ff. secs.1193-7. Aristotle begins from three parts, *Poetics* 7.3 = 1450b, 26f.; cf. 12.1 = 1452b, 14-16: μέρη δὲ τραγῳδίας... τάδε ἐστίν, πρόλογος ἐπεισόδιον ἔξοδος. The χορικόν as a fourth part can be left out of account as far as the *fabula* is concerned. Horace, *De arte poetica*, 189, strictly demands five acts for the *fabula* and adds (191): *nec deus intersit, nisi dignus vindice nodus/ inciderit*. Standaert, op.cit. (n.13), 50f., posits an underlying rhetorical scheme of (introduction), narration, argumentation, dénouement (conclusion): (1.1-13;) 1.14-6.13; 6.14-10.52; 11.1-15.47 (;16.1-8); here in turn he divides the middle section into three units: 6.14-8.21; 8.22-9.29; 9.30-10.52 (148, 172, 298ff.). However, I cannot see such a decisive break in 6.13, as 6.30 is directly attached to it. All attempts at division are in danger of being exaggerated for the sake of the cohesion of the scheme.

22. *Poetics* 7.2 = 1450b, 37f. Cf. already Jülicher, *Einleitung* (n.12), 297: 'Mark has the best τάξις of all the Gospels.'

23. F.G.Lang, op.cit. (n.13), 21, even wants to understand the ἐφοβοῦντο γάρ at the end in this sense. Cf. also Standaert, op.cit., 102ff.

24. Cf. e.g. J.Wellhausen, *Das Evangelium Marci*, ²1909, 84: 'The ἀπολύτρωσις by the death of Jesus finds its way into the Gospel only here; immediately before this, he has not died *for* the others and in their place, but has died *before* them.' This is to misunderstand the climactic significance of 10.45, and makes the death of Jesus meaningless. P.Vielhauer, *Aufsätze zum NT*, ThB 31, 1965, 200, is an example of the false verdicts one arrives at by failing to note Mark's arrangement of his material: 'The conception of the atoning death of Jesus... is not determinative for Mark's christology. It occurs only twice (Mark 10.45; 14.24), and is missing completely where one would most expect it, in the passion narrative proper and the announcements of the passion. The dominant thought here is of the divine δεῖ, the foreknowledge of Jesus and his readiness to accept suffering; that is determined by scriptural proof and the idea of the fulfilment of prophecy.' In reality Mark 10.45, as the conclusion and climax of all the instruction of the disciples from 8.31 onwards, is the first passage to put the career of Jesus in the right light; here the negative contrast saying in 8.37 prepares for the decisive concluding saying (see 36 above). Similarly, 14.24 illuminates the whole of the subsequent passion narrative. The tearing of the curtain of the temple in 15.38 is similarly best understood in the light of Lev.16, the sacrifice on the Day of Atonement. Mark 14.21, 49, the concluding saying of Jesus at his arrest, ἀλλ᾽ ἵνα πληρωθῶσιν αἱ γράφαι, shows that the divine δεῖ is not to be understood as a contrast to 'scriptural proof' and 'the fulfilment of prophecy', but rather that the two belong indissolubly together. J.R.Donahue is right here, in W.H.Kelber (ed.), *The Passion in Mark*, 1976, 13: 'The leitmotiv of his whole Gospel', and 77, 'a saying (10.45) which summarizes the theology of 8.27-10.52'. For the tradition history and originality see P.Stuhlmacher, 'Existenzstellvertretung für die Vielen: Mk 10,45 (Matt.20,28)', in *Werden und Wirken des Alten Testaments, Festschrift für Claus Westermann zum 70.Geburtstag*, 1980, 414-27, and M.Hengel, *The Atonement*, London 1981, 34ff., 42, 49ff., 71ff.

25. For the flight of the women, which corresponds to that of the disciples in Gethsemane (14.50 and 16.8: ἔφυγον), see M.Hengel, 'Maria Magdalena und die Frauen als Zeugen', in *Abraham unser Vater. Festschrift für Otto Michel zum 60. Geburtstag*, 1963, 253.

26. For the connection beween faith and history see the worthwhile comments by H.Weder, 'Zum Problem einer "christlichen Exegese"', *NTS* 27, 1981, 64-82, and id., *Das Kreuz Jesu bei Paulus*, FRLANT 125, 1981, 49-119: 'At all events it is inadmissable simply on the basis of their (viz. the Gospels') kerygmatic character to argue for their historical unreliability. Unreliability can only be established in individual instances and by means of a *documentary* argument' (59ff.). Here the concept of 'historical unreliability' must primarily be measured against ancient standards and not by the lofty ideals of modern criticism.

27. Standaert, op.cit. (n.13), 486-91, 619ff., 'De façon générale on peut affirmer que Marc est, dans l'histoire de l'éloquence chrétienne, un des tout

premiers témoins du *sermo humilis*, tel que l'a défini plus tard Augustin' (488). F.G.Lang, op.cit. (n.13), 18, already came to the conclusion: 'If it is demonstrated that Mark makes use of a developed technique of composition, then of course his Gospel comes close to "high literature". That then presupposes a degree of literary training in the author.' He goes on to presume in 22 n.48 that while Mark had not studied Aristotle's *Poetics*, he was familiar with the nature of the Hellenistic theatre. This was not impossible even in Jerusalem. As the exagoge from the Hellenistic Jewish poet Ezekiel shows, dramatic theatre was even performed in Jewish circles. But such a hypothesis is unnecessary for understanding Mark as a writer. Dramatic story-telling and writing could also be learned from Old Testament and Haggadic writings and novels.

28. Standaert himself has produced a comparative analysis in the light of the Book of Judith, op.cit., 392ff. Certainly this dramatic novella from the time of the successful Maccabaean revolt reflects the influence of Hellenistic literary conventions. Nevertheless it would be basically wrong to presuppose that the author had a thorough training in rhetoric, since in all probability the work derives from a Hebrew original. For this see A.M.Dubarle, *Judith*, AnBib 24, Rome 1966, I, 80-110, and E.Zenger, *Das Buch Judit*, JSHRZ I 6, 1981, 430f. Cf. also there, 436ff., on Judith as a 'Hellenistic romance'.

29. The coincidence of the *peripeteia* of a narrative and a recognition scene can also be found in the Joseph novella, Gen.45.1-15, cf. J.G.Williams, *JBL* 101, 1982, 435: ' "composite artistry" of a high order.' The verdict by H.Donner, *Die literarische Gestalt der alttestamentlichen Josephsgeschichte*, SHAW.PH ²1976, is similar, cf. especially 10ff., 36, on the principle of doubling in the composition. The Saul and David narratives up to the account of the latter's succession to the throne offer masterpieces of admirably arranged, dramatic narrative art, in which the moment of knowledge on each occasion forms the climax of the narrative (cf. e.g. I Sam.9.16ff.; 20.25ff.; 28.15ff.; II Sam.12.5ff.; 18.19-32). For the Elijah narrative in I Kings 17-19 see now R.L.Cohn, 'The Literary Logic of I Kings 17-19', *JBL* 101, 1982, 333-50: 'An excellent example of a carefully woven literary tissue... the richness of its structural and thematic texture. At the same time that the story develops linearly, it establishes three parallel episodic sequences' (333, 349). At the same time, these examples show that artistic arrangement, tense narrative and historical account need not necessarily be fundamentally opposed.

30. Therefore we can hardly assume that the author of the Second Gospel was an avid theatregoer or had advanced rhetorical training in the Hellenistic school. In my view there is no evidence that his very simple style, which Matthew and Luke improve, is simply a matter of adaptation to the hearer and is not his natural way of speaking. For the language, marked with semitisms, see N.Turner in Vol. 4 of J.H.Moulton, *A Grammar of New Testament Greek*, 1976, 11-29, which he himself wrote: 'On the one hand, it is felt that Mark's style is unpretentious, verging on the vernacular; on the other, that it is rich in Aramaisms. The latter are so much in evidence that early in this century scholars were convinced that Aramaic sources had been translated' (11). However, all his Greek is simple: '...he is manipulating none too skilfully

but with a curious overall effectiveness, a stereotyped variety of Greek, rather inflexible and schematized, adhering to simple and rigid rules' (28). In addition there is the fact that we have no literary work in Greek which has as many Aramaic expressions and formulae as the Second Gospel. See H.P.Rüger, 'Die lexikalischen Aramaismen im Markusevangelium', in H.Cancik (ed.), *Markus-Philologie*, WUNT 33, 1984, 73-84: 'The large number of lexical Aramaisms in the Gospel of Mark and the relative uniformity of the way in which they are reproduced by means of the Greek alphabet suggests that Mark could cope with Aramaisms.' M.Reiser, op.cit. (125 n.70) 131-63, refers to the parallels in style and narrative method in the popular Alexander romance from the end of the third century. Only fragments have come down to us from what was certainly an abundant Jewish Hellenistic literature - apart from Philo and Josephus and some 'apocryphal texts'. The pseudo-Philonic sermons *De Jona* and *De Sampsone*, which have both been preserved in Armenian, give us some impression of synagogue preaching, cf. F.Siegert, *Drei hellenistisch-jüdische Predigten* I, 1980. It can hardly be doubted that Greek-speaking Judaism had its own schools for the study of scripture, apologetics and liturgical rhetoric. Evidence of this, even in Jerusalem, is the well-known Theodotus inscription, CIJ II, no.1404, cf. M.Hengel, *Between Jesus and Paul*, 1983, 17f.: ᾠκο/δόμησε τὴν συναγωγὴν εἰς ἀν[άγν]ω/σ [ιν] νόμου καὶ εἰς [δ]ιδαχ[ὴ]ν ἐντολῶν.

31. See S.J.D.Cohen, *Josephus in Galilee and Rome. His Vita and Development as a Historian*, 1979, 24-47: 'On the whole Josephus was faithful to his sources: he neither invented new episodes nor distorted the essential content of those previously narrated. However, he did not confuse fidelity with slavish imitation. Like all ancient historians, he molded his material to suit his own tendentious and literary aims... the language of the source was not reproduced but was entirely recast' (47).

32. Typical of this ominous false opposition which even now pervades the literature is W.Marxsen, *Mark the Evangelist*, ET 1969, 131: 'It is a gospel. From the outset that means that his work is to be read as proclamation, and as such is an address and not "a report about Jesus". From this aspect, it is almost accidental that something in the way of a report also appears. In any case, it is only raw material. Paul can largely disregard this raw material.' Here W.Schadewaldt, the famous classical scholar (see above, 89–113), takes quite a different view.

33. For criticism of the widespread docetic attitude which is hostile to history, see H.Weder, *NTS* 27, 1981, 74-8. As Weder rightly stresses, message of salvation and historical event are not simply identical. The history of Jesus points beyond itself because faith recognizes in this Jesus that God has come in him to us men. 'If we bear in mind how the Synoptic Gospels refer to the history of Jesus, it is striking that they are not simply concerned with telling the story of Jesus. Rather, they keep leaving the historical sphere by narrating the history of Jesus as the history of the coming of God into the world... The fascinating thing here is that faith has nevertheless never left the historical behind' (op.cit., 75f.). Here it should be remembered that for earliest Christianity, as for Judaism, history embraces a wider area than it does for

us today. The heavenly world participates in earthly history (Luke 15.7, 10), and earthly history is directly dependent on what happens in heaven and is related to it (Luke 10.18; Mark 14.62). Our – premature – division of immanence and transcendence is therefore not to be found here.

34. For being-present-with Jesus and historical distance see J.Roloff, *Das Kerygma und der irdische Jesus*, 1969, 110ff., 205ff.

35. In connection with the Pauline theology of the cross. On this see H.Weder, *Kreuz* (n.26), 12 n.1, 40ff., 123ff., 154f., 165 n.164, 179f., 224ff. and id, *NTS* 27, 1981, 76: 'Paul never limited himself to giving only historical expression to the death of Jesus – say as the martyrdom of a prophet. He understood the death of Jesus on the cross as the action of the love of God (cf. Rom.5.8). However, for him the cross never became a mere theological cipher. Rather, it denotes the particular, specific death of Jesus, and this character is decisive (cf. e.g. Gal.3.13)': see also M.Hengel, *Crucifixion*, 1977, 88ff.; *Atonement*, 1981, 33ff., 65ff.

36. Cf.H.Weder, *Kreuz* (n.26), 56 n.22.

37. E.Jüngel, *Gott als Geheimnis der Welt*, 1977, 413: 'There is a compelling hermeneutical reason why the eschatological event of the identification of God with the crucified Jesus became the integral element in the life of Jesus as he lived it, and thus a concentrated narrative which in turn called for explanation. In this sense no theology of the crucified one can and may dispense with a narration of the life and suffering of Jesus as a life in the *action of the word* which tells of God's humanity' (author's italics). Cf. also 413f.

38. Mark 1.22: ἦν γὰρ διδάσκων αὐτοὺς ὡς ἐξουσίαν ἔχων and 27, διδαχὴ καινὴ κατ᾽ ἐξουσίαν presuppose among the congregation hearing the Gospel read in the service the knowledge of such teaching by Jesus with messianic authority. Matthew 7.28 has with good reason related the formula in Mark 1.22 to the audience of the Sermon on the Mount. The Gospel of Mark, as a passion narrative with extended introduction, does not claim to cover the whole of the tradition of Jesus which was available to the community. To some degree it was concerned to supplement the traditional 'Jesus halachah' with an account of the 'Jesus haggada', which narrated the saving event and was necessary for faith. For the difficulty of the problem see M.Devisch, 'La relation entre l'évangile de Marc et le document Q', in *L'Evangile selon Marc*, ed M.Sabbe, BETL 34, 1974, 59-91. The conclusions which W.Schenk, 'Der Einfluss der Logienquelle auf das Markusevangelium', *ZNW* 70, 1979, 141-65, draws on the basis of very hypothetical literary and form-critical considerations, namely that 'Pre-Mark is primary to Q' but that the 'Mark redaction is secondary to Q' (see ibid., 161) are not convincing. The most thorough investigation by R.Laufen, *Die Doppelüberlieferung der Logienquelle und des Markusevangeliums*, BBB 54, 1980, 386f., comes to the conclusion that neither Q nor Mark is literally dependent on the other but that in the case of the nine parallel traditions investigated, Q seems earlier in four cases and Mark in two, whereas in three cases both Mark and Q show partially earlier features. However, his analyses have not convinced me where he claims a priority for

Mark, e.g. 93ff. on Matt.3.11/Luke 3.16 in comparison with Mark 1.7f., and 302ff. on Mark 10.38/Luke 14.27 and Mark 8.34.

39. The question is whether in view of the complete destruction of the temple by Titus, 13.1f. could be a new construction by the evangelist. I think this improbable. The expectation of a possible destruction of the temple was earlier than this. Moreover 13.14ff. does not refer to specific events in the Jewish war but to an early Antichrist tradition from Jewish-Christian apocalyptic. Those who fled into the 'hill-country' of Judah before the Roman advance in AD 70 ran directly into the hands of the Romans or the fanatical Sicarii in and around Massada. The experience depicted in the account of the messianic woes in 13.14-18 basically goes back to the period of the religious distress under the Seleucids. There is no mention of the destruction of Jerusalem and the concrete events of the Jewish war in 13.14-18, in contrast to the Matthaean and Lucan parallels (Matt.24.15, ἑστὸς ἐν τόπῳ ἁγίῳ, cf. 22.7; Luke 21.20, cf. 17.31; 19.43f.). Elsewhere, too, Mark has no reference to the siege and conquest of Jerusalem by the Romans. See now 'The Gospel of Mark: Time of Origin and Situation', above, 1–30. The Gospel was presumably written in Rome in 69.

40. The basic study is now H.Räisänen, *Das 'Messiasgeheimmnis' im Markusevangelium*, 1976, 159: 'Wrede's study raises the basic question whether the theological view of the Gospel of Mark is based on a *unitary* theology of mystery. Analysis shows that the answer must be... negative. Nor of course is it enough to separate the "contradictions" which Wrede also established from the theology of mystery. It has come to light that the material brought together by Wrede also does not have the homogenous unity which he and most interpreters after him have supposed.' Cf. also the excursus by R.Pesch, op.cit. (n.1), II, 36-47. I cannot, however, accept Pesch's view that Mark can reconcile a 'christology with a variety of conceptions, expressed in different kinds of traditional material with a christology oriented on the different honorific titles; ...indeed he does not have a christological conception of his own' (45). The question is what Pesch wants to understand by 'a christological conception of his own'. Our modern understanding of theological 'originality' is alien to Mark. He simply wants to give expression to the work and status of Christ, Son of Man and Son of God, in a way which corresponds to the truth that has been handed down. But he does this in a deliberately reflective way and has a christology of suffering and exaltation with an independent stamp which has contacts partly with Paul and above all with I Peter. Individual themes of it are developed further in Hebrews.

41. Mark 1.24f.; 1.34; 3.11f.; 5.7.

42. Mark 1.44 (cf. already 1.35ff.); 5.43; 7.36; 8.30; cf. also 9.30. This will have historical roots. Jesus the miracle healer did not see any propaganda for his person in the healings, and at times he had to ward off the masses.

43. H.Räisänen, *Die Parabeltheorie im Markusevangelium*, Helsinki 1973. This is presumably a secondary construction which need not, of course, come from the evangelist himself. The saying about the hardening of Israel's heart in Isa.6.9f. = Mark 4.12 was in fact circulated widely in earliest Christianity (see John 12.40; Acts 28.26ff.; Rom.11.8; II Cor.3.14).

44. All are affected by the hardening of heart. The leaders of the people (3.5): συλλυπούμενος ἐπὶ τῇ πωρώσει τῆς καρδίας αὐτῶν; the crowd (4.12); the disciples (6.52): ἀλλ᾽ἦν αὐτῶν ἡ καρδία πεπωρωμένη, and 8.17: οὔπω νοεῖτε οὐδὲ συνίετε; πεπωρωμένην ἔχετε τὴν καρδίαν. This twofold stress on the hardening of the disciples' hearts gives the reason why the way of suffering revealed in 8.31 is necessary for Jesus. From 8.32 on, the rejection of Jesus' suffering is the expression of such hardening.

45. R.Bultmann, *Theology of the New Testament* 1, ET 1952, 26-32: 'The attempt to understand the Messiah-secret not as a theory of the evangelist but as historical fact (Schniewind), falls to pieces against the fact that its literary location is in the editorial sentences of the evangelist, not in the body of the traditional units'(32). Precisely that view is no longer tenable. Redaction and 'old tradition' cannot be separated so easily. Therefore there is a growing tendency today to see only 'redaction' almost everywhere, and to make Mark a 'theologizing romancer' or 'didactic poet' so that he can then be interpreted allegorically. In this way Mark is handed over even more to the whim of exegetes (see above, 32–34).

46. See the accounts of research in H.Räisänen, op.cit. (n.40), 18-49.

47. See J.Jeremias, *New Testament Theology, Part 1. The Proclamation of Jesus*, ET 1971, 250-99. For the messiahship of Jesus in the trial see A.Strobel, *Die Stunde der Wahrheit*, WUNT 21, 1980, and O.Betz, 'Probleme des Prozesses Jesu', in *ANRW* II, 25,1, 1982, 565-647; see now also, in the same volume, the contributions by R.Leivestad, 'Jesus-Messias-Menschensohn', op.cit., 220-64, and H.Bietenhard, 'Der Menschensohn...', op.cit., 265-350.

48. J.Jeremias, op.cit., 120, 256f.

49. Here I cannot go beyond the basic insights of Martin Werner's investigation, *Der Einfluss paulinischer Theologie im Markusevangelium*, BZNW 1, 1923, even if he stresses the differences in rather too pointed a way. Cf. already P.Wernle, *Die synoptische Frage*, 1899, 199ff., and also G.Delling, *Der Kreuzestod Jesu in der urchristlichen Verkündigung*, 1972, 57: 'When all is said and done, Mark is not a pupil of Paul, i.e. has no direct contact with Pauline theology.' Cf. 57f., 'We meet Mark as a representative of a *theologia crucis* in the time after Paul and his community..., as the witness to a *theologia crucis* alongside Paul; since all in all the Marcan community can hardly have shaped its traditional material on its own, the developed interpretation of the cross which we find here points us back, at all events in its beginnings, to the time before Paul.' Could we not replace the unknown 'Marcan community' here with a 'teacher of Mark'? K.Romaniuk, 'Le Problème des Paulinismes dans l'évangile de Marc', *NTS* 23, 1977, 266-74, is relatively critical.

50. K.Niederwimmer, 'Johannes Markus und die Frage nach dem Verfasser des zweiten Evangeliums', *ZNW* 58, 1967, 172-88, wants to see the author as an unknown Gentile Christian,'to whom Judaism is basically alien' (185). However, one can only infer from Niederwimmer's arguments that Judaism in the time of Jesus (and the problems of geographical knowledge in antiquity and the reliability of polemical descriptions in ancient texts) are basically alien to him. S.Schulz, *Die Stunde der Botschaft*, 1967, 127f., 139, believes on the basis of the chronological detail in 14.12 'that as a Gentile Christian Mark was

no longer familiar with the complicated passover regulations' (ibid., 127), cf. E.Lohse, *Die Geschichte des Lebens und Sterbens Jesu Christi*, 1964, 43. In reality, the author, who is writing for Gentile Christian readers, has adapted the Jewish calculation of the day, not at all easy to understand, in which the day begins at sunset, to what is presumably the Roman calculation of time, and has moved the beginning of the feast to dawn. A.Strobel, *Ursprung und Geschichte des frühchristlichen Osterkalenders*, TU 121, 1977, 49, sees here 'clearly the colouring of Christian terminology'.

51. His alleged ignorance of the geography of Palestine serves in a stereotyped and uncritical way to justify the assertion that the author could not have been a Palestinian Jew. Thus Niederwimmer, op.cit., 178: 'At some points the Gospel reveals conceptions of the geography of Palestine which could only be found in one who was a stranger to the country.' In recent times only F.G.Lang, ' "Über Sidon mitten ins Gebiet der Dekapolis." Geographie und Theologie in Markus 7,31', *ZDPV* 94, 1978, 145-60, has seen the problem in the right terms. Accordingly hardly anyone has taken account of his arguments. See also my study 'Luke the Historian and the Geography of Palestine in the Acts of the Apostles', in *Between Jesus and Paul*, ET 1983, 97ff. In addition to the modern example which I quote at the end, here is an even more topical one. When I visited my distinguished colleague A.Kuschke (to whom I had dedicated the above article on his seventieth birthday) in Kusterdingen, south-east of Tübingen, we were able to admire Pfrondorf to the north, beyond the Neckar. A colleague who had lived for many years in Tübingen asked me, 'Is that beyond Wankheim?' 'No,' I had to tell him, 'it's in the opposite direction.' Should we not forgive the author the doubtful sequence of Bethphage/Bethany in Mark 11.1 (see Niederwimmer, 181), especially as the Roman road ran directly only to Bethphage and left Bethany on the left, to the south? Mark introduces it to show its approximate position, as he mentions it often later (11.11f.; 14.3). Perhaps critical New Testament scholars, too, need to learn that a Gospel is neither a geographical handbook of Palestine nor an exact account of Jewish customs. As many and as few mistakes are made in the Gospels as in monographs on the New Testament.

52. Niederwimmer, op.cit., 185, wants to conclude from 7.3f. 'a lack of familiarity with Judaism'. In reply, my question would be: what is our more accurate knowledge of Palestinian and Diaspora Judaism on the basis of which we can level such charges at the author of the second Gospel? For the 'hand-washing' see my article 'Mk 7,3 πυγμῇ: Geschichte einer exegetischen Aporie und ihrer Lösung', *ZNW* 60, 1969, 182-98. For 7.4 see Billerbeck 1,934ff. and 2.14; Pesch, op.cit. (n.1), I, 371. Presumably we should follow Nestle/Aland[26] in reading βαπτίσωνται and referring to the bath to restore levitical purity which could be infringed by dealings with Gentiles in the market. The whole insertion has the character of a typical polemical exaggeration for the information of Gentile Christians. It is meant to take the Pharisaic Jewish παράδοσις τῶν πρεσβυτέρων ad absurdum. However, J.Neusner, *The Rabbinic Traditions about the Pharisees before 70*, 1971, 3, 304, shows how much for all its inexactitude it has a good historical background: 'Approximately 67% of all legal pericopae deal with dietary laws: ritual purity for meals and

agricultural rules governing the fitness of food for Pharisaic consumption.' The Pharisaic paradosis before the catastrophe and the intrinsic transformation of Palestinian Judaism was not least concerned with ritual purity at mealtimes. Cf. also Mark 7.15 and Gal.2.11f. Mark, who did not set out to be a scholar, should be excused this polemically exaggerated account, and we should not draw senseless conclusions from it. The absurd closing sentence by Niederwimmer shows that even New Testament scholars are not immune from such exaggerations (188): 'If this supposition is correct, then it would mean that the note by Papias appears as a prime example of that dogmatic ideology with which the second-century(?!) church sought to conceal its own origins and provide a secondary interpretation.'

53. See S.J.D.Cohen (n.31), index 276 s.v. 'Josephus' exaggerations; inconsistency and sloppiness; corrupt transmission of names and numbers.'

54. The dating of this work is disputed. A.v.Harnack, *Geschichte der altchristlichen Literatur bis Eusebius, 2.Teil: Die Chronologie der altchristlichen Literatur bis Eusebius*, I, 1897, 721, cf.356ff., puts it in the period between 145 (140) and 160, though the year in which Papias was born was 'hardly later than 80' (ibid., 358). He is followed rather more cautiously by P.Vielhauer, *Geschichte der urchristlichen Literatur*, 1975, 759: towards the end of or after the reign of Hadrian (10.7.138); he wants to regard him as a contemporary of Justin, 785, cf. 254: 'about the middle of the second century... his contemporary and compatriot Justin.' In reality a gulf separates the two. Justin is hardly interested in oral tradition any more and keeps to the *written* 'recollections of the apostles', even if he quotes them relatively freely. See also L.Abramowski, ' "Die Erinnerungen der Apostel" bei Justin', in *Das Evangelium und die Evangelien*, ed. P.Stuhlmacher, WUNT 28, 1983, 341ff. On the other hand, the new investigation by U.H.J.Körtner, *Papias von Hierapolis. Ein Beitrag zur Geschichte des frühen Christentums*, FRLANT 133, 1983, 88-94, 225f., has produced good arguments for an early date round about 110. However, I cannot go back further in this connection than Fragment XI of the Church History of Philip of Side (Funk/Bihlmeyer, *Apostolische Väter*, 1924, 138f.), which explicitly refers to the time of Hadrian (117-38). In accordance with the title Papias interpreted what he regarded as the authoritative 'Sayings of the Lord' – in the widest sense. In contemporary literature λόγιον almost always means a divine saying, see Bauer/Arndt/Gingrich, *Lexicon*, s.v., or Plutarch, *Theseus*, 32.4; *Romulus*, 14.1; *Numa*, 9.3; *Aristides*, 9.2; 15.3; *Camillus*, 4.1.3 and so on. Cf. also the fixed terminology of λόγια θεοῦ or κυρίου in the LXX Psalter; Rom.3.2; Acts 7.78; Heb.5.12; I Peter 4.11; Polycarp 7.1; Justin, *Dialogue* 18.1; Irenaeus, *Adv.Haer.* 1 preface; 8.1 etc. Here for Papias it can refer also to anecdotes and brief narratives. He has a higher estimation of oral tradition (see n.61 below). The attempt by U.H.J.Körtner, op.cit., 143ff., to define these λόγια by genre is mistaken. Papias is concerned with the religious sound of the term λόγιον as opposed to the everyday word λόγος. See now also the collection of articles and fragments with extended bibliography by J.Kürzinger, *Papias von Hierapolis und die Evangelien des Neuen Testaments*, Eichstätter Materialien 4, 1983. However, I cannot agree with his interpretation of the fragments about Mark and Matthew.

55. This important fact (καὶ τοῦθ᾽ὁ πρεσβύτερος ἔλεγεν) is overlooked or unreasonably questioned in the 'critical' literature, cf. e.g. Niederwimmer, op.cit. 185f., 'his alleged informant'. In connection with the proemium Eusebius reports (HE 3,39,7) of the presbyter: 'But Papias says that he himself heard Aristion and the presbyter John. Therefore he often mentions them by name and reproduces their traditions in his writing.' Cf.14, immediately before the Mark tradition: 'He reports still other things in his writing from the interpretations of the Lord's sayings by the above-mentioned Aristion and the traditions of the presbyter John. After we have pointed this out to the curious, we think it necessary to add to his remarks made so far a tradition which he has handed down about Mark, the author of the Gospel.' Here Papias is not advancing something that he has made up himself, but an old tradition guaranteed by the presbyter, which goes back to a time towards the end of the first century.

56. The claim that Papias invented the link between Mark the evangelist and Peter on the basis of his reading of I Peter 5.13, which has proved particularly popular, is nonsense. J.Regul, *Die Antimarcionitischen Evangelienprologe*, 1969, who discusses the notes by Papias in detail on pp.113-60, but in part with pettifogging arguments which lead him astray, and without historical understanding, claims without any justification (96) that Papias' testimony about Mark was 'spun out of I Peter 5.13, the key passage for connecting Mark and the Gospel attributed to him with the apostle Peter'. Papias certainly knows I Peter (and I John, HE 3,39,17), but the date of his tradent is synchronous with the origin of I Peter under Domitian (81–96) or soon after him). Both traditions are independent and provide reciprocal confirmation. It is also an unprovable assertion that only the first clause of the quotation is the tradition of the presbyter and that the rest is only interpretation of Papias. Papias reproduces this tradition in his own words and the exact wording can no longer be reconstructed. Cf. already A.Jülicher, *RE* XII, 291: 'In no way does Papias provide here a literal protocol about a communication from his main authority the presbyter (John)... and it is no less arbitrary to seek to distinguish Papias' additions from what the presbyter says. Rather, Papias is completely responsible for the wording; in fact he is convinced that he is merely handing on what he received from a well-informed personality of the previous generation. As we have no reason to mistrust Papias, we note his judgment as that of a respected figure from the church in Asia Minor between about 90 and 130.' My colleague Frau Abramowski, in P.Stuhlmacher (ed.), *Das Evangelium und die Evangelien*, 350 n.35, appeals for support for her view that the notes by Papias are unreliable to the judgment by E.Schwartz, op.cit. (see n.59), 76f., and to his indication that even in the case of Origen, and far more elsewhere in his literary history, Eusebius had only written sources at his disposal. However, one can hardly compare Eusebius, a man of letters with a giant library at his disposal, with Papias, a collector of predominantly oral tradition. The nearest parallels to the Papias traditions, which also have a marked Jewish-Christian stamp, are to be found in rabbinical sources. They have a bizarre hyperbolical character in common with these (cf. fr.I,III, XI, Funk/Bihlmeyer).

57. Cf. e.g. K.L.Schmidt, 'Die Stellung der Evangelien in der allgemeinen Literaturgeschichte', EYXAPIΣTHPION. FS H.Gunkel, 2, 1923, 57f. = *Neues Testament – Judentum – Kirche*, ThB 69, 1981, 46f., on Papias, arguing with E.Meyer: 'Mark is presented as the first proclaimer and literary author of the story of Jesus, but the literary character of the Gospel of Mark excludes so individual an origin.' Here on the one hand Papias is interpreted wrongly, and on the other this presupposition has become questionable. E.Meyer, *Ursprung und Anfänge des Christentums*, I, *Die Evangelien*, ⁴⁻⁵1924, reprinted 1962, 157ff., 245ff., had some correct insights which were buried under the form-critical wave; see the reviews by K.L.Schmidt, *CW* 35, 1921, 114-20, and M.Dibelius, *DLZ* 42, 1921, 225-35, which in my view are excessively sharp in their abrupt criticism and therefore are again in turn partly misleading.

58. Op.cit. (n.1), 1,5f. Pesch also speaks of an 'apologetic commentary on the remark by the presbyter' (6) and wants to see I Peter 5.13 as 'the bridge towards an identification' (7f.). Cf. also R.Pesch, 'Die Zuschreibung der Evangelien an apostolische Verfasser', *ZTK* 97, 1975, 56-71. By contrast, W.Bauer, *Orthodoxy and Heresy in Earliest Christianity*, ET 1972, 107, is right here: 'Both personalities (i.e. Peter and Mark) appear to be so closely associated in Rome already in the first century (I Peter 5.13) that I can hardly doubt that it was here that the origin of Mark's gospel was first attributed to the influence of Peter and that the "elder" derived from this source what he passed on to Papias.' The question is whether this oral 'source' was reliable. I would say that it was. For the Mark-Peter tradition see also U.H.J.Körtner, 'Markus der Mitarbeiter des Petrus', *ZNW* 71, 1980, 160-73, with very worthwhile considerations. However, because he puts too much confidence in the untenable theories of Niederwimmer (171 n.54a), he arrives at a false conclusion.

59. Thus already with good reasons J.B.Lightfoot, *Biblical Essays*, ²1904 (1893), 63-70, and E.Schwartz, 'Über den Tod der Söhne Zebedaei', in *Gesammelte Schriften*, 5. *Zum Neuen Testament und zum frühen Christentum*, 1963, 78ff. = AGG NF VII, 5,1904, 23ff. Cf. also A.Jülicher and E.Fascher, *Einleitung in das NT*, ⁷1931, 284f.; H.Merkel, *Widersprüche zwischen den Evangelien*, WUNT 13, 1971, 46ff.: 'So Papias seems to have known the differences between the chronology of John and that of Mark and opted undisguisedly for John' (48f.). Cf. now F.Siegert, 'Unbeachtete Papiaszitate bei armenischen Schriftstellern', *NTS* 27, 1981, 605-14. For the argument whether Papias knew the Gospel of John see in detail J.Regul (op.cit. n.56), 143ff., who challenges this view bitterly, but not very convincingly. His main argument, that Eusebius would have mentioned such an acquaintance, is wrong because Eusebius tendentiously and notoriously unreliably also says nothing of the use of Revelation by Papias, which is clearly established by the fragment of Andrew of Caesarea (F IV). In addition one can assume with W.Heitmüller, *ZNW* 15, 1914, 200, that Papias said things about the Gospel of John and Revelation which did not please Eusebius. I believe that the Fourth Gospel was adopted by the Great Church in Asia Minor precisely at the time of the presbyter and Papias, somewhere between 90 and 120. Some decades later it played a very important role there, as is evident from the dispute over

Easter and the Montanist movement. Regul leaves completely unexplained the origin of the many-layered tradition of John in Asia Minor. The fragment of an interpretation of the Prologue of John by Valentinus contained in Irenaeus, *Adv.haer.* I.8.5 (Harvey I, 75, 78), suggests that the Valentinians already described the author of the Fourth Gospel as Ἰωάννης ὁ μαθητὴς τοῦ κυρίου. The attribution of the Gospel to John is connected with its reception into the church, which, as Harnack already conjectured, took place in Asia Minor.

60. Eusebius, HE 3,39,4: 'What Andrew or what Peter said, or what Philip or what Thomas or what James or what Matthew or another of the Lord's disciples.' Cf. J.B.Lightfoot, op.cit. 69, and A.Ehrhardt, 'The Gospels in the Muratorian Fragment', in *The Framework of the New Testament Stories*, 1964, 11-36 (= *Ostkirchliche Studien* 2, 1953, 121-38); however, he goes on to refer to the special stress on Andrew in connection with the origin of the Gospel of John in the Muratorian Canon (13ff., 19ff.). Of the thirteen fragments printed in Funk/Bihlmeyer, nine mention John in some way. That may largely rest on secondary tradition, but it is impossible to overlook the connection between the Bishop of Hierapolis and the Johannine tradition. Cf. also the interpretation of the Gospel of John by the presbyter in Irenaeus, *Adv.Haer.*.2,22,5 (Harvey, 1,331f.) = John 8.56, and 5,36,1 (Harvey 2,428) = John 14.2, which probably goes back to Papias.

61. The picture that W.Bauer, op.cit.(n.58), 184ff., and index s.v.Papias, draws of the Phrygian bishop is completely misleading. As elsewhere, Bauer works too much with the questionable argument from silence. There is nothing in the little that has been handed down of Papias' work to give the impression that he is deliberately writing to combat heresy. His polemic in the Preface against 'those who write much' which delights 'the many' and against the 'strange commandments' is largely literary convention. Luke already wrote the πολλοί in 1.1 with a sharp pen. The fact that Papias still prefers the living oral tradition to 'books' in principle and not just verbally (see n.65 below) distinguishes him from those who attack the heretics in literature from the middle of the second century onwards. Anti-gnostic polemic is nowhere to be seen in the fragments. There is no basis for the statement that 'the criticism of Mark and Matthew has its basis in the controversy with heretics and the gospel writings they supported (which?)' (W.Bauer, op.cit., 185). K.Niederwimmer, op.cit (n.50), 186, makes Bauer's conjecture even cruder in his distinctive way: '...that Papias' apologia in favour of the Gospel of Mark is aimed at Gnostic circles. He is concerned to defend the Gospel of Mark (and of Matthew, cf. Eusebius, HE III, 39,16) against the charges of the Gnostics and even perhaps against the *advantages* (author's italics) of the Gnostic Gospels.' For a criticism of this theory of a clearly anti-gnostic attitude on the part of Papias see U.H.J Körtner, op.cit. (n.54), 154–9. He thinks, rather, of heretics like the mysterious Nicolaitans (Rev.2.6,15). For Irenaeus and the Gnostic predilection for Mark see *Adv.haer.* 3,11,7: *Qui autem Jesum separant a Christo et impassibilem perseverasse Christum, passum vero Jesum dicunt, id quod secundum Marcum est praeferentes Evangelium,* cf. 3,10,6.

62. Cf. A.von Harnack, *Marcion*, ²1924 reprinted 1960, 26-70*.

63. H.F.von Campenhausen, *The Formation of the Christian Bible*, 1972, 156, makes perhaps an over-pointed comment:'So far as we know, he never polemised against particular gospels. Instead, what he is attacking in the Great Church is the teaching of the first, judaising apostles.'

64. Scholars are fond of referring in this connection to Clement of Alexandria, *Strom.* 7,106,4: '...and only later, at the time of the emperor Hadrian, did the founders of heresies appear – and remained until the time of the older Antoninus, as is the case with Basilides, though he also claims as his teacher Glaucias, who, as they themselves boast, was the interpreter of Peter. They also affirm that Valentinus had listened to Theodas. Now this last had been a pupil of Paul.' The decisive passage cannot be interpreted simply, since here there is a clear distinction between Basilides, who calls Glaucias his teacher (καθάπερ ὁ Βασιλείδης, κἂν Γλαυκίαν ἐπιγράφηται διδάσκαλον), and the plural of those who boast of Glaucias as Peter's interpreter (ὡς αὐχοῦσι αὐτοί, τὸν Πέτρον ἑρμηνέα). Stählin therefore gives an interpretative translation of this: 'who, as the supporters of Basilides themselves boast, was the interpreter of Peter.' Of course the plural could also be a general reference to the heretics, cf. 7,108,1 on them: κἂν τὴν Ματθίου αὐχοῦσι προσάγεσθαι δόξαν: 'Even if they claim to present the view of (the apostle) Matthias.' However, on the basis of the break in wording we must take into account that the Basilidians were the first to claim that Glaucias was the interpreter of Peter. Therefore the historical circumstances are stood on their head, when E.Schwartz, op.cit.(n.59), 74 = 20f., assumes that in his note on Mark (which in reality goes back to the presbyter John) Papias is dependent on Gnostic assertions, a view which P.Vielhauer, op.cit. (n.54), 764 n.11, quotes with approval. Rather, the opposite is the case, that the Gnostics imitated the old Mark-Peter tradition for their aims. In contrast to the Basilidians, Papias does not in fact claim any tradition which connects Peter with Mark, as his own legitimation. Nor does he make any claim to secret tradition.

65. With him it already has a 'nostalgic' character. Here the fragments of the Jesus tradition which have been preserved fall back before the Gospels. See also H.F.von Campenhausen, op.cit. (n.63), 130 n.109: the high estimation of the *viva vox* 'is especially characteristic of early Christianity'. Cf. also Irenaeus to Florinus in Eusebius, HE 5,20,6f. and *Adv.haer.* 3.2.1: *non enim per literas traditam illam, sed per vivam vocem*: sc. the *traditio* of the church, which alone guarantees the true use of scripture which the heretics lack. Irenaeus could be dependent on Papias, whom he knew, for this formulation. His aim is essentially different from that in Papias (see n.61 above). Aristides, *Apol.* 15.3 (Goodspeed): ἔχουσι τὰς ἐντολὰς αὐτοῦ τοῦ κυρίου Ἰησοῦ Χριστοῦ ἐν ταῖς καρδίαις κεχαραγμένας... For personal oral tradition which goes back over several generations cf. Plutarch, *Mark Antony*, 28.2-7 and 68.4f.; *Kimon* 1.2-2.5; see also Josephus, *Vita* 3f., and Dio Cassius (born c.160) 69,1,3 on the death of Trajan and the adoption of Hadrian in August 117.

66. In his mistaken attempt to make Papias an untrustworthy apologist, P.Vielhauer, op.cit. (n.54), 260, interprets the statements far too positively, given their wording: 'He cannot challenge these objections, of which the

second – that Mark was not an eye-witness account of a disciple – was particularly painful for his point of view (how does the author know that?) but seeks all the more energetically (?) to rob them of their force by asserting that the book simply contains the accurate and complete account of the teaching of Peter.' There can be no question of that. Mark only wrote some things down as he remembered them (ἔνια γράψας ὡς ἀπεμνημόνευσεν). The concluding clause only says that Mark took trouble (ἐποιήσατο πρόνοιαν) not to leave out or falsify anything that he had heard. However, that may be presupposed in any student's seminar paper.

67. See S.J.P.Cohen (n.31), 24f., especially on the universal formula, 'Adding nothing and leaving nothing out' (27f.), which originally derives from legal terminology but was at that time taken over by the historians. See already H.Cancik, *Mythische und historische Wahrheit*, SBS 48, 1970, 24ff., 85ff., 99-103. For its frequency see e.g. also Plutarch, *Lycurgus*, 6.4; 13.2; 25.4; Theopompus, FGrHist 115 T 31 = Photius bibl. 176 p.121a 35; Dionysius of Halicarnassus, *Thuc.* 5 (LCL Vol.465, p.472) and 8 (p.478), on Thucydides: πλείστην ἐποιήσατο πρόνοιαν, οὔτε προστιθεὶς τοῖς πράγμασιν οὐδὲν ὃ μὴ δίκαιον οὔτε ἀφαιρῶν, οὐδὲ ἐνεξουσιάζων τῇ γραφῇ.

For the later Christian terminology see the anonymous author against the Montanists (Eusebius, HE 5,16,3) and Polycrates of Smyrna, ibid., 5,24,2. The decisive concepts and formulae which Papias uses appear in a slightly different form in Josephus, *Antt*. 1.17: τὰ μὲν οὖν ἀκριβῆ τῶν ἐν ταῖς ἀναγραφαῖς προϊὼν ὁ λόγος κατὰ τὴν οἰκείαν τάξιν σημανεῖ. τοῦτο γὰρ διὰ ταύτης ποιήσειν τῆς πραγματείας ἐπηγγειλάμην οὐδὲν προσθεὶς οὐδ᾽ αὖ παραλιπών. Directly before this we have the affirmation of the credibility of Moses, which is commended to the reader for examination. As he is speaking about such a distant past, he 'had a great freedom for lying falsifications' (1.16: πολλὴν εἶχεν ἄδειαν ψευδῶν πλασμάτων). The whole text 'consists of historiographical commonplaces' (Cohen, op.cit., 28). For the selection of ἔνια see Lucian, *Demonax*, 12: Βούλομαι δὲ ἔνια παραθέσθαι; for 'recollection' see ibid. 67: ταῦτα ὀλίγα πάνυ ἐκ πολλῶν ἀπεμνημόνευσα.

By contrast, the lack of τάξις is a real criticism: the notion corresponds to the καθεξῆς of Luke 1.3. Both the Preface and the note on Mark show us that, after Luke, Papias was the second author known to us who was most familiar with Greek literary usages, as was already stressed by E.Schwartz, op.cit. (n.59), 70 =18, on the account of Mark: '...these statements betray an elegant literary style'. The charge of deficient τάξις is also part of this literary jargon and is no light one. It automatically also indicates erroneous arrangement, see H.Lausberg, op.cit (n.16), 241 sec. 443, 507 sec.1055; in our case, however, it is not a matter of literary but of historical arrangement. In the case of a 'historian' who describes 'the words and acts' of a historical figure (for the formulation cf. Polybius 2,56,10; Gellius, *Noct.Att.* 14.3.5), a false arrangement of chronology and subject matter is a basic error. For Lucian, therefore, part of the once-for-allness of historiography (*Quom.hist.conscr.6*) is: καὶ τάξιν ἥντινα τοῖς ἔργοις ἐφαρμοστέον, cf. also Josephus, *Antt*.1.17; *BJ* 1.15. For Papias and his informant it is a question of the right 'historical' ordering of the material – orientated on John – which they cannot find in Mark.

68. P.Wernle, to whom we owe what is still the basic study, *Die Synoptische Frage*, 1899, devotes himself at length to the question of Mark and the Peter tradition (195-208). He comes to what sounds to modern ears to be a bold conclusion: 'Rather, the Gospel of Mark is the most valuable source for the "theology" of Peter' (ibid., 200). Similarly E.Meyer, *Ursprung und Anfänge des Christentums*, I. *Die Evangelien*, [4-5]1924, 147-60. I would not go as far as this, but one should no longer completely deny any connection between Peter and Mark.

69. *Dial.* 106.3, after the renaming of the apostle Peter: καὶ γεγράφθαι ἐν τοῖς ἀπομνημονεύμασιν αὐτοῦ (= Πέτρου) γεγενημένον καὶ τοῦτο, μετὰ τοῦ καὶ ἄλλους δύο ἀδελφούς, υἱοὺς Ζεβεδαίου ὄντας, ἐπωνομακέναι ὀνόματι τοῦ Βοανεργές, ὅ ἐστιν υἱοὶ βροντῆς. Cf. also 103.8: the reminiscences were composed by his apostles and their 'successors' (cf. Papias on Mark as 'Peter's successor': in both cases we have the verb παρακολουθεῖν, i.e. Mark and Luke. The concept of ἀπομνημονεύματα in Justin is usually – and rightly – derived from the ἀπομνημονεύματα Σωκράτους of Xenophon, which Justin knew (cf. *Apol.* II,11,3). See also L.Abramowski, 'Die "Erinnerungen der Apostel" bei Justin', in *Das Evangelium und die Evangelien*, ed.P.Stuhlmacher, WUNT 28, 1983, 341ff. However, the term appears in contemporary literature, e.g. as a collection of gleanings from reading in five books by Favorinus (c.80-150), and in his friend Plutarch, whose ἀπομνημονεύματα have unfortunately not survived. Plutarch, *Cato Major*, 9,7, uses it in the sense of 'famous comments' by Cato.

70. For the difficulties of the 'barbarians', who could not speak Greek unexceptionably, see M.Hengel, *Jews, Greeks and Barbarians*, ET 1980, 76f.

71. The *inscriptiones* and *subscriptiones* of the Gospels are very old – as is evident from the fact that there is complete unanimity over them towards the end of the second century, from Egypt to Lyons and from Africa to Antioch. Thus H.F.von Campenhausen, rightly, against the view widespread today, op.cit.(n.63), 173 n.123: 'But these ancient and presumably original titles were already long established, as Papias indicates and indeed Justin as well…, and could no longer be altered arbitrarily at a later stage.' See 'The Titles of the Gospels', below, 64–84. In all probability the Mark mentioned in the NT (I Peter 5.13; Philemon 24; Col.4.10; II Tim.4.11) and John Mark (Acts 12.12,25; 15.37; 15.39) which only has Μάρκος, are identical. The second Gospel was not written anonymously by just anyone, but by a theological teacher with authority, behind whom there was an even greater authority: see below, 50ff.

72. A survey of the mentions of Peter in Mark shows that they occur more frequently at the key points of the Gospel: at the beginning, in the *peripeteia* and then at the beginning of the passion narrative. This is hardly a coincidence, but is connected with the general arrangement.

Ch. 1	2	3	4	5	6	7	8
1.16:2xS		3.16:2xS+P		5.37 P			8.29 P
1.29 S							8.32 P
1.30 S							8.33 P
1.36 S							

Ch. 9	10	11	12	13	14	15	16
9.2 P	10.28 P	11.21 P		13.3 P	14.29 P		16.7 P
9.5 P					14.33 P		
					14.37 P+S		
					14.54 P		
					14.66 P		
					14.67 P		
					14.70 P		
					14.72 P		

A striking feature here is, moreover, the clear division between the original name Simon and the Peter which was added by Jesus. The first disciple is called Simon up to the list of names (3.16) and then again in the special, familiar address in Gethsemane (14.54). Here the other Gospels do not distinguish so exactly in the nomenclature. This reveals a greater proximity to the Petrine tradition. The tendency of Mark is continued most closely by Matthew. He builds on the Gospel of Mark and adds further, more legendary traditions about Peter (14.28ff.; 16.16ff.; 17.25ff.). For the whole question see the appendix by R.Feldmeier, 59ff.

73. Cf. Mark 3.16ff.; 5.37; 9.2; 13.3.

74. Cf in addition, 8.29; 9.5; 10.28; 11.21; 13.3; 14.29,37.

75. Cf. P.Wernle, op.cit (n.68), 197: 'He is the leading figure in the circle of disciples at all the important points from the beginning to the end of the narrative. He is the first to be called, the first in the catalogue of apostles, whom Jesus calls the rock when he chooses him, the first to confess Jesus as Mes siah and to see his glory; despite the denial, the disciple who follows him longest, the first to be vouchsafed an appearance.' H.-H.Stoldt, *Geschichte und Kritik der Markushypothese*, 1977, 180f., has protested against this interpretation. He may be right that we cannot derive the protophany to Peter directly from 16.7 – though it could at least be an indication there to the community which knows about it (cf.I Cor.15.4; Luke 24.34) – but he cannot give an explanation for the concentrated stress on Peter in Mark. In the parallel, Matt.28.7f., the reference to Peter is deleted. The hypothesis of Schmithals, *ZTK* 77, 1980, 164, that here Mark is giving 'an outline of the exemplary disciple or Christian which was self-contained from the start and only understandable in such a context', is correct only with some essential qualifications. In the first place, Peter's conduct is very often anything but exemplary, and secondly, some scenes (1.29, cf. I Cor.9.5; 8.32f. or 14.66ff.) are much too specific for an abstract construction of this kind. Mark is not working – as Schmithals would like – freely to create a romance, or in a theologically abstract way, but is shaping tradition about Peter which is obviously close to him. James and John, the sons of Zebedee, also to some degree take on a profile of their own, though of course it is much more limited: 1.19f.; 3.17; 10.35ff.

76. W.H.Kelber, *Mark's Story of Jesus*, 1979, 90, is somewhat off the mark: 'In sum, Mark's combined critique of the Twelve, the Three, Peter, Jesus' family, and the Galilean women is directed against people who are identifiable

as representative figures of the Jerusalem Church.' Unbridled redaction criticism makes everything possible in this way.

77. For the various Peter traditions see T.Smith, *Petrine Controversies in Early Christianity*, a London dissertation supervised by G.N.Stanton which is soon to appear in WUNT; see further R.Pesch, 'Simon Petrus', *Päpste und Papsttum* 15, 1980, 138-49, and the unfortunately unsatisfactory joint study *Peter in the New Testament*, ed.R.E.Brown, K.P.Donfried and J.Reumann, 1974, 54-129. For Peter in the four Gospels and the significance of Mark as the starting point see the excursus by R.Feldmeier, below 59ff.

77a. On James, see my article in the forthcoming Festschrift for the 80th birthday of W.G.Kümmel, 'Jakobus, der Herrenbruder – der erste "Papst"?'

78. J.G.Herder, *Vom Erlöser der Menschen, Sämtliche Werke*, ed. B.Suphan, 19, 1880, has recognized the decisive features of Mark's work: 'His Gospel is arranged to be read aloud; it ends and abbreviates the discourse for heart and ear' (216). 'In short, the Gospel of Mark is a *Gospel of the church* written from living narrative for public reading in the community' (217). So when Herder speaks of the Gospels as a '*sacred epic*' (199) and describes this more closely as 'the presentation of the Gospels in composition and aim' (author's italics), this applies quite specifically to the second Gospel. And when he calls the evangelists 'rhapsodists' (214), of whom could that be said with more justification than of Mark, the 'living rhapsodist of this history'(217)? In his little noted commentary, *The Gospel of Saint Mark*, 1936, by arranging the text into sense units, i.e. short *Cola et Commata*, the American Jesuit and classical philologist James A.Kleist gives the reader the impression of the way in which the Gospel was presented; here the evangelist's sense of rhythm and speech melody is particularly striking (91-127), cf. 125f. on Mark 4.2: 'The very rhythm, even apart from the meaning of the words, puts the hearer in a solemn and attentive mood.' See also the observations of G.Lüderitz on 'poetic rhythm' in the second Gospel, in H.Cancik, op.cit. (n.39), 168ff.: 'Kola und Rhythmik', 183: 'The similarity in diction... with books which are read in worship, could be an indication that the Gospel was written for such a use.' B.H.M.G.M. Standaert, op.cit. (n.13), 496-618, conjectures that the original Sitz im Leben of the Gospel was liturgical usage at baptism and Christian Easter celebrations on Easter Day in Rome. This is certainly to restrict the use of the work too much. It is in no way limited to one day in the year. On the other hand no Gospel leads up to Easter morning so clearly as Mark, and the exceptional, abrupt conclusion in 16.8 makes a liturgical response in the confession of the community plausible. On this see now also E.Trocmé, *The Passion as Liturgy*, 1983.

79. The discussions by O.Cullmann, *Peter: Disciple, Apostle, Martyr*, ET 1962, 66-70, show how little we know. I would agree with Cullmann that Peter was presumably not *all that* remote theologically from Paul, and also that the interpretation of the death of Jesus as an expiatory death was particular significant for him. The Deutero-Petrine I Peter also indicates this. For Peter as the first Easter witness see R.Pesch, op.cit. (n.77), 48ff.

80. See above, 32ff. S.Schulz, 'Die Bedeutung des Markus für die Theologie-geschichte des Urchristentums', in *Studia Evangelica* II, TU 87, 1964, 135-45,

has rightly pointed out that the 'Evangelium' at the same time represents a 'historia between Galilee and Jerusalem' to which 'constitutive elements', including 'geographical connections, chronological sequences and biographical details' (136) belong. However, his derivation of this 'consecutive, integrated historia Jesu' 'from the popular tradition of the θεῖος ἀνήρ lives, as for example those of Apollonius of Tyana, Alexander of Abonuteichos and Peregrinus Proteus' (143), is unfortunate. Popular θεῖος ἀνήρ lives of this kind cannot be demonstrated as a specific genre, and the Gospels have little to do with the later high-literary and partly polemical works of Lucian and Philostratus about these 'heroes'.

81. 1.1 is to be understood as the introduction to the book. The 'contents' are εὐαγγέλιον Ἰησοῦ Χριστοῦ. The content of the work is the whole εὐαγγέλιον Ἰησοῦ Χριστοῦ from the appearance of John the Baptist to the Parousia (Mark 13). The ἀρχὴ τοῦ εὐαγγελίου... relates to the appearance of John the Baptist and the baptism and temptation of Jesus (1.1-13), i.e. it comprises the event of the public activity of the Son of God. Only a semicolon should be put between vv. 1 and 2, but a full stop after v. 3. 'The beginning of the gospel of Jesus Christ (happened) as it is written...' The account of Jesus proper begins in 1.14.

82. The perfect ἤγγικεν is to be understood like the Aramaic mt' as present: cf. Mark 14.42: ἰδοὺ ὁ παραδιδούς με ἤγγικεν, 'Behold he who betrays me is here.' Cf. also J.Jeremias, The Parables of Jesus, ET ³1972, 230: 'The hour of fulfilment is come.'

83. Cf. R.Pesch, op.cit. (n.1), 2,285, and G.Schneider, 'Der Missionsauftrag Jesus in der Darstellung der Evangelien', in Mission im Neuen Testament, ed. K.Kertelge, QD 93, 1982, 84f. The saying has been inserted 'redactionally' by Mark, though in terms of content it is 'traditional'. In my view the formulation derives from Greek-speaking Jewish Christian circles which, parallel to Paul, advocated the idea of a world-wide mission before the parousia. This was a group to which Peter is to be added in his later period, after his departure from Jerusalem (cf. Acts 12.17b) or in the years after the Apostolic Council. Cf. M.Hengel, Acts and the History of Earliest Christianity, 92-8: 'Peter and the Mission to the Gentiles'. Peter was not the slave of the Law that Marcion and the Tübingen school wanted to make him. See n.90 below. The mission charge in Matt.28.18-20 takes this line further, but it is significant that there, in accordance with the understanding of the first evangelist, the place of the proclamation of the gospel is taken by the extension of discipleship among the Gentiles and the teaching of the commandments of Jesus.

84. Here the evangelist has changed the narrative to suit his purpose. In my view we can only reconstruct the original version of the logion very hypothetically. See R.Pesch, op.cit. (see n.1), 2,34f., and J.Jeremias, Abba, 1966, 115-20. This text is the Marcan climax to the story of the anointing and stands at the beginning of the passion narrative proper (the fifth act), immediately before the betrayal by the disciple Judas – the contrast is made quite deliberately. As such it has a key position in the Gospel. It is understandable that on the basis of his presuppositions Schmithals has to take particular exception to it. His hostility reaches such a pitch that he claims that 14.3-9 is 'an originally redactional unit' which the dumb fool Mark formed

on 'historical and biographical grounds' without any 'specifically theological interest', in order to 'make it possible to divide passion week into days' (cf. id., 593 n.3). The 'theologically coherent original version of the narrative' is in Luke 7.36-47, and Mark's bungled effort is simply 'a bad copy' (595). Here Schmithals refers to M. Goguel, *The Life of Jesus*, ET 1933, 458, whose judgment is, however, much more cautious. Behind Mark and Luke there is 'a simpler archetype'. Luke's account comes 'closest' to this. Schmithals' verdict on 14.9 is similarly expressed with dogmatic zeal: 'The theological lack of taste in turning attention away from Jesus at the climax of the story, though the service of the woman is directed towards him, is also to be attributed to the historicizing bias of the evangelist' (590). *De gustibus non disputandum*. In my view it is a sign of the theological greatness of the evangelist and the enthusiastic humanity of his Gospel that in this pericope, which is framed by the resolve to kill Jesus and Judas' betrayal, he ventures to report that Jesus looked on an unknown woman, in order to connect the worldwide proclamation of the message of victory with a narrative remembrance of her loving action.

85. For the tradition history of εὐαγγέλιον in the 'Hellenistic Jewish-Christian community' see the basic work by P.Stuhlmacher, *Das paulinische Evangelium*, FRLANT 95, 1968, 254-86, also id., *Das Evangelium und die Evangelien*, WUNT 28, 1983, 157ff. Cf. also M.Hengel, *Between Jesus and Paul*, ET 1983, 26.

86. Ignatius, *Philad.* 5.1f.; 8.2; 9.2: ἐξαίρετον δέ τι ἔχει τὸ εὐαγγέλιον, τὴν παρουσίαν (here in the sense of the advent of Jesus in the incarnation, cf. Bauer/Arndt/Gingrich, *Lexicon*, s.v. 2b) τοῦ σωτῆρος... τὸ πάθος αὐτοῦ καὶ τὴν ἀνάστασιν; Sm.5.1; 7.2. Cf. below, 71. In the Didache, in accordance with a community ordinance, εὐαγγέλιον refers more markedly to the word and commands of Jesus 8.2; 11.3; 15.3.

87. Cf. also Joel 3.5; Nahum 2.1; Isa. 41.27; 52.7; 61.1; Ps.86.12. The original meaning, 'message of victory', appears above all in II Sam. 18.19-32, cf. also II Sam.4.10; II Kings 7.9. For the event see also Plutarch, *Demetrius*, 17, where at the end (17.5) εὐαγγέλιον appears with the meaning of reward for a message (for the message of victory).

88. Cf. Luke 7.22 = Matt.11.5 Q. Also 4.18, from the Lucan special material, where the evangelist puts Isa.61.1 on the lips of Jesus himself in a way which is completely appropriate. For the Targum of Isa 53.1, cf. O.Betz, 'Jesu Evangelium vom Gottesreich', *Das Evangelium und die Evangelien* (n.85), 55ff.

89. Cf. P.Stuhlmacher, op.cit. (n.85), 266ff. Peter, the Twelve, James and all the apostles agree with the traditional εὐαγγέλιον which is expressed in I Cor.15.3f., see v.11.

90. Like Paul, Peter too is entrusted by God (divine passive) with 'the gospel' (πεπίστευμαι τὸ εὐαγγέλιον), but he proclaims it to the Jews. This restriction to the Jews may still have applied for the Apostolic Council about 48. As the Peter party in Corinth shows, there is no longer mention of such a restriction about five years later. Now Peter can also become the apostolic authority for Gentile Christians.

91. Cf. Mark 1.14b and Luke 4.15; Mark 8.35 and Luke 9.24; Mark 13.10

and Luke 21.13f. Luke 18.30 is most striking; here Mark 10.29, ἕνεκεν ἐμοῦ καὶ ἕνεκεν τοῦ εὐαγγελίου, is replaced by a ἕνεκεν τῆς βασιλείας τοῦ θεοῦ. By contrast, Luke uses the verb εὐαγγελίζεσθαι relatively frequently in his Gospel, presumably taking up the language of LXX, cf. 4.18 = Isa.61.1; 1.19; 2.10; 8.1; 16.16; 20.1. Apart from 7.22 = Matt.11.5 Q (καὶ πτωχοὶ εὐαγγελίζονται, cf. again Isa.61.1), all the passages could be 'redactional'. Matthew takes over three examples from Mark: 4.23 which is identical with 9.35; 24.14; 26.13). In the first three passages he defines the word εὐαγγέλιον by the genitive attribute τῆς βασιλείας. The term is completely absent from the Johannine corpus as also from the logia source. In Rev. 14.6 it does not have the specific meaning of 'message of salvation'.

92. For this enumeration, which can be demonstrated for the first time in the second century, see Billerbeck 1,900; 3,542; 4,438, and Targ.Jerus.I on Gen.1.27.

93. Above all in Greek-speaking Judaism the Pentateuch could also be understood as a *vita Mosis* prefixed by an 'extended introduction' in Genesis. Plutarch's double lives of Lycurgus and Numa and of Solon show in turn that Greek biography could contain extended passages of laws or religious ritual. In addition, Moses was 'the best-known personality in Jewish history' (I.Heinemann, *PRE*16,1 [1933], col.361). For Philo, who wrote an extended biography of Moses, he is 'the πάνσοφος and ἱεροφάντης' (col.369), and as such 'the perfect man par excellence' (col.371). In Josephus, *Antt.* 2,201-4,331, we have a detailed life of Moses with a marked apologetic stamp; it ends with an encomium (4,327-31) which describes him as the most significant prophet, whose word was as good as the voice of God (329).

94. Before the well-known passage about Elijah, Malachi 3 (+ EVV 4), another text which is essential for Mark (cf. Mal.3.1; Ex.23.20: Mark 1.2; Mal.3.23f.[EVV 4.5f.]: Mark 9.11f.), has a reference to the revelation of the Torah on Horeb to Moses as a binding saving event; the 'shift' ushered in by Elijah, which brings salvation from judgment, amounts to repentance and obedience to the Torah (3.22, EVV 4.4): 'Remember the law of my servant Moses, the statutes and ordinances that I commanded him at Horeb for all Israel. Behold, I will send you Elijah the prophet before the great and terrible day of the Lord comes. And he will turn the hearts of the fathers to their children and the hearts of children to their fathers, lest I come and smite the land with a curse' (3.22-24, EVV 4.4-6).

95. Ex.14.31: *wyyr'w h῾m 't-yhwh wy'mynw byhwh*: Mark 1.15b μετανοεῖτε καὶ πιστεύετε ἐν τῷ εὐαγγελίῳ (= τοῦ θεοῦ, v.14). Cf. on this the old Tannaitic commentary Mekilta on Ez.14.31 (ed. Lauterbach 1,252f.). The faith of Israel brings about the gift of the spirit and thus confession, in the Song of Moses, 15.1-18. The redemption from Egypt is simply the reward of this faith.

96. Cf. K.Haacker and P.Schäfer, 'Nachbiblische Traditionen vom Tod des Mose', in *Josephus Studien. Festschrift O.Michel*, 1974, 146-74. Cf. Josephus' comment in *Antt.* 4.325, which rejects the idea of transportation. In Ps. Philo, *Lib.Ant.* 19.16, Moses dies *in gloria*. In AssMos 10.12, a *receptione* has found its way into the text, probably 'as a variant to *morte*' (160). In the Samaritan *Memar Marqa* God makes sleep come on Moses, who lay down in a cave on

Gerizim, 'and his soul left him without pain, indeed without his noticing it' (163).In Targ.Jer.I on Deut.34.5 the death of Moses *'l-pi yhwh* is interpreted as a death 'by a kiss of the Memra of God', as it also is in some midrashim (169f.). For the transportation and return see 170ff. Here Moses can be connected with Elijah.

97. Probably Mark and Matthew were from the beginning written for reading in worship (see above, 52). The liturgical reading of the OT as scripture and preaching is already presupposed in I Tim.4.13. Rev.1.3 contains the earliest clear reference to the reading of a Christian 'scripture of revelation' in worship. But cf. already I Thess.5.27; Col.4.16. There is then evidence in Justin, *Apol.* 1,67,3 of the reading of the Gospels in worship as a custom which everyone can understand: καὶ τὰ ἀπομνημονεύματα τῶν ἀποστόλων ἢ τὰ συγγράμματα τῶν προφητῶν ἀναγινώσκεται. Here it is striking that reading the Gospels is put first. In my view, the reading of scripture in communities with an originally Jewish-Christian stamp, who parted company with the synagogue, say in Rome, Antioch and perhaps also in Corinth, goes back to the beginning of these communities. Without relatively regular reading of scripture in worship, Paul could never have argued in his letters with the help of the OT. How otherwise would the newly-won Gentile Christians have been able to understand his often complicated scriptural arguments? II Corinthians 3.14 certainly presupposes that Moses was also read in Christian worship (as a prophet with other prophets), but that here for Christians 'the veil was taken away' and the prophetic saying was understood, in accordance with the Spirit, as promise. For the significance of scriptural reading see also my study 'The Titles of the Gospels', below 64ff.

98. Cf. Luke 16.16 = Matt.11.12 Q; Luke 7.26ff. = Matt.11. 9ff. Q; Luke 11.30ff. = Matt.12.41f. Q, etc.

Excursus: The Portrayal of Peter in the Synoptic Gospels

1. I have not taken into account the additions at the end of the Gospel of Mark, which in terms of textual criticism are to be judged secondary.

2. In Mark 1.16 the designation of Andrew as 'brother of Simon' is counted as an independent naming, because here we have an unusual closer definition of Andrew in relation to his brother (and not – as is usual – in relation to his father, as in the case of the sons of Zebedee). On the other hand, the change of Peter's name to Simon was only counted once.

3. The double name Simon Peter was counted once (cf. Matt.16.16; Luke 5.8), as were similar formulations (Matt.4.18; 10.2: 'Simon, who is called Peter').

4. The numbers are taken from the statistical synopsis by R.Morgenthaler, 1971, 89.

5. Only Matt.18.21 was disputed; cf. A.Polag, *Fragmenta Q*, ²1982, 76f. (where there is a further bibliography).

6. μαθητής is used only once for the disciples of John the Baptist (Matt.11.2 par. Luke 7.18) and once in a saying about the master-disciple relationship

(Matt.10.24 par. Luke 6.40). The saying Matt.19.28 par. Luke 22.30 probably refers to the Twelve as disciples; here Jesus promises those who follow him that they will sit on twelve thrones and judge the twelve tribes of Israel. Otherwise the disciples are not mentioned either as a totality or as individuals.

7. After the call of the disciples Matthew first of all portrays the 'Christ of the word' (chs.5-7) and then the 'Christ of action' (chs.8f.). He has either omitted (Mark 1.23-28) or integrated into ch.8 (Mark 1.29-31 par. Matt.8.14f.; Mark 1.32-34 par. Matt.8.16f.) the actions of Jesus reported by Mark 1.21-34. The departure from Capernaum (Mark 1.35-38) and the subsequent search for Jesus had to develop from there.

8. Cf.J.Schniewind, *Das Evangelium nach Matthäus*, 195f.; E.Lohmeyer/ W.Schmauch, *Das Evangelium des Matthäus*, 275f.; R.Bultmann, *The History of the Synoptic Tradition*, ET ²1968, 34f.; E.Schweizer, *Good News according to Matthew*, ET 1976, 355-60, etc.

9. J.Gnilka, *Das Evangelium nach Markus*, I, 88.

10. A further reason for the omission could be the incorporation of Luke 22.43ff., which on the basis of intrinsic criteria belongs to the original text (cf. G.Schneider, 'Engel und Blutschweiss', *BZ* NF 20, 1976, 112-16) and the associated reworking of the text. That does not alter in any way the fact that here Luke has strongly toned down the failure of the disciples.

11. Cf. I.H.Marshall, *The Gospel of Luke*, 1978, 385.

12. It is particularly clear in the case of John that this stress is caused by the later significance of the apostles. On important occasions, in contrast to the Gospel of Mark, John is mentioned by Luke before his brother James, who was executed in 44 (cf. Luke 8.51 with Mark 5.37; Luke 9.28 with Mark 9.2).

13. R.Bultmann, op.cit., 217f.

III. The Titles of the Gospels and the Gospel of Mark

1. This article goes back to a lecture given for the first time on 17 October 1981 to the Philosophical and Historical Section of the Heidelberg Academy of Sciences. I have merely expanded it at some points and added notes. At present I am working on a larger study on the theme of 'The One Gospel and the Four Gospels', and in this connection hope to deal with the whole subject at much greater length.

2. A. von Harnack, *Geschichte der altchristlichen Litteratur bis Eusebius. Zweiter Theil: Die Chronologie. I Band: Die Chronologie der Litteratur bis Irenäus nebst einleitenden Untersuchungen*, Leipzig 1897, 681 (authors' italics). Cf. Irenaeus, *Adv.haer*. 3,11,8: τετράμορφα γὰρ τὰ ζῶα, τετράμορφον καὶ τὸ εὐαγγέλιον καὶ ἡ πραγματεία τοῦ Κυρίου.

3. *Das Markusevangelium*, 1.Teil, 1976 (³1980), 4.

4. H. von Campenhausen, *The Formation of the Christian Bible*, ET 1972, 173 n.123: 'But these ancient and presumably original titles were already long established, as Papias indicates and indeed Justin as well... and could no longer be altered arbitrarily at a later stage.'

5. A. von Harnack, op.cit (n.2), 681-700: id., *Entstehung und Entwickelung der Kirchenverfassung und des Kirchenrechts in den zwei ersten Jahrhunderten nebst*

einer Kritik der Abhandlung R.Sohm's 'Wesen und Ursprung des Katholizismus' und Untersuchungen über 'Evangelium', 'Wort Gottes' und das trinitarische Bekenntnis, Leipzig 1910, (222-32) 225ff.; T.Zahn, *Einleitung in das Neue Testament* II, ³1924, 176-86; id., *Geschichte des neutestamentlichen Kanons, I. Das Neue Testament vor Origenes, 1.Hälfte,* Erlangen 1888, 150-92 (164ff.); id., *Das Evangelium des Matthäus,* ⁴1922, 5-9. The most thorough discussion of the problem in more recent times, in P.Vielhauer, *Geschichte der urchristlichen Literatur,* 1975, 252-8, is on the whole unsatisfactory, despite a number of correct insights.

6. T.Zahn, *Das Evangelium des Matthäus,* ⁴1922, 6.

7. Harnack, op.cit. (n.2), 681f.

8. The text II Macc.2.13, which is often quoted as an example, is not a real book title. The periphrastic form of expression to be found there indicates an unknown apocryphon. But cf. *Corpus Medicorum Graecorum* IV (ed. J.Ilberg), 1927, 175: ΙΠΠΟΚΡΑΤΟΥΣ ΓΕΝΟΣ ΚΑΙ ΒΙΟΣ ΚΑΤΑ ΣΩΡΑΝΟΝ (the reference comes from W.Speyer) and ΒΙΟΓΡΑΦΟΙ. *Vitarum scriptores Graeci minores* (ed. A.Westermann), Brunswick 1845, 398: Ἀριστοτέλους βίος [κατ' Ἀμμώνιον], according to others κατὰ Φιλόπονον (p.xx); both attributions are doubtful. In the two cases mentioned here there are several biographies of the same man, which are attributed to different authors. Eustathius (twelfth century), *Commentarii ad Homeri Iliadem et Odysseam,* Tom. II, Leipzig 1828 (facsimile reprint Hildesheim 1960), 633 (the Roman edition) [97 line 3]: ἐν τῇ κατ᾽ Εὐριπίδην Φαίδρα; Johannes Lydus (sixth century), *de magistratibus populi Romani* 3.46 (ed. R.Wünsch, 1967, 136,10-12); ὡς ὁ Πολέμων ἐν πέμπτῇ ἐξη(γ)ήσεων τῆς κατὰ Λουκανὸν τὸν Ῥωμαῖον ἐμφυλίου συγγραφῆς ἀπεφήνατο). Here the periphrasis, which is unusual, is used only to avoid the ugly double genitive.

9. W.Bauer/W.F.Arndt/F.W.Gingrich, *Lexicon,* ²1979, 408 (7c); similarly id., *Orthodoxy and Heresy in Earliest Christianity,* ET 1972, 50. Bauer refers, in my view wrongly, to G.Rudberg, *'Ad usum circumscribentem praepositionum Graecarum adnotationes', Eranos* 19, 1919/20, 173-206; there matters are expressed in a much more complicated way. For the question see, however, F.Blass/A.Debrunner/R.W.Funk, *A Greek Grammar of the New Testament,* ET 1961, 224.2, p.120: 'In the superscriptions to the Gospels... the author of this form of the Gospel is designated by κατά.' It is stressed (163, p.90) against Bauer that 'in the superscriptions of the Gospels τοῦ Μαθθαίου does not designate "the (special) Gospel of Matthew"', as Josephus, *c.Apionem* I, 3,18 τὴν καθ᾽αὑτὸν (sic) ἱστορίαν means 'his history work'.

10. Cf. op.cit. 224,2 n.4. See already Jacobus Wettstein, *Novum Testamentum Graecum,* Tom.I, reprint of the 1752 edition, Graz 1962, 223, on the titles of the Gospels; *Patres Graeci, quando vetus Testamentum ejusque varias Conversiones citant, solent dicere* κατὰ τοὺς ἑβδομήκοντα, κατὰ Ἀκύλαν, κατὰ Σύμμαχον. However, it should be noted here that what we find in the fathers are not 'titles', but an academic-exegetical terminology; in my view this is expressed by the use of the article before the name of the translator. Wettstein does indicate this, but sometimes omits the article.

11. While Sinaiticus always has the short form in the inscriptions, in the case of Mark, Luke and John the subscriptions, which were normative in the

case of ancient books, have the long form. In Matthew this was omitted, presumably as a result of the scribe's carelessness.

12. In the papyrus codices the first and last leaves, the covers, with the *inscriptio* and *subscriptio*, were easily destroyed. This was not the case with the scroll, where the *subscriptio* on the inside was especially protected. The papyri of the Gospels are always codexes – an early Christian characteristic (see below, 78f.). For the title page in the codex see Jürgen Scheele, 'Buch und Bibliothek bei Augustinus', *Bibliothek und Wissenschaft* 12, 1978, (14-114) 22-24,32. Augustine, *Ep.* 40,2, to Jerome, shows how easily such a title page could get lost. The case in question is Jerome's work *De viris inlustribus*. On this cf. H.Lietzmann, 'Zur Entstehung der Briefsammlung Augustins', in *Kleine Schriften* I, 1958, 287. Cf. *Ep.* 75.3 and op.cit., 289. Epistles 68,72,73,82 in the correspondence with Jerome (see op.cit., 287-9) show that in the copying of letters the *subscriptio* was left out, which led to doubt as to their authenticity. Cf. also G.Kloeters, *Buch und Schrift bei Hieronymus*, Diss.phil. Münster 1957, 160f.,217ff., 235ff.

13. V.Martin, *Papyrus Bodmer, II, Évangile de Jean, BBod V*, 1956, pl.1. On this see K.Aland, 'Repertorium der griechischen christlichen Papyri. 1. Biblische Papyri', *PTS* 18, 1976, 296ff. For the dating see also J. van Haelst, *Catalogue des papyrus littéraires juifs et chrétiens*, Paris 1976, no.426, between 150 and the beginning of the third century.

14. R.Kasser/V.Martin, *Papyrus Bodmer XIV-XV, BBod 1961*, Vols. I/II, pl.61; see K.Aland, op.cit. (n.13), 309f.; J van Haelst, op.cit (n.13), no.406.

15. K.Aland, 'Neue neutestamentliche Papyri II', *NTS* 12, 1965/66, (193-210) 214; cf. K.Aland, op.cit. (n.13), 219, 293, and J. van Haelst, op.cit. (n.13), nos.336, 403.

16. C.H.Roberts, *Manuscript, Society and Belief in Early Christian Egypt*, The Schweich Lectures of the British Academy 1977, London 1979, 8, 13 (no 8 = P.Barc.Inv.1 + P.Magdalen College, Oxford Gr. 18 + P.Paris, Bibl.Nat.Suppl Gr. 1120). The papyrus is 'on palaeographical grounds' (23) to be dated to the later part of the second century. The text is already divided into sections, like the Bodmer Papyrus of Luke and John. 'Once again we find in a manuscript of this early period a characteristic that appears to be not specifically Egyptian but of wider application' (23). This indicates a fixed and widespread Christian practice of writing in the second century, see below 78ff.

17. *Itala. Das Neue Testament in altlateinischer Überlieferung* (ed. A.Jülicher), I. Matthäusevangelium, ²1972, 1:

g¹: *Initium evangelii secundum Matthm* (sic)
q : *Initium sancti evangelii secundum Matheum*
k = *Afra: Incipit cata Mattheum feliciter* (sic).
Cf. the *subscriptiones*, p.214.

18. Ed. E.Preuschen, *Analecta. Kürzere Texte zur Geschichte der Alten Kirche und des Kanons. II Teil. Zur Kanonsgeschichte*, ²1910, 27 line 2: *tertio euangelii librum (!) secundo lucan*. Here the Gospel is evidently seen as a writing with different books. But cf. the plural *euangeliorum*, 27 line 9; 28 line 17.

19. *Apol.* 61.4 ≙ John 3.3-5: cf. W.von Loewenich, *Das Johannes-Verständnis*

im zweiten Jahrhundert, BZNW 13, 1932, (39-50) 47: 'The clearest proof of all that he knows John.' His pupil Tatian uses the Fourth Gospel as the basis for the order of his Diatessaron.

20. Thus e.g. Irenaeus, *Haer.* 3,11,9. For the whole question see now S.G.Hall, 'Aloger', *TRE* 2, 1978, 290-5.

21. *Geschichte des neutestamentlichen Kanons. II. Urkunden und Belege zum ersten und dritten Band, 1.Hälfte*, Erlangen und Leipzig 1890, 364ff.

22. K.Aland, op.cit. (n.13), (269ff.) 270.

23. C.H.Roberts, op.cit. (n.16), 61f. Here it is striking that the four Gospels, in contrast to other writings, never appear 'in a "mixed" codex' (61) with canonical and non-canonical writings. This indicates a pre-eminence of the Gospels. For the problem cf. also id., *The Birth of the Codex*, 1983, 62-6. The numbers given by Roberts must now be changed as a result of POxy.50, 1983, 2523, see n.97 below.

24. The plural appears once in a fragment of Apollinarius of Hierapolis contained in the *Chronicon Paschale* (ed. Dindorf I, 13f.) according to which the synoptic date of the Last Supper is in conflict with 'the Gospels' (!), and once in Justin, see n.26 below. For Aristides see E.Hennecke, *Die Apologie des Aristides. Recension und Rekonstruktion des Textes*, TU 4,3,1893, ch.16, p.41: καὶ ἵνα γνῷς, βασιλεῦ, ὅτι οὐκ ἀπ᾽ἐμαυτοῦ ταῦτα λέγω, ταῖς γραφαῖς ἐγκύψας τῶν Χριστιανῶν εὑρήσεις οὐδὲν ἔξω τῆς ἀληθείας με λέγειν. It follows from the context that Aristides here was thinking principally of the Gospels, cf. also ch.17 beginning, p.42. For εὐαγγελικὴ γραφὴ see ch.2, pp.9f., in the Greek text; the Syriac reads: 'This is to be learned from that Gospel (*hd' mn sbrt' hy*) which a short time ago, (as) is told among them, was proclaimed (*d'tkrzt*), the power of which you too will experience when you read in it'. For Aristides the Christian writings and the Gospels are in practice identical.

25. *Apol.* I, 66.3; 67.3; *Dial.*100.4; 101.3; 102.5; 103.6,8; 104.1; 105.1,5f.; 106.1,3f.; 107.1. In the *Dialogue with Trypho* the mentions are concentrated in the story of Jesus which is bound up with the exegesis of Ps.22. Here too in 100.1 we have the first appearance of the term εὐαγγέλιον as 'holy scripture' (ἐν τῷ εὐαγγελίῳ... γέγραπται), see now L.Abramowski, 'Die "Erinnerungen der Apostel" bei Justin', in *Das Evangelium und die Evangelien*, ed.P.Stuhlmacher, WUNT 28, 1983, 341-53. His knowledge of Xenophon follows from *Apol.* II,11,2f., cf. op.cit., 346f. *Apomnemoneumata*, in contrast to *Hypomnemata*, were not a relatively fixed and widespread genre. The (ἀπο)μνημονεύειν already appears in the note about Mark in Papias, Eusebius, HE 3,39,15; cf. my 'Problems in the Gospel of Mark', above 47ff., 155 n.69.

26. *Apol.*66.3. Εὐαγγέλιον in the singular above appears only twice elsewhere: *Dial.* 10.2, where the Jew Trypho is saying that 'wonderful divine commandments appear ἐν τῷ λεγομένῳ εὐαγγελίῳ', and *Dial.* 100,1, see above, n.25.

27. *Dial.* 103,8.

28. Cf.*Apol.* 42.4; 45.5; 49.5; 50.12; 53.3; *Dial.*114.4; 119.6. It is significant that Justin never designates the apostles' proclamation of the word as gospel. For him the gospel is exclusively a writing.

29. A.von Harnack, *Marcion: das Evangelium vom fremden Gott. Eine Mono-*

graphie zur Geschichte der Grundlegung der katholischen Kirche, TU 45, ²1924, reprinted Darmstadt 1960, 26. For the Gospel of Marcion see 177*-255*.

30. Tertullian, *Adv.Marc.* 4,2,3: *Contra Marcion evangelio scilicet suo nullum adscribit auctorem, quasi non licuerit illi titulum quoque affingere cui nefas non fuit ipsum corpus evertere. Et possem hic iam gradum figere, non agnoscendum contendens opus quod non erigat frontem, quod nullam constantiam praeferat, nullam fidem repromittat de plenitudine tituli et professione debita auctoris.* Cf. the argument by the Marcionite Megethius in Adamantius, ed. Bakhuyzen, GCS 1901, pp.8/10, against the authorship of Luke and Matthew.

31. For Marcion's controversy with Matt.5.17 in the 'antitheses' see A.von Harnack, op.cit. (n.29), 261*f., cf. 259*. An influence of Matthew on his Gospel cannot be ruled out, cf. 251*f.

32. Tertullian *Adv.Marc.* 4,11,1.

32a. Tertullian, *Adv.Marc.* 4,4,4: *Si enim id evangelium quod Lucae refertur penes nos (viderimus an et penes Marcionem) ipsum est quod Marcion per Antitheses suas arguit ut interpolatum a protectoribus Iudaismi ad concorporationem legis et prophetarum.* Cf. A. von Harnack, op.cit. (n.29), 42.

33. For the Papias notes in Eusebius HE 3,39,15f., see above 47ff.

34. See the quotation in H.von Campenhausen, above n.4.

35. Eusebius, HE 3,39,7: Ἀριστίωνος δὲ καὶ τοῦ πρεσβυτέρου Ἰωάννου αὐτήκοον ἑαυτόν φησι γενέσθαι; 14f.: καὶ ἄλλας δὲ τῇ ἰδίᾳ γραφῇ παραδίδωσιν Ἀριστίωνο ... καὶ τοῦ πρεσβυτέρου Ἰωάννους παραδόσεις. There follows the note about Mark with the introduction: καὶ τοῦθ' ὁ πρεσβύτερος ἔλεγεν.

36. See above, 150 n.56.   37. See above, 151f. nn 59, 60.

38. Eusebius, HE 3,39,4: οὐ γὰρ ἐκ τῶν βιβλίων τοσοῦτόν με ὠφελεῖν ὑπελάμβανον ὅσον τὰ παρὰ ζωσῆς φωνῆς καὶ μενούσης, see above, 48f. The rivalry between different Gospel *traditions* underlies the rivalry between Peter and the beloved disciple in John 13.23f.; 20.1-9; 21.7, 15-24.

39. See the table of contents to E.Hennecke/W.Schneemelcher/R.McL.Wilson, *New Testament Apocrypha* I, *Gospels*, ET 1963. When Origen, *Homilies on Luke* (ed. M.Rauer, GCS 35, ²1959, *Homilia* 1, p.4f.) interprets the πολλοὶ ἐπεχείρησαν of Luke 1.1 polemically in terms of apocryphal Gospels, κατὰ Αἰγυπτίους, τῶν Δώδεκα, κατὰ Βασιλείδην, κατὰ Θωμᾶν, κατὰ Ματθίαν καὶ ἄλλα πλείονα, he is deliberately using an anachronism to stress the 'many' over against 'the four which the church alone recognizes'.

40. Hennecke/Schneemelcher/Wilson, op.cit., I, 117-65. The conjecture by W.Bauer, *Orthodoxy* (n.9), 50, that 'the designation *Gospel of the Egyptians* points back to a time in which the Christians of Egypt used this gospel, and only this gospel, as their "life of Jesus"', is quite unfounded, as is the even more precise claim that it was the Gospel 'of the Gentile Christians in Egypt'(53), since we have very little certain knowledge apart from some quotations in Clement of Alexandria. We may doubt whether this Encratite gnosticizing work ever contained a life of Jesus at all. How loose such a designation became is clear from the title on the Nag Hammadi Gospel of the Egyptians, which is clearly a secondary accretion (Cod.III 2 and IV 2), ed. A.Böhlig and F.Wisse, *Nag Hammadi Studies* IV, 1975, 166. The Gospel (of the) Egyptians ΠΕΥΑΓΓΕΛΙΟΝ ‹Ν› ΝΡΜΝΚΗΜΕ (III, 69, 6), see 18-23.

41. *Didache* 8.2; 15.3f.

42. II Clement 8.5: λέγει γὰρ ὁ κύριος ἐν τῷ εὐαγγελίῳ. There follows a quotation of Luke 16.11, slightly varied, and then a literal quotation of Luke 16.10a. It is striking that the author adduces four apocryphal quotations from the New Testament sphere: 4.5; 5.2-4; 12.2; 13.2. K.Wengst, *Schriften des Urchristentums* II, *Didache (Apostellehre), Barnabasbrief, Zweiter Klemensbrief, Schrift an Diognet*, Darmstadt 1984, 221ff., conjectures that along with the quotations which have a synoptic ring they all come from one Gospel writing which in turn is a redaction of Luke and Matthew. However, this does not seem to me to be very probable. There are too many possible explanations here. Perhaps the author goes back to a catechetical collection which he had made himself. Oral tradition may also play a role. The significant concept for the author is not yet the term εὐαγγέλιον, which he only uses once, but 'the word of the Lord': cf. 4.5; 5.2; 6.1; 8.5; 9.11; 13.2 (Isa.52.5); 15.4; 17.3,4 (Isa.66.18). The sayings of Jesus predominate, but the OT is also cited twice.

43. οὐκ ἔπεισαν αἱ προφητεῖαι οὐδὲ ὁ νόμος Μωϋσέως, ἀλλ᾿ οὐδὲ μέχρι νῦν τὸ εὐαγγέλιον.

44. πρέπον οὖν ἐστὶν... προσέχειν δὲ τοῖς προφήταις, ἐξαιρέτως δὲ τῷ εὐαγγελίῳ, ἐν ᾧ τὸ πάθος ἡμῖν δεδήλωται καὶ ἡ ἀνάστασις τετελείωται.

45. Cf. Matt.3.15 = Smyrn. 1.1; Matt.10.16/Luke 6.32 = Pol.2,1f.; Matt.19.12 = Smyrn 6.1; cf. E.Massaux, *Influence de l'Évangile de saint Matthieu sur la littérature chrétienne avant saint Irénée*, 1950, 94ff., 133f.; John 3.8 = Phil.7.1; John 4.10ff. and 7.38f. = Rom.7.2; John 6.33 = Rom.7.3; cf. op.cit., 112ff., and W.von Loewenich, op.cit. (n.19), 25ff.: 'The spiritual affinity seems to be strengthened by literary acquaintance' (38).

46. For the sources and his teaching see E.Mühlenberg, 'Basilides', *TRE*, 1980, 296ff. For Basilides the Gospel is greater than ἡ τῶν ὑπερκοσμίων γνῶσις (Hippolytus, *Haer.* 7,27,7), basically identical with Gnosis. It descends from heaven to Jesus, cf. *Haer.* 7,23-26 and 27,6-13. For the Gospel according to Basilides see Origen (n.39). In addition to the known Gospels Basilides (or his disciples) referred to secret revelations which go back to the apostle Matthias (*Haer.* 7,20,1) and to Glaucias, an alleged interpreter of Peter (Clement, *Strom.* 7,106,4). In my view he here presupposes knowledge of the Peter-Mark tradition, which he imitates. Presumably Basilides commented on his own 'Gospel'. According to Hegemonius (*Act.Archelai* 67, 5 [GCS 16, ed. C.H.Beeson, p.96]), in Book 13 of his commentary he mentioned the parable of the rich man and poor Lazarus (Luke 16.19ff.). An echo of the Gospel of Luke appears in Clement (*Strom.* 1,146, 1-3, cf. Luke 3,1, and for the length of Jesus' ministry as one year, Luke 4.19). Hippolytus bears witness that in the view of the pupils of Basilides, 'everything happened in connection with the saviour precisely as it is written in the Gospels' (*Haer.* 7,27,8): that may go back to the teacher himself. Cf. 7,22,4 = John 1,9; 7,26,9 = Luke 1.35; 7,27,5 = John 2.4; see Clement, *Strom.* 3,1,1 = Matt.19.11ff. and above 153 n.64.

47. For the ending of Mark see R.Pesch, op.cit. (n.3), 41-4; II, 1977, 544-56; W.R.Farmer, *The Last Twelve Verses of Mark*, SNTS.MS 25, 1974; K.Aland, 'Der Schluss des Markusevangeliums', in *Neutestamentliche Entwürfe*, ThB 63, 1979, 246-61; J.Hug, *La finale de l'évangile de Marc*, 1978. The secondary conclusion

to Mark was perhaps already known to Tertullian: *Apol.* 21.23,25 = Mark 16.8,20; *Praescript.Haer.* 30,16 = 16,17 cf. 20; *Adv.Prax.* 2,1: *et in caelum resumptum sedere ad dextram Patris* = Mark 16.19. There is a clear quotation in Irenaeus 3,10,6 = Mark 16.19; Tatian's Diatessaron probably already presupposes the extended conclusion, cf. K.Aland, op.cit., 261 n.20; J.Hug, op.cit., 201; cf. also Justin, *Apol.* 45.5: ἐξελθόντες πανταχοῦ ἐκήρυξαν and Mark 16.20, ἐξελθόντες ἐκήρυξαν πανταχοῦ. W.R.Farmer, op.cit., 31f., conjectures that the designation of the first eyewitness Mary Magdalene as γυνὴ πάροιστρος in Celsus (Origen, *c.Cels.* 2,55) is dependent on 16.9. There could perhaps be an allusion in Hermas 102.2 = 16.15,19; the same goes for the Gospel of Peter 14: ἡμεῖς δὲ οἱ δώδεκα(!) μαθηταὶ τοῦ κυρίου ἐκλαίομεν καὶ ἐλυπούμεθα = 16.10.

The connections with the *Epistula Apostolorum* are particularly striking. Here, as M.Hornschuh, *Studien zur Epistula Apostolorum*, PTS 5, 1965, 14, stresses, the account of the resurrection 'is closest to the so-called inauthentic conclusion to Mark in respect of its structures'. Cf. op.cit., 15, 'The basic pattern of the account is thus derived from the inauthentic conclusion to Mark.' As the *Epistula Apostolorum* is to be put at the latest in the middle of the second century, and very probably earlier, the addition of Mark 16.9-20 must be dated to the first decades of the second century. Hornschuh, op.cit., 118, conjectures that the *Epistula Apostolorum* was even written 'in the first fifth of the second century'. The significance for the history of the canon of the *Epistula Apostolorum*, which knows all four Gospels - again, it is especially familiar with John – and uses them intensively, along with Acts, does not seem to me to have been recognized clearly enough. The ὄφεις ἀροῦσιν of Mark 16.18 could presuppose acquaintance with Acts 28.3-6, but also with Luke 10.19; the following κἂν θανάσιμόν τι πίωσιν οὐ μὴ αὐτοὺς βλαψῃ recalls the Papias note (Eusebius, HE 3,39,9) on Justus Barsabbas: ὡς δηλητήριον φάρμακον ἐμπίοντος καὶ μηδὲν ἀηδὲς διὰ τὴν τοῦ κυρίου χάριν ὑπομείναντος, cf. also the fragment from Philippus Sidetes, Fragment no.16 (= 11 Funk-Bihlmeyer) in J.Kürzinger, *Papias von Hierapolis und die Evangelien des Neuen Testaments*, Eichstätter Materialien 4, 1983, 116: ὑπὸ τῶν ἀπίστων ἰὸν ἐχίδνης πιὼν ἐν ὀνόματι τοῦ Χριστοῦ ἀπαθὴς διεφυλάχθη.

Perhaps the information in the Armenian Ejmiadsin Evangeliar about the inauthentic ending to Mark 'by Arist[i]on the Presbyter' should in fact be taken seriously, see F.Siegert in J.Kürzinger, op.cit., 138. In that case Mark 16.9-20 would possibly go back to an informant of Papias. By contrast, the conjecture by E.Lohmeyer, *Das Evangelium des Markus*, [11]1951, 361, that the inauthentic conclusion was an originally 'independent epitome', is as improbable as the hypothesis of J.Hug, op.cit., who categorically denies a dependence on the other Gospels and conjectures the use of exclusively oral tradition. The use of the accounts from other Gospels, with forced harmonization and marked abbreviation, is unmistakable: cf. John 20.14,17f.; Luke 8.2; 24.11 with Mark 16.9-11; Luke 24.13-35 with Mark 16.12; Luke 24.36ff. see also John 20.19ff.,29; Matt.28.17b with Mark 16.15; Matt.28.19f. (cf. Luke 24.27) with Mark 16.15f. For Mark 16.16 see also Acts 2.18; for Mark 16.17 cf. Acts 2.43; 5.12; 8.6f. etc., and, especially on speaking with tongues,

Acts 2.4; 10.46; 19.6. In my view the ascension tradition in 16.19 is a contraction of Luke 24.50b; Acts 1.11 (on ἀνελήμφθη see also 1.2,22) and 2.33f. (cf. 5.31 etc.). The age of the conclusion to Mark emerges from the great freedom with which the harmonizer and epitomator uses the Gospels and Acts along with other material for his purposes.

48. For the *Epistula Apostolorum* see C.Schmidt, *Gespräche Jesu mit seinen Jüngern nach der Auferstehung. Ein katholisch-apostolisches Sendschreiben des 2.Jahrhunderts*, 1919 reprinted 1967, esp. 213ff. on its use of the NT. Schmidt comes to the conclusion 'that our author possessed the canon of the four Gospels' (216). It would probably be more correct to say that the author knew the four Gospels, but did not yet regard them as 'canonical' in the strict sense; otherwise he would not have been able to write his work. It is also worth noting that 'in none of the second-century writings before Irenaeus which have come down to us is the Gospel of John used so strongly as here' (224f., cf.241). Alongside this, apocryphal texts, at least the Infancy Gospel of Thomas, are used (226ff.). For Acts see the detailed account; the relationship to the letters of Paul remains obscure (246ff.). I think it likely that the work comes from Asia Minor, which was theologically the most active province in the second century (366ff.). M.Hornschuh, op.cit. (n.47), (116ff.) 118, has demonstrated convincingly that to put it in the period between AD 160 and 170 is too late (399-402); he suggests that it comes from Egypt (99ff.). Cf. also H.Duensing in Hennecke/Schneemelcher/ Wilson, *New Testament Apocrypha* I, 1963, 191: 'first half of the second century'. The references made to it in P.Vielhauer, op.cit. (n.5)., 407, vary remarkably: 'about the first half of the second century'; 'about the middle of the second century', with a misleading reference to Hornschuh (684).

49. For the dating and the location of the Gospel of Mark in Rome in the crisis year of AD 69, see 1–30 above.

50. For εὐαγγέλιον in Mark see above, 53ff. I wonder whether there could not be a Petrine understanding of the term εὐαγγέλιον here.

51. Mark 8.35: ἕνεκεν ἐμοῦ καὶ τοῦ εὐαγγελίου

Luke 9.24 (and Matt.16.25) ἕνεκεν ἐμοῦ

Mark 10.29 ἕνεκεν ἐμοῦ καὶ ἕνεκεν τοῦ εὐαγγελίου

Luke 18.29 ἕνεκεν τῆς βασιλείας τοῦ θεοῦ

Matt. 19.29 ἕνεκεν τοῦ ὀνόματός μου

Mark 13.10: …δεῖ κηρυχθῆναι τὸ εὐαγγέλιον.

Luke omits the verse between 21.13 and 14, whereas Matt.24.14 puts the mission saying immediately before the beginning of the end-events: καὶ κηρυχθήσεται τοῦτο τὸ εὐαγγέλιον τῆς βασιλείας… Could this Lucan aversion to the noun in the Gospel (as opposed to the verb εὐαγγελίζεσθαι) be a 'Pauline rudiment'? Can the earthly Jesus not yet preach the full gospel? Or does Luke have an aversion because of a possible misuse of the term? In Acts 15.7 he puts τὸν λόγον τοῦ εὐαγγελίου on the lips of Peter and in 20.24, τὸ εὐαγγέλιον τοῦ θεοῦ τῆς χάριτος (!) on the lips of Paul. He does not to want to suppress it completely, but he uses it first for the post-Easter mission to the Gentiles.

52. εὐαγγέλιον τῆς βασιλείας: Matt.4.23 cf. Mark 1.14; 9.35; Matt. 24.14 = Mark 13.10; τὸ εὐαγγέλιον τοῦτο, Matt.26.13; cf. Mark 14.9.

53. Only Revelation, which can be counted as part of the Johannine corpus only with many reservations, has the term in an 'archaic' form (14.6) which is untypical of the NT elsewhere. See P.Stuhlmacher, *Das paulinische Evangelium, I. Vorgeschichte*, FRLANT 95, 1968, 210ff.: Stuhlmacher's work has made clear the derivation of the terminology in the history of religion. It is completely misleading to derive the term from usage in the emperor cult, which at present is being excessively over-valued, especially as in the few relevant instances we only find the plural, which was usual among the Greeks.

54. See M.Hengel, 'Anonymität, Pseudepigraphie und "literarische Fälschung" in der jüdisch-hellenistischen Literatur', in *Pseudepigrapha I, Entretiens sur l'Antiquité Classique XVIII*, 1972, (229-308) 234; id., *Judaism and Hellenism*, ET 1974, I, 131ff.

55. Gal.2.9; cf.1.18f. It is striking how much the authority of individual missionaries, teachers and other people in service for the good of the communities is stressed in the letters of Paul (cf. I Cor.1.12ff.; 9.5f.; 15.5ff; 16.15ff.) and the prescripts to the Pauline letters and the lists of greetings generally. The catalogues of apostles and other names in the Gospels and Acts – including the lists of women in Luke 8.2ff.; Mark 15.40ff. etc. – confirm this deliberate stress on particular authoritative leading personalities in the communities and contradict the excessive emphasis on anonymous collectivity in the communities among the form critics. The numerous lists usually at the same time indicate degrees of rank, see my 'Maria Magdalena und die Frauen als Zeugen', in *Abraham unser Vater. Festschrift O.Michel zum 60. Geburtstag*, AGSU 5, 1963, (243-56) 248ff.

56. I Clement itself makes no reference to the personality of the author; rather, the author represents the Roman community and therefore writes in the first person plural. Nevertheless, there is no reason for doubting the attribution of authorship which is already attested by Dionysius of Corinth and Hegesippus (Eusebius, HE 4,23,11; 4,22,1, and Irenaeus, *Adv.Haer.* 3,3,3), as by the title, which was probably already given to the letter when copies were made for its circulation in the communities, see below. 80f.

57. Of course there were exceptions, for example letters (or tractates) of which only the address, 'To the Hebrews' or 'To Diognetus', is preserved, but they were the exception that proves the rule. The examples from the correspondence between Augustine and Jerome (see n.12 above) show how easily in a codex, the format which also tended to be used in longer letters, the title page or the *subscriptio* could be lost. It is probably no coincidence that the Letter to Diognetus had no significance in the early church and that the Letter to the Hebrews first became established in the East, where on the basis of ch.13 it was attributed to Paul – thus already in the earliest manuscript P 46, cf. Pantaenus according to Clement of Alexandria (Eusebius 6,14,4) and the still more artificial explanation by Clement himself (6.14.2f.). Tertullian attributes it to Paul's companion Barnabas (*De pud.* 20.2f.). 'Once the letter was accepted into the canon, a process which was still not complete everywhere at the beginning of the fifth century, the acknowledgment of Pauline authorship in the manuscript inscriptions and subscriptions also

generally prevailed' (A.von Harnack, *Die Briefsammlung des Apostels Paulus*, 1926, 16; cf. also O.Michel, *Der Brief an die Hebräer*, KEK [12]1966, 38f.). The letter evidently circulated very early, 'as still today, with the address cut off' (A. von Harnack, op.cit., 15f.). It is all the more striking that despite the confusion over the authorship of the letter, the *inscriptio* (and *subscriptio*) ΠΡΟΣ ΕΒΡΑΙΟΥΣ in the old and good manuscripts remains relatively constant and is not changed or even removed arbitrarily (see C.Tischendorf, *Novum Testamentum Graece* II, 780, 839, cf. Nestle/Aland[26], p.587). The mention of Pauline authorship in the manuscript inscriptions and subscriptions also appears relatively late and rarely. In my view this suggests that the title was added very early and remained in a fixed form. See below 78ff. Eusebius, HE 5,27, lists a large number of church writers at the time of Septimius Severus and adds that – presumably in the library of Caesarea – there are also writings 'of many others whose names he could not name... because the name of the author was not given'. However, of these he cites only one against Artemon (5,28,1); later, in Theodoret of Cyrus (*Haeret.fab. comp.* 2.5, PG 83, 392 B1), it has the title ὁ σμικρὸς Λαβύρινθος and by some is attributed wrongly to Origen; today the author is usually thought to be Hippolytus. Photius (*Bibl.cod.* 46, ed.R.Henry, 1,33ff.), however, mentions the Roman presbyter Gaius as its author. The anonymity of a writing hampered its effectiveness and therefore people were fond of remedying this by attributing it to someone. On the other hand, with simple papyrus codices the first and last leaves with the *inscriptio* and *subscriptio* could easily be lost. Jerome conjectures that the letter of Augustine brought to him by Sisennius after a five-year delay was a forgery, as this did not have Augustine's signature (*Ep.* 40; 68; 72); see H.Lietzmann, op.cit. [n.12], 287f. and G.Kloeters, op.cit. [n.12], 235f. Cf. II Thess.3.17). The difficulties which could arise from a secondary attribution of author and addition of a title are clear from the writing 'On the Universe', mentioned by Photius, loc.cit. It was presented as the work of Josephus, but from a learned marginal note Photius discovered that it also derived from Gaius. Others are said to have conjectured Justin, Irenaeus and Origen as authors of the ἀνεπίγραφον. In reality it also derives from Hippolytus, cf. A.von Harnack, *Die Geschichte der altchristlichen Litteratur bis Eusebius* I, 2, 622f.; II, 2, 219f. Quite apart from the question of authorship he mentions four different titles; the title which Hippolytus *Haer.* 10,32,4 (GCS 26, ed. Wendland, 288) himself gives it, περὶ τῆς παντὸς οὐσίας, differs from the list of writings on his statue, πρὸς Ἕλληνας καὶ πρὸς Πλάτωνα ἢ περὶ τοῦ παντός. Sometimes titles of books were also deliberately removed, or a work was put into circulation anonymously. Jerome, *Ep.* 73.1, reluctantly comments on a work which the presbyter Euangelus had sent him with the request that he should refute it: *misisti mihi volumen* ἀδέσποτον *et nescio, utrum tu de titulo nomen subtraxeris an ille, qui scripsit, ut periculum fugeret disputandi, auctorem noluerit confiteri* ('You have sent me a book without an author and I do not know whether you have removed the name from the title or whether the person who wrote it did not want to indicate its authorship in order to avoid the danger of critical discussion'). See G.Kloeters, op.cit. (n.12), 218. These are just some examples among many. The problem of book titles in patristics needs a thorough investigation. For the variants in titles and double titles see also below, 74f.

58. It should not be forgotten here that Jōhanan\Ἰωάννης was one of the most frequent Palestinian names at that time. In the NT we find five or six different people who bear this name: 1. John the Baptist; 2. the son of Zebedee; (3. the seer of Revelation); 4. the father of Simon Peter (John 1.43; 21.15-17); 5. John Mark and 6. the high priest (Acts 4.6). In addition, one could also mention the presbyter John in Papias. Josephus knows seventeen people by this name, see A.Schalit, *Namenswörterbuch zu Flavius Josephus*, 1968, 66; Billerbeck VI, *Verzeichnis der Schriftgelehrten...*, ed. J.Jeremias and K.Adolph, 1961, 84-88 mentions fifteen. Confusion was easily possible here.

59. The title ran Ἔλεγχος καὶ ἀνατροπὴ τῆς ψευδωνύμου γνώσεως; see A.Rousseau/L.Doutreleau, *Irénée de Lyon, Contre les Hérésies, Tome I*, SC 293, 1982, 199. The two terms come from rhetorical legal terminology. In the first book Irenaeus had unmasked and convicted his opponent, and in the second book he presented a devastating refutation. It follows from the prologue to the second book that he himself gave the work this title, loc.cit., 24: *Quapropter quod sit et detectio et euersio* (ἔλεγχος καὶ ἀνατροπή) *sententiae ipsorum, operis huius conscriptionem ita titulauimus.* Cf. also Clement of Alexandria, *Stromateis*, 6,2,1; 7,18,3, who gives detailed reasons for the title of his work, στρωματεῖς, which he himself gave it and which had already been used by Plutarch. As the first sheet of the book is missing, we do not know whether he also went into it there. See H.Zilliacus, op.cit. (n.60), 26f.

60. For reasons of space, at this point I cannot go more closely into the development of the book title in antiquity; I shall just mention some literature: E.Schmalzriedt, ΠΕΡΙ ΦΥΣΕΩΣ. *Zur Frühgeschichte der Buchtitel*, Munich 1970, and the critical review by C.W.Müller, *Gnomon*, 50, 1978, 628-38. Basic studies are still: E.Nachmanson, *Der Griechische Buchtitel. Einige Beobachtungen*, Göteborgs Högskolas Årsskrift XLVII, 1949, 19; H.Zilliacus, 'Boktiteln in antik Literatur', *Eranos* 36, 1938, 1-40; cf. also R.P.Oliver, 'The First Medicean MS of Tacitus and the Titulature of Ancient Books', *TPAPA* 82, 1951, 232-61. For descriptions of ancient books and their role in the determining the form of libraries see C.Wendel, *Die griechisch-römische Buchbeschreibung verglichen mit der des vorderen Orients*, HM 3, 1949; for the titles see 106ff. For titles of books put on the outside of scrolls, the so-called σύλλιβος, see already T. Birt, *Die Buchrolle in der Kunst*, 1907 (reprinted 1976), 237ff., and index s.v. *sittybos*; for the book in early Christianity and antiquity generally see L.Koep/S.Morenz/I.Leipoldt, 'Buch I/II', *RAC* 3, 1954, cols. 664-717, for the title 674f., 685; all too briefly, D.Fouqet-Plümacher, *TRE* 7, 1981, 275-8, 288f. (lit.)

61. *FGrHist* 1 F1: Ἑκαταῖος Μιλήσιος ὧδε μυθεῖται. τάδε γράφω ὥς μοι δοκεῖ ἀληθέα εἶναι. This is already the expression of a rationalistic and critical personality. Similarly Herodotus, Prologue, and Thucydides 1,1.

62. T.Kleberg, *Buchhandel und Verlagswesen in der Antike*, ³1969 (1967); H.Widmann, 'Herstellung und Vertrieb des Buches in der Antiken Welt', *Archiv für Geschichte des Buchwesens* 8, 1967, cols.540-640; id., *Geschichte des Buchhandels vom Altertum bis zur Gegenwart* I, ²1975, 1-23.

63. For the libraries in antiquity, in addition to the literature mentioned in

n.60 cf. C.Wendel, 'Bibliothek', *RAC* 2, 1954, cols.231-74, and now basically for the Hellenistic period: R.Blum, 'Kallimachos und die Literaturverzeichnung bei den Griechen', in *Archiv für Geschichte des Buchwesens* 18, 1977, cols.1-360; E.Plümacher, 'Bibliothekswesen (Antike) II 1', *TRE* 6, 1980, 413-15. For libraries in the early church see H.Leclercq, *DACL* 2, 1, 1910, cols. 842-904; J.Scheele, 'Buch und Bibliothek bei Augustinus', *Bibliothek und Wissenschaft* 12, 1978, 14-114; G.Kloeters, *Buch und Schrift bei Hieronymus*, Diss.phil. Münster, 1957 ,162-9. There is an urgent need for a monograph on the nature of books and libraries in the early church.

64. C.W.Müller, op.cit. (n.60), 628f.

65. For two or more titles see H.Zilliacus, op.cit (n.60), 38ff.; Nachmanson, op.cit (n.60), 10ff. The double title could be deliberately chosen by the author, as in Lucian and Philo, or simply be a result of carelessness, but usually it arises from the fact that writings were given different names at different places and different times. See also E.Nachmanson, op.cit., 6ff., 12 (on Plato): 'There is often a rich flora of variations'. Great authors like Aristotle or Galen (see below, n.67; cf. Hippolytus, above n.57) could quote works which they themselves had written by different titles. Cf. also C.Wendel, *Buchbeschreibung* (n.60), 30ff. For the later development of the double title see A.Rothe, *Der Doppeltitel. Zu Form und Geschichte einer literarischen Konvention*, AAMz 1969, (8ff.) 10.

66. My colleague Hartmut Stegemann of Göttingen was kind enough to explain the complicated situation in Qumran to me. There is neither *inscriptio* nor *subscriptio* on the scrolls there, but book titles appear as 'tables of contents', so that there are numerous references to individual prophetic books, to the 'books of the prophets' or 'the Torah' (CD 7.15,17) or the 'Book of Moses' (2Q 25,1,3) and the 'Book of the Torah' (CD 5,2; cf. 6Q 9,21,3), as to other works, e.g. the Book of Jubilees (CD 16.3: *spr mḥlqwt hʿtym* = 'book of the divisions of the times', or the mysterious *spr hhgw(y)* 1QSa 1,7 etc.). These book titles partly appear as the first line of a work (1QS 1,1: *spr srk hyḥ'd*). The external description of the scrolls was given by an external designation on the scroll which has been preserved in two cases: 1. in the 'Paroles des luminaires', *DJD* VII, Qumran Cave 4, III (ed. M.Baillet), 1982, p.138; 4Q 504 fr.8 verso = pl.XLIX with the title: *dbry hm'rwt*. The scroll begins with Fr.8 verso. The title goes across the text of the scroll on the inside. 2. A special 'handle sheet' appears in J.T.Milik, DJD I, Qumran Cave I, 1955, 107 = pl.XXII; it belongs to the scroll with the Rule, 1QS and Sa and Sb, and, as certain traces show, was sewn on to this on the outside. We can also see such traces in 1QIsᵃ. I quote the explanation by H.Stegemann, 'If the scroll was rolled up with the beginning of the text on the outside and the end on the inside, as was necessary for an orderly "library", then this inscription was on the outside; it began about 3cm from the lower margin of the scroll and then ran on the back of the scroll in such a way that one could read it immediately on taking out and holding up the scroll lying on the shelf with the upper part to the rear.' The inscription of the scroll which contains the Rule of the sect runs [*sr*]*k hyḥd wmn*[. It evidently contained a 'Table of Contents', which could include the titles of several works in one scroll. It is striking that in Qumran

– quite against the spirit of the time – the individual personality of the author was still insignificant. The only exceptions were the inspired authors of the holy scriptures.

67. E.Nachmanson, op.cit. (n.60), 25, cf.27f., Porphyry's changes in the edition of Plotinus' writings. J.Wettstein, op.cit.(n.10), 224, had already referred to the Galen passage in connection with the titles of the Gospels.

68. For the dedication see K.Diatzko, *PW* 3, 1897, col. 967. J.Ruppert, *Quaestiones ad historiam dedicationis librorum pertinentes*, Diss. Leipzig 1911; T.Janson, *Latin Prose Prefaces*, 1964; T.Kleberg, op.cit (n.62), 29f., 54f. For the edition see T.Birt, *Das antike Buchwesen in seinem Verhältnis zur Literatur*, 1882 (reprinted 1974), 342-70. K.Diatzko, *Untersuchungen über ausgewählte Kapitel des antiken Buchwesens*, 1900, 149-78; H.I.Marrou, 'La technique de l'édition à l'époque Patristique', *VC* 3, 1949, 208-24, with a critical supplement by H.L.M. van der Valk, *VC* 11, 1957, 1-10; G.Kloeters, op.cit. (n.63), 93-104. It is striking that from Luke 1.1 and Acts 1.1 on we find numerous prologues with dedications in early Christian literature, though these are only partially preserved in the fragments of second-century authors; here it is not always possible to make a clear distinction between theological tractate and letter. See the Papias prologue (Eusebius, HE 3,39,3); Marcion (see A.von Harnack, *Marcion* 77, 256); Justin, *Dial.* 141,4, dedicated to Marcus Pomponius, cf.8.3 – the dedication is broken off at the beginning; Diognetus 1; the anonymous anti-Montanist, Eusebius, HE 5,16: to Avirkios Markellos; Irenaeus, *Ad.haer.*, Prologue (this does not contain the name). *Demonstration of the Proclamation of the Apostles* 1 (SC 62, 1959, trans. Froidevaux, 27): Marcianus; Melito, Ἐκλογαί (Eusebius, HE 4,26,12 = Fr.3, ed S.G.Hall, OECT, p.66): Onesimus; Theophilus: *ad Autolykon*. Thus even apart from the Apologists and their writings dedicated to the emperors after Hadrian (or the 'Romans', Justin, *Apol.* II, or 'Greeks', Tatian), the literary convention of the time can be demonstrated continuously throughout the second century, after Luke.

69. See A.Vögtle, *Das Evangelium und die Evangelien, Beiträge zur Evangelienforschung*, 1971, 31-42.

70. M.Dibelius, *Studies in the Acts of the Apostles*, ET 1956, 135f., cf.147: 'The book had two market outlets: it was intended as a book to be read by the Christian community as the εὐαγγέλιον Ἰησοῦ Χριστοῦ', and 'only where there were several books of this kind would the name of the author have been added: κατὰ Λουκᾶν', but through Theophilus it was to be 'the private reading of people of literary education', distributed through the book trade, 'and if we may be permitted to draw a conclusion in reverse from the title of the second book, then the title of the first was Λουκᾶ ('Αντιοχέως) πράξεις Ἰησοῦ'. In my view, in that case some trace of a double title should have been left. Dibelius' theory has been rejected almost unanimously, though H.von Campenhausen, op.cit., 128 n.101, is positive. For criticism see A.D.Nock, *Gnomon* 25, 1953, 501f. However, Dibelius is right in commenting, op.cit., 136, that 'it would have been strange indeed if the person to whom the book was dedicated had been named, but not the dedicator', see also von Campenhausen, op.cit., 126 n.92.

71. Tertullian, *De test. anim.*1.4: 'So much is lacking that people make the

acquaintance of our writings to which no one has access who is not already a Christian' (*tantum abest, ut nostris litteris annuant homines, ad quas nemo uenit nisi iam christianus*). Statements like Matt.28.18; Luke 4.5-7 and the Synoptic apocalypse must have had a provocative effect. However, Christian books were systematically destroyed only in the Diocletian persecution, see W.Speyer, *Büchervernichtung und Zensur bei Heiden, Juden und Christen*, Bibliothek des Buchwesens 7, 1981, 74,76ff., 127ff. Still, we can assume that even in earlier persecutions, books of Christians were destroyed as a side-effect. The governor who asks the martyrs in Scili in North Africa about their books will hardly have given them back to the Christians, see below 78.

72. See the penultimate verse of the Gospel of John, 21.24: the reference to the author marks an address now not just to the Johannine school but to the whole church. The commission to Peter (21.15-17) and the reference to his martyrdom (21.18f.) show the ecumenical breadth of the editor(s). In that case the riddle of 21.24 was solved when the name of the beloved disciple could be inferred from the title. III John clearly shows that the 'head of the school', the 'presbyter', is leader of a supra-regional *ecclesiola in ecclesia*, who was concerned to circulate the theological conceptions of his school throughout the church. However, that was not possible through anonymous writings. The problem in the later attempts at identification was simply that John was an all too frequent name in contemporary Jewish Christianity (see above, n.58), and this could easily lead to confusion.

73. See Tertullian's verdict on Marcion, above 166 n.30, and the stress on orthodoxy in the anonymous writings in the library of Caesarea, above 171 n.57. Even in the esoteric Gnostic library of Nag Hammadi, to which the public had no access, the majority of the tractates in the codexes are given titles, some of them secondary, which often of course have a deliberately mysterious ring. It is in the nature of the milieu that here pseudepigraphical attributions to Christian authorities (Peter, James, John, Philip, Thomas, Paul, Mary) and figures from primal, 'mythical' times (Adam, Shem, Seth, Zostrianos) or even titles relating to content predominate. Ordinary authors' names were hardly in place in this illustrious company, and are therefore rare. Among the genres named in the titles we often find apocalypses and gospels, and in addition apocrypha, apostolic acts, letters and dialogues. The question of titles in the Nag Hammadi texts needs a thorough investigation. It seems to me important that this was a private collection of writings, made relatively indiscriminately, which was not used for public reading in worship (see below, 176 nn.76, 77).

74. It is therefore already contested in the letters of Paul, cf. I Cor.15.3ff.; 11.23ff.; Gal.1.11ff.; 2.7ff.; Rom.6.17, etc.; i.e., this question dogged the church right from the beginning and did not first become acute at the time of 'early Catholicism'.

75. See already Neh.8.4ff.; Luke 4.17-20; Acts 13.15; 15.21; Billerbeck 4,154-65 and the Theodotus inscription from Jerusalem, CIJ 1404, lines 3ff.: ...ὠκο/δόμησε τὴν συναγωγὴν εἰς ἀν[άγν]ω/σ [ιν] νόμου καὶ εἰς [δ]ιδαχ[ὴ]ν ἐντολῶν... Here in my view the allusion is to the reading of scripture and the exposition of the Torah which followed it in synagogue worship. The so-

called 'Hellenistic community' grew out of this milieu of the Greek-speaking synagogues in Jerusalem. In my view, they had scripture reading in worship from the beginning. Cf. *Between Jesus and Paul*, 1983, 17ff. Cf. above, n.72.

76. *Apol.* I, 67,3. For scripture reading in early Christianity see P.Glaue, *Die Verlesung heiliger Schriften im Gottesdienst* I, 1907, passim; R.Knopf, *Das nachapostolische Zeitalter*, 1905, 233-6; J.Leipoldt/S.Morenz, *Heilige Schriften* 1953, 106ff., 112f. The consequences which Leipoldt draws from the late attestation of scripture reading are, however, false; cf. also K.Aland, *Studien zur Überlieferung des Neuen Testaments und seines Textes*, ANTT 2, 1967, 29: the reading of a scripture presumably first took place in worship in the community in which the author lived, and if it was recognized there, it was circulated more widely.

77. Cf.17.3f., the reference to preaching and on it R.Knopf, 'Die Anagnose zum zweiten Clemensbriefe', *ZNW* 3, 1902, 266-79; against this, K.P.Donfried, 'The Setting of Second Clement in Early Christianity', *NTS* 38, 1974, 55f. However, Donfried puts II Clement at least twenty years too early in connection with I Clement. On the other hand, Donfried (89) rightly points out the affinity of 19,1 to I Tim.4.11-16. See now also K.Wengst (ed.), *Schriften des Urchristentums. Didache. Barnabasbrief. Zweiter Klemensbrief. Schrift an Diognet*, 1984, 215f.

78. Ἕως ἔρχομαι πρόσεχε τῇ ἀναγνώσει, τῇ παρακλήσει, τῇ διδασκαλίᾳ. See C.Spicq, *Saint Paul. Les épitres pastorales*, 1969, 514ff.: 'En attendant, Timothée donnera tous ses soins dans les assemblées liturgiques à la dispensation de la parole de Dieu et des prescriptions apostoliques (v.11), sous les trois formes traditionelles de la lecture, de l'exhortation, de l'enseignement; l'article répété devant ces substantifs indique que ces fonctions sont définies et bien connues.'

79. In Rev.1.4f. the author adds a letter prescript to the seven churches, which shows that Revelation is to be understood as a letter and was circulated as such in the communities. The blessing in 22.21 also points to this. However, in contrast to the other NT letters, Revelation for the first time claims to be a written revelation given by God, communicated through Christ (1.1) and therefore sacrosanct (22.18). For the – extended – warning formula see my 'Problems', 154 n.67. Its immediate model is to be found in Deut.4.2; 13.1ff. It is not yet a 'canonization formula', as it only protects the work and does not yet guarantee its general recognition; however, it represents an essential step on the way to the formation of the New Testament canon.

80. Cf. Col.7.16; Eph.3.4; II Cor.1.13; 3.1; later II Peter 3.16; I Clem.47.1; Ign.12.2. From the end of the first century we can presuppose the reading of letters of Paul in numerous communities. The prescripts and endings of Paul's letters are deliberately formulated for liturgical use. The 'holy kiss' at the end of the letter, in Rom.16.16; I Cor.16.20; II Cor.13.12; I Thess 5.26; I Peter 5.14, marks the transition to the Supper at the end of the reading of the letter: see Justin, *Apol.*I, 65,2; Tertullian, *De oratione* 18; Hippolytus, *Apostolic Tradition* 4.21, ed. B.Botte, *La tradition apostolique de Saint Hippolyte*, LWQF 39, 1962, 10, 54; Athenagoras, *Suppl.* 32.6 etc. See K.Thraede, 'Friedenskuss', *RAC* 7, 1972, 505-19, and G.Stählin, φιλέω κτλ.', *TDNT* IX, 140ff. Against

Thraede I would say that in its basic form primitive Christian worship was more uniform than is usually assumed today. The chaos in Corinth, which at all events still presupposes a certain degree of order, should not be made the rule. Otherwise the development of relative order later, which points to synagogue worship, becomes completely incomprehensible.

81. Eusebius, HE 4,23,11. Cf. Hegesippus according to HE 4,22,1f.: the reading of I Clement in Corinth seems to be a sign of the ὀρθὸς Λόγος of the community. The collection and the exchange of letters and corpora of letters among the communities, like the Pauline corpus, the letters of the Johannine corpus, the letters of Ignatius, indeed even the letters of Dionysius of Corinth two generations later, served above all to enrich worship. The early acts of martyrs also have the external form of letters (circular letters) and were composed with the aim of being read in worship. However, this reading is not just edifying, but is at the same time a piece of church politics, see P. Nautin, *Lettres et écrivains chrétiens des IIe et IIIe siècles*, 1961, 27f.: 'Omettre cette lecture était une injure à l'évêque expéditeur; cela signifiait qu'on ne le tenait pas pour légitime', with reference to Cyprian, Ep. 65. But by the 'letter of Clement' he understands a previous letter which Dionysius had received from the Roman community. He does not consider (see 28 n.1) that we might well follow Eusebius in seeing it as I Clement (see also HE 3, 16 and Hegesippus' comment in HE 4, 22, 1f.)

82. Ἡ μὲν γραφὴ τῆς Ἑβραϊκῆς ἐξόδου ἀνέγνωσται, cf. G.Zuntz, *HTR* 36, 1943, 299-315 = *Opuscula Selecta* 1972, 293-309, and the conflicting interpretation by S.G.Hall in *Kyriakon, Festschrift J.Quasten*, 1970, 236-48. Cf. also Justin, *Dial*. 59.2; ἐν τῇ βίβλῳ ἣ ἐπιγράφεται Ἔξοδος, 59.1; 75.1; 126.2. For Moses as author see 79.4; 90.4.

83. 4.17: καὶ παρεδόθη αὐτῷ βιβλίον προφήτου Ἰσαίου. Leaving aside the fact that here Luke is speaking, in terms of his own experience, of a scroll which is rolled up, and from which the reader read standing at the desk (cf.4.20), we can imagine the readings taking place in Christian worship in an analogous way. However, at a very early stage the codex took the place of the scroll. In both instances it was impossible not to mention the name of the writing.

84. Cf. Did.8.2: ἐκέλευσεν ὁ κύριος ἐν τῷ εὐαγγελίῳ αὐτοῦ, see above, nn.41, 42. The reference to the Kyrios alone – which was traditional and very popular – did not tell the community whether this was the Old Testament or a saying of Jesus.

85. We very much need a comprehensive investigation of the Jewish, early Christian and Gnostic libraries. The investigations into ancient libraries as a rule pay niggardly attention to Christian libraries, see n.63 above. All too briefly, and only for the later period, see E.Plümacher, 'Bibliothekswesen 1.3: Christliche Bibliotheken', *TRE* 6, 1980, 414f.; C.Wendel, 'Bibliothek B. Christliche Bibliotheken Ia. Kirchliche Bibliotheken vor Konstantin', *RAC* 2, 1954, 246ff.: 'It goes without saying that the Christian communities needed a certain supply of books for their services and for the instruction of catechumens.' See also the survey by H.Leclercq, 'Bibliothèques', *DACL* II,1, 1925, 854ff., which, though very uncritical in places, contains a large amount of material. For Augustine's library see the excellent work by J.Scheele, op.cit.

(n.12); for Jerome and Caesarea, G.Koeters, op.cit. (n.63), 162-9; for Rome, E.D.Roberts, 'Notes on Early Christian Libraries in Rome', *Speculum* 9, 1934, 190f.; for Tertullian, A.von Harnack, 'Tertullians Bibliothek christlicher Schriften', *SPAW* 1914, 303-34 = *Kleine Schriften zur Alten Kirche*, 1980, I, 227-258; cf. there also 334 = 258 the reference to Cyprian's limitations on himself.

86. Eusebius, HE 6,20,1.

87. Irenaeus deliberately collected the writings of the heretics and must have owned a formidable library of them; see his own testimony, *Adv.Haer.*I,31,2: *Iam autem et collegi eorum conscriptorum* (sc. of the Cainites). Cf. *Adv.haer.* I, Prol.2.: ἐντυχὼν τοῖς ὑπομνήμασι τῶν ὡς αὐτοὶ λέγουσιν Οὐαλεντίνων μαθητῶν.

88. For the school of Justin see *Mart.Justini* ch.3, (ed. H.Musurillo, *The Acts of the Christian Martyrs*, OECT 1972, 44); W.Bousset, *Jüdisch-christlicher Schulbetrieb in Alexandrien und Rom*, 1915 reprinted 1975, 382ff. In addition to the writings of the Old and New Testament he also had access to the Sibylline books, the oracles of Hystaspes (*Apol.* 20.1; 44.12), Xenophon's *Memorabilia* (*Apol.* II, 11,3), Dialogues of Plato, Homer and apocrypha like the Gospel of Peter and the Protevangelium of James.

89. Cf. II Tim.4.12. I would regard the μέμβρανα as notebooks made of parchment, see C.H.Roberts/T.C.Skeat, *The Birth of the Codex*, 1983, 22, 60. They were the forerunners of the parchment codex. For the whole subject see C.Spicq, op.cit. (n.78), 2,814ff. Melito of Sardes brings back from his journey to Palestine an exact list of the writings of the 'old covenant', from which he made 'extracts' in six books; see his letter to Onesimus, Eusebius, HE 4,26,13-14. On his journey to Syria and Mesopotamia, Abercius always took 'Paul in his carriage'. This is the probable reading, see W.Wischmeyer, *JAC* 23, 1980, (23-47) 25 line 12: '"Paul" as *pars pro toto* of the Christian sacred writings' (41); cf. Acts 8.28ff. In the *contestatio* of the recipients of the *Kerygmata Petrou* 3.3 (*PsClemHom*, ed. B.Rehm, GCS 42, 1953, 3), these commit themselves when on journeys either to take all the books with them or to entrust them to a bishop of orthodox belief.

90. *De Morte Peregrini* 11: καὶ τῶν βίβλων τὰς μὲν ἐξηγεῖτο καὶ διεσάφει, πολλὰς δὲ αὐτὸς καὶ συνέγραφεν. See also above, 165 n.24, the request of the apologist Aristides to the Emperor to read the books of the Christians.

91. For the collection of the letters of Ignatius and the letters of Polycarp see P.Vielhauer, op.cit. (n.5), (540-66) 543ff., 562f.; A. von Harnack, *Die Briefsammlung des Apostels Paulus*, 1929, 28-35; for the substance now also C.P.Hammond-Bammel, 'Ignatian Problems', *JTS* 33, 1982, 62-97; P.N.Harrison, *Polycarp's Two Epistles to the Philippians*, 1936. For the collection of Dionysius' letters see P. Nautin, op.cit (n.81), 10–32, 90f.

92. Ignatius, *Philad.* 8.2: ἐπεὶ ἤκουσά τινων λεγόντων, ὅτι, ἐὰν μὴ ἐν τοῖς ἀρχείοις εὕρω, ἐν τῷ εὐαγγελίῳ οὐ πιστεύω. See on this C.P.Hammond-Bammel, op.cit., 74, who, following a suggestion from E.Bammel, sees ἐν τῷ εὐαγγελίῳ as a gloss. This would make the text more understandable. For ἀρχεῖα cf. H.Leclercq, *DACL* II, 1, 1925, 853: ''Αρχεῖα ne désigne pas seulement les livres… mais le local dans lequel on les conserve..' However, I regard as completely erroneous his suggestion that this refers to the synagogue

archives. The opponents call for proof through the holy scriptures (of the Old Testament) which are laid up in the community libraries: Ignatius, ibid.: καὶ λέγοντός μου αὐτοῖς, ὅτι γέγραπται, ἀπεκρίθησάν μοι, ὅτι πρόκειται. By contrast, Ignatius refers to the saving event which is present in the oral tradition, ibid.: ἐμοὶ δὲ ἀρχεῖά ἐστιν Ἰησοῦς Χριστός, τὰ ἄθικτα ἀρχεῖα ὁ σταυρὸς αὐτοῦ καὶ ὁ θάνατος καὶ ἡ ἀνάστασις αὐτοῦ καὶ ἡ πίστις δι᾽ αὐτοῦ, ...

93. HE 3,39,3: οὐ γὰρ τοῖς τὰ πολλὰ λέγουσιν ἔχαιρον ὥσπερ οἱ πολλοί: this polemic is directed against contemporary literary production. According to the extant fragments, Papias knows Matthew and John, I John, I Peter, Revelation and in my view also the Gospel of John and Acts, and in addition perhaps the Gospel of the Hebrews (3,39,17) and τοῦ κυρίου λόγων διηγήσεις of Aristion. The τοῦ πρεσβυτέρου Ἰωάννου παραδόσεις (3,39,14) are hardly likely to be a written source. Possibly here Papias is giving written designations he has collected himself.

94. H. Leclercq, op.cit., 854: 'On peut supposer que les anciennes églises chrétiennes réservèrent d'abord une armoire, ensuite une chambre, pour la conservation des livres liturgiques et des documents relatifs à l'administration des communautés chrétiennes. Malheureusement nous ne savons rien de précis et qui sorte du domaine trop libre de la conjecture.' For the book chest see E.G.Budde, *Armarium* und Κιβωτός, Diss.phil. Münster 1939, and the various investigations by C.Wendel on the ancient book chest, *armarium legum* and Torah shrine in *Kleine Schriften zum antiken Bibliothekswesen*, Cologne 1974, 64ff., 93ff., 108ff.

95. Ed. Musurillo, op.cit. (n.88), 88 = ch.12: *Saturninus proconsul dixit: Quas sunt res in capsa vestra? Speratus dixit: Libri et epistulae Pauli viri iusti.*

96. For the following see the thorough investigation by C.H.Roberts, *Manuscript, Society and Belief in Early Christian Egypt*, Schweich Lectures 1977, 1979; cf. also C.H.Roberts and T.C.Skeat, *The Birth of the Codex*, 1983, 38ff., 45ff. The early Christian writers usually did not produce their texts by dictation to groups or by others, but as individual copyists – even in later times (if we leave out of account the decades after the Edict of Galerius on religion in 311 and the shift under Constantine, when many texts were mass-produced). Here, of course, self-dictation will have been the usual pattern, see A.Dain, *Les Manuscrits* 1949, [2]1964, 40-5, and the critical supplement by Klaus Junack, 'Abschreibepraktiken und Schreibgewohnheiten', in *New Testament Textual Criticism, its Significance for Exegesis. Festschrift B.M.Metzger*, 1981, 277-95. The 'more than seven stenographers who were at work at particular times' and the 'not inconsiderable number of calligraphers along with the maidens practised in calligraphy', whom Origen's rich patron Ambrosius paid for, are a unique exception (Eusebius, HE 6,23,2). People were certainly less generous in the second century. For the single copy and the danger of forgery see the adjuration by Irenaeus in his Anti-Valentinian writing *On the Number Eight*, in Eusebius, HE 5,20,2.

97. For the codex, in addition to the literature mentioned in n.96, see E.G.Turner, *The Typology of the Early Codex*, 1977. According to C.H.Roberts and T.C.Skeat, op.cit., 37, cf. 38-44, the number of codexes among the literary Greek texts on papyrus amounts to the following: in the first century 0%; in

the second century 2%; in the second and third centuries 1.5%; in the third century 4.5% (37); by contrast, of the eleven Christian biblical papyri from the second century, all have the form of a codex (40f.). In addition there is the fragment of an apocryphal Gospel in P.Egerton 2, P.Oxy 1.1, a fragment from the Gospel of Thomas, both similarly on one codex; P.Mich.130, a fragment from the Shepherd of Hermas, on the other side of a papyrus scroll, and P.Oxy. 3,405 (the fragment of Irenaeus, *Adv.Haer.*, similarly on a scroll. The most recently published fragment of John, P.Oxy 50,1983, 3523, the writing on which is very similar to P.Egerton 2 and P.Oxy 4,656 (codex, according to Bell and Skeat still in the second century), again comes from a codex. For Suetonius see *Vit.Caes.* 1,56,6; cf. A.Wallace-Hadrill, *Suetonius*, 1983, 87.

98. C.H.Roberts, *Manuscript*, 26-48; cf. T.C.Skeat, 'Early Christian Book Production', in *The Cambridge History of the Bible*, 1969, (54-79) 72f.; J.O'Callaghan, *Nomina sacra in papyris graecis saeculi III neotestamentariis*, 1970; C.H.Roberts and T.C.Skeat, *Birth*, 57ff. A *nomen sacrum* ĪĊ is also contained in the new John papyrus from the second century (above, n.97), P.Oxy.50, 3523 (2.36).

99. C.H.Roberts, *Manuscript*, 14: 'they are the work of men not trained in calligraphy and so not accustomed to writing books, though they were familiar with them: they employ what is basically a documentary hand but at the same time they are aware that it is a book, not a document on which they are engaged. They are not personal or private hands; in most a degree of regularity and of clarity is aimed at and achieved. Such hands might be described as "reformed documentary" '. One of the practices of those who write documents is the marking of new paragraphs or sentences and the abbreviation of cardinal numbers by symbols. The emphasis on new paragraphs also occurs in P.Oxy 50, 3523.

100. T.C.Skeat, in *The Cambridge History of the Bible* 2, 73, quoted in C.H.Roberts and T.C.Skeat, *Birth*, 57. The authors continue: 'It may be further noted that, whether or not this was the intention, *nomina sacra* share the same characteristic with the codex of differentiating Christian from both Jewish and pagan books.' The same could also be said of the designation of a book or its content as εὐαγγέλιον.

101. For the Lord's day see already Rev.1.10; cf. Rev.20.7ff.; I Cor. 16.2; Did.14.2. Cf. W.Rordorf, *Sunday*, ET 1968, 38-42 and bibliography. For the synagogue see W.Schrage, 'Ekklesia und Synagoge', *ZTK* 60, 1963, (178-202) 196ff. In my view these differentiations go back to the Hellenists in Jerusalem (Acts 6.1ff.), see *Between Jesus and Paul*, 27f.

102. See above, 176 n.76. For Justin on the reading of Gospels and prophets see 'Problems in the Gospel of Mark', above, 57f.

103. Tertius was probably the stenographer who wrote Romans. His salutation tells against the argument that Romans 16.1-23 was orginally a separate letter with greetings addressed to the community in Ephesus. Having done the hard work of writing the letter, he too wants to have a word. His intervention would be incomprehensible in a very short work. For the question cf. C.E.B.Cranfield, *The Epistle to the Romans*, ICC, II, 1979, 806: 'one

might understand Tertius to be expressing by this ἐν κυρίῳ a certain awareness of the importance of that in which he had played a vital part.' Cranfield further conjectures 'that he had some connexion with Rome and would be known to some of the Christians there.'

104. Since the much-discussed investigation by G.Theissen, 'Wanderradikalismus. Literatursoziologische Aspekte der Überlieferung von Worten Jesu im Urchristentum', *ZTK* 70, 1973, 245-71 = *Studien zur Soziologie des Urchristentums*, WUNT 19, ²1983 (1979), 79-105 (bibliography, 344), interest has turned above all to the Christian itinerant teachers who appear e.g. also in the Didache and in III John. Over against this we need a more thorough investigation of the problem of exchanges between communities through messengers and the numerous thorough accounts of the journeys of Christian figures between the first and third centuries. Of course journeys to and from Rome are mentioned particularly frequently, as Tacitus (*Ann.* 15,44,3) and Juvenal (*Sat.* 3.60ff.) complain in their well known way. Here the way to Rome often led through Asia Minor. In addition to this, Alexandria and Palestine later played a great role (Melito, see above, n.89; Peregrinus Proteus, see above, n.90; Alexander, the later bishop of Jerusalem, comes from Cappadocia: Eusebius, HE 6,11,2, cf. also Ps.Clem.Hom.1,7,7; 8.1: ἀλλ' εἰς Ἰουδαίαν ὁρμήσω). We have numerous accounts from itinerant Gnostic teachers. The fact that many people travelled explains the special value attached to hospitality, see A.von Harnack, *The Mission and Expansion of Christianity*, I, ET 1908 reissued 1962, 177-82. His excursus on 'Travellers: The Exchange of Letters and Literature', I, 369-80, is still unsurpassed. For the difficulty in finding good messengers in later times see G.Kloeters, op.cit. (n.12), 138-48. See also the details in C.Andresen, *Die Kirche der alten Christenheit*, 1971, 17, 43ff. Here the starting point was the missionary journeys of the apostles, which were portrayed in the imaginary descriptions of the romances about the apostles.

105. Ignatius was visited during a lengthy stay in Smyrna, when he was a prisoner on the way to Rome, by emissaries of the communities in Ephesus, Magnesia and Tralles, each of which was led by the bishops. He gave them letters to the communities, with special stress on the Ephesians (Eph.1.3; 2.21; Magn.2.15; Trall.1.1; 13.1). In the letter to the Romans, which he sent from Smyrna, he mentions Syrian Christians who had already travelled to Rome; presumably in Smyrna he had news of the situation in Rome; perhaps that the community there wanted to prevent his martyrdom. The letters to the communities in Philadelphia and Smyrna, and the personal letter to Polycarp, were written in Troas; there Ignatius had received news by messengers from Antioch that the persecution was at an end (cf. Philad. 10.1; 11.1; Smyrn.11.1; Polycarp 7.1). The letters were brought back by Burrus, a temporary companion organized by the communities in Smyrna and Ephesus (Philad.11.2; Smyrn.12.1). The sudden departure from Troas to Neapolis prevents him from writing further letters. He therefore asks Polycarp to delegate a messenger to Antioch by means of a meeting of the community, and by letter to involve other communities from Asia Minor in the delegation, whether through letters or further messengers (Polycarp 7.2; 8.1f.). The

community in Philippi sent on such a letter to Polycarp which was to be forwarded to Syria; he promises to do this, and for his part sends to the Philippians the collection of letters by the martyr bishop. At the same time he asks for further news about the fate of Ignatius (Polycarp, ad Phil. ch.13).

106. Rom. 16.1; I Cor.1.11; 4.17; 5,9; 7.1; 16.12,17; II Cor.1.13; 7.5; 8.16, 22; Phil. 2.19, 25ff. The Pauline mission is inconceivable without this interchange between the communities.

107. *Martyr.Polyc.*, Prologue = Eusebius HE 4,15,3. Cf. *Mart.Polyc.* 22.2f. Some of the notes may be fictitious, for example the reference to the famous Irenaeus and to (Pseudo-) Pionius, but they nevertheless show how such writings were copied and therefore changed, and further circulated. See H. von Campenhausen, *Bearbeitungen und Interpolationen des Polykarpmartyriums*, SAH.PH 1957, 5-48 = *Aus der Frühzeit des Christentums*, 1963, (253-301) 291f. However, his reconstruction generally does not seem to me to be very convincing, see B.Dehandschuter, *Martyrium Polycarpi. Een literair-kritische Studie*, BETL 52, 1980, 139ff. For the letter form see 157ff. The account by the communities in Lugdunum and Vienna of the persecutions of the year 177 sent to the communities in Asia and Phrygia also takes the form of a letter (Eusebius, HE 5,1,3).

108. Col.4.16: Clement of Rome, in Rome: quotes not only from Romans but also from I Corinthians and Philippians (cf. 47.1-3; 37.5; 49.5); Polycarp, *ad Phil.* 7.1, not just from the Pauline corpus but also from I John 4.2f. (or II John 7) and at least three times from I Peter (1.2 = 1.8; 8.1 = 2.22; 10.2 = 2.12). Both letters were also known to Papias, see above n.93.

109. Cf. C.Andresen, *Die Kirche der alten Christenheit*, 1971, 43f. A striking feature in the formula of the letter is the stress on 'being alien', cf. I Peter 1.1 (παρεπίδημοι); 1 Clem., inscr.; Polycarp, Phil., inscr.; Mart. Polyc., inscr.; Mart Lugd., inscr. = Eusebius, HE 5,1,3 (παροικεῖν): cf. also the letter of Dionysus of Corinth: καὶ τῇ ἐκκλεσίᾳ δὲ τῇ παροικούσῃ Γόρτυναν ἅμα ταῖς λοιπαῖς κατὰ Κρήτην παροικίαις ἐπιστείλας... καὶ τῇ ἐκκλησίᾳ δὲ τῇ παροικούσῃ Ἄμαστριν ἅμα ταῖς κατὰ Πόντον, Eusebius, HE 4,23,5f. Here in my view Eusebius is quoting from the *inscriptio*.

110. Hermas had received and written out the heavenly letter from the old woman (the pre-existent church) after her question, 'Can you proclaim this to the elect' (5.3f. = Vis.2,1,3f.). In an additional vision a youth asks him whether he has already read the writing to the elders of the community. When he says no, he is praised: 'You have acted rightly, for I still have words to add. When I have completed all the words, they are to be made known by you to all the elect. Now you are to take two copies and send one to Clement and one to Grapte. Clement is then to send them to the cities outside, for that is his task (πέμψει οὖν Κλήμης εἰς τὰς ἔξω πόλεις, ἐκείνῳ γὰρ ἐπιτρέπεται). Grapte is to exhort the widows and orphans. But you yourself are to read it in this city before the elders who preside over the community', 8.2f. (*Vis.* II, 4,2f.). Evidently Clement was responsible for communication with the outside communities.

111. See the multiplicity of variants in the title of Joseph and Asenath, which probably go back to two basic forms: C.Burchard, *Untersuchungen zu*

Joseph und Aseneth, WUNT 8, 1965, 50ff. The titles of the Protevangelium of James are almost beyond counting, see K. von Tischendorf, *Evangelia apocrypha*, Leipzig ²1876 (reprinted 1966), 1f.; cf. E.de Strycker, 'La forme la plus ancienne du Protévangile de Jacques', *SHG* 33, 1961, 211f. See further the variants of the so-called *Apocalypsis Mosis* or *Vita Adae et Evae* in K.von Tischendorf, *Apocalypses Apocryphae*, Leipzig 1866 (reprinted 1966), 1. The variation in title is understandably the greatest where the manuscript tradition shows a certain breadth and is not just limited to a very few textual witnesses. A sometimes amazing range is evident even in the LXX, as can easily be seen from the volumes which have appeared in the Göttingen edition.

112. See 'Literary, Theological and Historical Problems in the Gospel of Mark', above 54–8.

113. For the historical setting of the second Gospel see 'The Gospel of Mark: Origin and Situation of Mark', 1–30 (28ff.) above.

Index of Biblical References

Old Testament

Index of Ancient Authors

Index of Modern Scholars

Subject Index

DATE DUE

FEB 17 '88			